Golf and the Law

Golf and the Law

A Practitioner's Guide to the Law and Golf Management

Thomas H. Sawyer

Carolina Academic Press
Durham, North Carolina

Library of Congress Cataloging-in-Publication Data

Sawyer, Thomas H.
Golf and the law: a practitioner's guide to the law and golf management / Thomas H. Sawyer.
p. cm.
Includes bibliographical references.
ISBN 0-89089-916-9
1. Golf—Law and legislation—United States. 2. Golf courses—United States—Management.

KF3989.S29 2001
796.352'06'9—dc21 00-050760

Carolina Academic Press
700 Kent Street
Durham, North Carolina 27701
Telephone (919) 489-7486
Fax (919) 493-5668
E-mail: cap@cap-press.com
www.cap-press.com

Printed in the United States of America.

Dedication

This book is dedicated to four very fine ladies who have influenced my way of thinking for years—Daughn, my mother and teacher; Kathi, my wife, companion, and partner for life; Meghan (Muffin), my daughter who has encouraged me to keep an open mind at all times; and Edie Godleski, a dear friend and colleague who never feared telling me what she thought and how I ought to do something... her thoughts have all been a breath of fresh air.

In Memory of...

"Sadie" Daly Sawyer II, a miniature Poodle Terrier, a wonderful and loving companion to the family for over ten years before her tragic death in the family swimming pool (November 1999); and Sargeant "Sarge" Montgomery Sawyer I, an AKC English Bull Dog, who in a short time became a wonderful companion who had won the hearts of every family member and then tragically drowned in the family pool at age two falling through the protective cover (February 2000).

Contents

Foreword

I remember my college days at Wake Forest University when a fellow student was setting records and making history in collegiate golf. These were the days of Arnold Palmer and his great rivalry with North Carolina's Harvey Ward. These were the days when there was little or no threat of expensive lawsuits in sport-related activities. These were the 1940s and '50s when people just didn't sue coaches, players, or schools. It just wasn't the thing to do. All this changed dramatically as damaging lawsuits entered the sport arena and multi-million dollar awards became the rule rather than the exception.

In the 1970s a popular TV sports reporter participated in the Greater Greensboro Open (GGO). At the pro-am, he sliced his drive off the tee and struck and injured a spectator. The woman filed a personal injury suit against the amateur golfer and the GGO. The reporter's attorney confidently predicted that the case would be dismissed because "anyone who plays golf or watches it on a golf course assumes the risk of injury and cannot hold anyone liable for injuries sustained in a golf environment." However, as Tom Sawyer found when he wrote *Golf and the Law*, there were hundreds of golf-related cases from 1962 to 1987. Since 1987 the number of cases has escalated as well as the enormous awards. Tom Sawyer reported cases in which injuries were caused by the following: golfers by other golfers, golfers in the same party and in another party, while taking instruction, golf carts, driving ranges, premises, club houses, non-golfers such as caddies, children, employees, spectators and residents adjacent to golf courses.

In *Golf and The Law*, Tom Sawyer, risk management expert, professor of recreation and sport management, author, renowned speaker and formerly an operator of a campus golf course, accepted the challenge to write about the law and golf management. His book exceeds the expectation of legal scholars for his attention to detail, thoroughness, accuracy and valuable information on law and how it relates to golf. The author, in essence, covers golf and the law from tee to green. Each chapter can stand alone and answer the many questions of the reader while offering solutions and strategies. In *Golf and The Law*, the author deals with discrimination, disabilities, contracts, employment practices, injuries, emergency action plans, lightning, risk management strategies and more.

Golf and The Law will become the definitive work in golf and legal issues. I commend and congratulate Tom Sawyer for accepting the challenge of such an important topic and feel confident that it will enhance the readers' understanding of the law and how it relates to golf.

Golf and The Law is a welcome addition to the series on sport law and sport management published by Carolina Academic Press. I recommend *Golf and The Law* to all who enjoy and love the game of golf.

Herb Appenzeller
Jefferson Pilot Professor of Sport
Management Emeritus, Guilford College

Preface

After serving as the golf course coordinator for Indiana State University's Stadium Golf Course for four years, it became abundantly clear there was a need for an operations guide relative to golf course liability for golf course managers. There was not a single day that went by that I did not have to concern myself with liability issues. Issues related to employees, passers-by, golfers, golf carts, golf cart maintenance, mowing equipment, chemical usage and storage, weather dangers, tree debris, cars hit by golf balls, houses hit by golf balls, and much more. I found two books on golf course liability that were helpful but I needed more. I decided that I would sit down and prepare a comprehensive golf course liability guide for golf course managers. The result of labor of love is this manuscript you are about to read.

I am sharing my experience as a former golf course manager and expertise as a sport law specialist to identify current issues confronting golf. The purpose of this book is to raise the risk and liability consciousness of the golf course manager, which will ultimately increase golf safety.

Those of you that are practicing golf course managers or superintendents know that golf-related litigation continues to grow rapidly. This will continue to be the case as long as golf course managers carelessly forget to do things that lead to personal injury and property damage or carelessly do things that cause damage, and employees, golfers, passers-by, and spectators are looking for a fast buck. Golf course managers or superintendents are human and make unintentional mistakes.

Golf and the Law: A Practitioner's Guide to the Law and Golf Management features a prologue, 11 chapters, and an epilogue. The prologue describes notable case law focusing on negligence issues. The first two chapters describe the foundations of law and the legal practitioner. The next chapter deals with defining negligence and a standard of care. Chapter 4 has a discussion centered on warnings and waivers. The next two chapters describe contracts and planning. Chapter 7 outlines safety concerns relative to severe weather conditions. The next chapter provides a discussion relating to employment issues, which has become a growing concern for employers. Chapter 9 talks about insurance issues related to golf course management. The tenth chapter describes what needs to done to a golf course to make it ADA compliant. The final chapter discusses a variety of OSHA issues and describes what should be done to comply with OSHA regulations. The epilogue focuses on risk management issues and golf course management. The appendices have been designed to provide some practical assistance to the golf course manager.

It is hoped that while you read this book, you will take the opportunity to evaluate the material and opinions of the author and the various courts, and compare these thoughts to current practices and policies. If, after reading this book, you decide to alter practices and policies to make your golf course safer and more golfer-friendly the book has been a success and the golf industry as a whole has become safer for millions of employees, golfers, passers-by, and spectators.

Thomas H. Sawyer

Acknowledgments

The author is indebted to Herb Appenzeller who was always there for support and encouragement during the development of the book. The author is also grateful to many undergraduate and graduate students over the years for providing valuable research assistance and in particular to Cathrine Tonner for her in depth research regarding negligence on the golf course. Further, I greatly appreciate the assistance of Michael G. Hypes for his research assistance and photographic expertise, my daughter-in-law Dani Sawyer who spent many an hour typing and re-typing the manuscript, and my wife, the 7th grade English teacher, for her editorial assistance.

This book would not have been possible without the foresight and encouragement of Herb Appenzeller. Herb has been, and continues to be, a leader in sport law and management. Our profession and my career have gained greatly because of Herb Appenzeller.

Finally, the author would be remiss if he did not mention the great support he received from his family Kathi, Shawn, Meghan, and Peter. They made the task easier and allowed me time away from them to complete the research and writing.

Thank You!

Thomas H. Sawyer, Ed.D.

Golf and the Law

Prologue

Golf Course Negligence

On average, people in American society spend as many waking hours at leisure as they do at work. Fewer households today have children in them, Americans are spending more of their lives unmarried, and people are retiring earlier and living longer after retirement. All of these conditions are positively related to the amount of leisure time one has.[1] With this increase in time, people tend to participate in sports and recreate more than before.

As the number of people who participate in sports grows more and more each year, so do the risks associated with these sports. Consequently, whether participation is for recreation or competition, the legal liability of these sports has long since been a concern for recreation and sport professionals alike.

The sport of golf is a popular choice for individuals looking to spend their increased free time. Golf is viewed as both a recreational and competitive sport, however, whatever the venue, the sport of golf has many more risks than the average recreation or sport professional may be aware of. These risks (e.g., personal injuries to the eyes, nose, face, head, legs, knees, ankles, as well as property damage to houses, cars, fences, satellite dishes, and windows), which often result in litigation, are costly in both time and money. What is most intriguing is that the litigation which golf courses and country clubs are often faced with can be avoided and prevented through sound risk management practices and programs. New golf courses are being built in the United States at the rate of more than one per day.[2] There are over 16,300 golf courses in the United States with another 1,069 courses under construction as of January 1, 1999.[3] The golf industry is booming. This rapid expansion, however, could be a problem since according to Floyd[4] each one is a complex business venture, which includes complex business-related problems. These problems typically include such things as real estate issues, employment matters, premises liability, discrimination, personal injury, and property damage as well as many other issues.

Golf used to be nothing more than a popular pastime. However, the golf industry today resembles a stand-alone business complete with its own legal issues. The golf industry will likely continue to grow as Baby Boomers age and retire.[5] With this increase in complexity on the business side, golfers, course managers, course designers, equipment manufacturers, and adjacent property owners need to pay close attention to risks that might be present that could lead to litigation.

1. Godbey, G.(1990). *Leisure in Your Life: An Exploration.* (3rd ed.) State College, PA: Venture Publishing Inc.
2. Floyd D.B. (1999). Bad shots and adjacent property owners. <www.golflaw.com>.
3. Id.
4. Id.
5. Id.

Of the areas identified, personal injury as the result of negligence, was the most profound area accounting for nearly 53% of all litigation concerning the sport of golf.[6] Other areas included concerns regarding taxes and taxation (17%), breach of contract (14%), discrimination issues (7%), nuisance (5%), and wrongful death suits (4%).[7] In addition there were a number of other areas, which would best be categorized as miscellaneous, including lien complaints, environmental protection, product liability, declaratory relief, property use, zoning, trademark infringement, as well as some employee-related issues such as wrongful termination and due process.

Negligence

A golf course environment is one of the most serene and spiritually relaxing experiences a person can enjoy. However, golf courses can also be dangerous to golfers, employees, and adjacent property users unless proper risk management practices are implemented. Some areas of potential risk include discrimination, errant golf balls, food and beverage concessions, general protection against environmental pests and varmints, golf carts, maintenance practices, steps and pavement, and wrongful death.[8] Keeping this in mind, legal claims involving golf-related injuries and damages are becoming almost a matter of course: Players sue other players, spectators sue players, and both players and homeowners sue golf course owners for a number of reasons.[9]

Player Injury Due to Errant Ball

One of the most prevalent areas in litigation concerning the sport of golf is personal injury as a result of negligence. Accounting for 53% of all litigation, it warrants attention.[10] The most commonly litigated situation occurs when a player hits a ball (unintentionally) and mistakes another player for the flag.[11] Airborne golf balls are a danger with which golf course personnel must pay close attention. Of all the cases researched, negligence concerning golf balls hitting players and spectators was the most frequent, comprising over 50% of all cases reviewed.[12]

Participants, spectators, and even employees have often been the unlucky recipient of a renegade golf ball, sometimes causing serious, if not fatal injuries. Generally, participants in sports, like golf, can only hold another player responsible for injuries that are intentionally, or in some cases, recklessly caused. Injuries that result from a merely accidental bad shot generally cannot be the basis for liability.[13]

---

6. Tonner, C., Sawyer, T.H., & Hypes, M.G. (1999). Golf litigation: A 25 year Review (1973-98). *Journal of the Legal Aspects of Sport*, *9*(3), 125.
7. Id.
8. Hurzan, M.J. (1990). Golf courses: Liability, luxury, or lifeline? *Journal of Parks and Recreation*, *25*(5).
9. Savell, L. (1998). Litigious links. *Golf Magazine*, *40*(2).
10. See Hurzan at 8.
11. Id.
12. Id.
13. Id.

Golfers (and, usually spectators) are viewed as having "assumed the risks" inherent in the sport, which includes the risk of being hit by an errant stroke. However, the rules and customs of the game must be followed. Therefore, if a golfer knows that another is in the line of flight of his or her shot and fails to yell the customary "Fore" the golfer might be liable (when such a warning would have made a difference).[14]

In some cases of player injury, it is alleged that a golfer neglected to warn players within the reasonable ambit of danger of his/her intent to tee off. In *Schmidt*,[15] a golf partner brought a negligence suit against a fellow golfer for injuries he sustained when he was hit in the eye by a golf ball. The court of appeals held that the defendant had no duty to issue an audible warning upon striking the ball, nor to protect a partner from injuries that might result from the ordinary and ever present risks of the sport of golf. Further, in *Bartlett*,[16] a golfer and his wife brought a negligence suit against a second golfer for injuries they sustained when they were hit by a ball struck by the second golfer. The court found that in a situation where a person is struck by a golf ball, the general rule is that a golfer is only required to exercise ordinary care for the safety of persons reasonably within the range of danger of being struck by the ball. If the golfer happens to drive a bad golf shot which causes injury to another this does not of itself, establish negligence.

However, a bad shot may constitute negligence in a situation where a golfer has a propensity to shank his golf shots. In a situation such as this, the golfer who has a habit of shanking his shots could reasonably foresee that this might happen, which therefore increases the ambit of danger to include the area where a shanked golf shot might be included. He then has a duty to warn any golfer that might be in that area of danger. In *Cook*[17], the plaintiff was struck in the eye with a golf ball hit by a member of his golfing foursome with an alleged propensity to shank his golf shot. In deciding this case, the court looked at whether a golfer with an alleged propensity to shank his golf shot owed a duty to warn a member of his golfing foursome about this problem and whether the shanker breached that duty. If the golfer knew of his propensity to shank his golf shots, he had a duty to warn those players around him. However, if the injured party also knew of this propensity and did not take precautions (e.g., ducking), his or her own lack of care might be used as a defense in a court of law.[18] As *Savell*[19] points out, the safest course of action is for players to announce their intention to hit the ball to those even remotely in the line of fire, and for those anywhere in range to keep in mind the navigational limitations of the human golfer.

Further, in *Cavin*,[20] a golf ball hit by another golfer struck a fellow golfer in a different foursome on a different green. The court of appeals decided that a golfer has no duty to give timely warning of their intention to strike a ball to any other persons within the foreseeable ambit of danger. There is generally no duty to warn persons, not in the intended line of flight of the shot, on another tee or fairway. If the golfer who was hitting the ball did not intend for the ball to travel over

14. Id.
15. *Schmidt v. Youngs*, 544 N.W. 2d. 743 (1996).
16. *Bartlett v. Chedubar*, 479 N.W. 2d. 321-323 (1992).
17. *Cook v. Johnston*, 688 P.2d. 215, 216 (1984).
18. See Hurzan at 9.
19. Id.
20. *Cavin v. Kasser*, 820 S.W.2d. 647, 650 (1991).

and into another fairway or green, then it is reasonable that he/she did not warn the players on that other fairway. Once again the court found in favor of the defendant following the general rule of thumb that a player cannot be held liable for anything more than a bad shot. The court followed this line of thought and found that the golfer did not breach any duty to a person on the tee or adjacent fairway, where the golfer and others yelled "fore" as soon as it was apparent that the drive was heading toward the other tee. In addition to this, the plaintiff in this case admitted that he had heard the warning before he was struck and did not pay attention to the warning. In *Jenks*,[21] a golfer was struck by a golf ball driven by another golfer who was on another tee 150 yards away. The court of appeals held that a golfer has a duty to give timely warning to other persons within the foreseeable ambit of danger; however, there is generally no duty to warn persons not in the intended line of flight of an intention to drive the ball. The defendant golfer teed-off while the plaintiff golfer was on another tee 150 yards away and about 25 yards from the intended line of flight. At the time the defendant was prepared to drive the ball, the plaintiff was behind a protective fence. Therefore, there was no duty on the part of the defendant golfer to yell "fore" prior to hitting the ball. Once again the court followed the general rule of thumb in holding that a golfer cannot be held liable for a shot that deviated from the intended line of flight. The court found that the mere fact that a golf ball does not travel the intended course does not establish negligence on the part of the defendant golfer.

There have been some instances where the courts have ruled against the general rule concerning a bad shot constituting negligence. In *Zurla*,[22] a golfer sued a fellow golfer for injuries received alleging that the defendant golfer negligently hit the golf ball which struck him as they played a round of golf. The appellate court found that golfing participants were not inherently, inevitably, or customarily struck by a golf ball. It was further upheld that golf was a contemplative and careful sport with emphasis placed on control and finesse rather than speed or raw strength, and that the physical dangers that existed were diminished by long standing traditions in which courtesy between players prevailed.

Spectator Injury Due to Errant Ball

Not only do players sue other players when a golf ball hits them, but spectators also have been known to bring negligence suits against players and course owners when they are the unfortunate recipients of a flying golf ball. In *Ludwikoski*,[23] a bystander who was sitting in a car in a driveway across the street from the golf course was hit in the face by a golf ball and consequently sued the golfer who hit the ball. The driveway was past the perimeter of the safety fence and a group of trees that were planted to prevent balls from leaving the course. In deciding this case, the court found in favor of the golfer reasoning that the mere fact that a golf ball driven by a person playing a game of golf strikes a person is not proof of negligence on the part of the golfer who hit the ball. A golfer is only required to exercise reasonable care for the safety of persons reasonably within the range of danger of being struck by a ball. Since the plaintiff was sitting in the car far outside

21. *Jenks v. McGranaghan*, 285 N.E. 2d. 876 (1973).
22. *Zurla v. Hydel*, 681 N.E. 2d. 148 (1997).
23. *Ludwikoski v. Kurotsu*, 875 F. Supp. 727 (1995).

the perimeter of the golf course, he was outside the foreseeable ambit of danger and was not entitled to a warning prior to the golfer's shot. Spectators and golfers alike have taken their concerns into the courtroom in the form of a lawsuit against the actual golf course, country club, or property on which the injury occurred, in some cases with success.

Similarly, in *Baker,*[24] a business invitee brought a negligence action against a country club and sponsor of a golf exhibition. The plaintiff was watching a featured golf celebrity search for a ball when a golf ball driven by another tournament player hit him. The plaintiff alleged that the country club and exhibition sponsor failed to take adequate precautions to prevent the invitee from being struck by a golf ball. The court held that the country club and sponsor of a golfing exhibition are required to use ordinary care to ensure that the premises are in reasonably safe condition for the invitee, guarding the invitee against all reasonably foreseeable dangers in light of the totality of the circumstances. It was reasonably foreseeable that the plaintiff and other spectators would focus their attention on the featured celebrity golfers, which would result in inattention to other golfers. The plaintiff was not warned that the other golfers were about to play their shots. Furthermore, the sponsor of the exhibition was not relieved of its nondelegable responsibility to make the premises of a country club reasonably safe for its invitees, where the sponsor: planned the exhibition, controlled admissions, collected admission price, and retained whatever profits were derived and had the right to use the golf course in order to invite the public to attend the event.

Lawsuits under this area of litigation usually involve negligent design, construction, maintenance, or operation. In *Knittle,*[25] the plaintiff was a spectator at an amateur golf tournament when he was struck by a golf ball and consequently filed a negligence suit against the golfer, the country club, the golf association, and the tournament sponsor. According to the court, a golfer has a duty to warn those persons within the foreseeable ambit of danger of his intention to strike the ball. However, one who is outside the zone of danger from a golf call or who is or should be aware of the impending shot is not entitled to a warning and if hit, cannot hold the golfer liable for failing to give any warning before making the shot. Since the plaintiff was in fact a spectator of the tournament, he should have been watching and therefore been aware that the defendant was going to strike the golf ball.

In *Duffy,*[26] a spectator claimed negligent construction by the country club and the golf association when she was struck in the eye with a golf ball while waiting in line at the concession stand. In deciding this case, the court reviewed why the plaintiff was on the property when the injury occurred. Since the plaintiff was purchasing something at the time she was injured, it was argued whether the spectator was a business invitee to whom the defendant owed a duty of care as owners and operators of the golf course or tournament. This seemed to be a defining factor in this case, since the owner of business premises has a duty to discover dangerous conditions existing on the premises and to give sufficient warnings to invitees to enable them to avoid harm. The defendant was considered to be negligent. In their defense the country club and golf association raised assumption of risk as a defense. However, the club and association had to prove that the spectator ap-

24. *Baker v. Mid Maine Medical Center*, 499 A.2d. 464 (1985).
25. *Knittle v. Miller*, 709 P.2d. 32, 34 (1985).
26. *Duffy v. Midlothian Country Club*, 415 N.E.2d. 1099, 1103 (1980).

preciated the danger of being struck by the golf ball while in the presumed area of safety at the concession stand at the golf course. It was reasonable for the spectator to assume that she was relatively safe from danger while waiting in line at the concession stand.

In a different approach, a spectator felt he had the right to sue based on where he stood as a spectator at a golf tournament.[27] In *Grisim*,[28] a spectator brought a personal injury action against golf tournament promoters, the country club, and an amateur golfer for injuries received from a flying golf ball. The courts held that the amateur golfer had no duty to shout a warning prior to teeing off. It was reasoned that the only duty owed to a spectator at a golf tournament was to provide reasonable opportunity to view the participants from a safe area. The amateur golfer playing in the tournament owed no duty to provide the spectator with a reasonably safe area for watching the tournament since he had no control over the arrangements for the spectators. It appears that the spectator in this case felt that the golfer who hit him with the golf ball was responsible for his standing where he was when he was hit. The court ruled in favor of the golfer, since he was not the one who decided where the spectators were going to stand during the tournament.

Swinging the Golf Club

The vast majority of the cases researched in this classification involved minors and their parents. Typically, the cases within this area involved the parents of one adolescent or minor bringing action against the parents of another child who was directly responsible for the injury of the first child. In *Mayer*,[29] the mother of the injured child brought action against the parents of another child to recover damages for injuries the first child suffered when the defendants' child struck her child with a golf club. The key to deciding this case hinged on whether the parents of the defendant child permitted their child to have access to the golf club and whether the parents should have anticipated injury to another through the child's use of the golf club. The court suggested that generally parents are not liable in damages for torts of their minor children merely because of the parent-child relationship. Likewise, in *Muse*,[30] the court held that a parent could not be held liable for injuries that resulted when a nine-year old child obtained a golf club from an unlocked storage building and in swinging the club, struck another child. Once again the court reasoned that where the injured party seeks to impose liability on a parent for the actions of a minor child, the facts of the case must impose on the parent a duty to anticipate injury to another through the child's use of the club. Furthermore, in *Poythress*,[31] action was brought against the parents of a sixteen-year-old for serious facial injuries that were sustained by a child who was struck by the head of a golf club. The injury occurred when the head of a golf club broke or slipped from the wooden shaft as it was used to hit a semi-deflated volleyball. Again the court decided that the parents of the sixteen-year-old knew nothing of

27. *Grisim v. Tapemark Charity Pro-AM Golf Tournament*, 415 N.W.2d. 874, 876 (1987).
28. Id.
29. *Mayer v. Self et al.*, 341 S.E.2d. 924 (1986).
30. *Muse et al. v. Ozment*, 264 S.E. 2d. 328 (1980).
31. *Poythress v. Walls et al.*, 259 S.E.2d. 177 (1979).

the golf club and that they had no reason to believe that the son would put the golf club to a reckless use. The court further found that the parents were not liable on the basis of negligent entrustment. The court took a slightly different approach in deciding the case of *Morrison*,[32] where a thirteen-year-old boy was struck in the head by a golf club which was swung by an eleven-year-old boy. The defendant in this case admitted to knowing at the time of the accident that a person should not swing a golf club when another is near. In addition to this, the defendant further admitted to not looking and not warning the plaintiff of his impending swing.

In *Thurston Metals and Supply Company Inc.*,[33] a golfer and his corporate employer were sued for the loss of an eye in a golfing accident. The verdict of this case hinged on whether the golfer exercised reasonable care toward a fellow golfer in rear when he performed a practice swing without a ball in place using as much velocity and gusto as he had employed when he was attempting to strike two previous shots. This caused the club, through the action of the wrist, to travel backward and strike the fellow golfer in the eye. In deciding this case, the courts looked at several different elements of the law: theaters and show, corporations, master servant, and insurance. However, the court found that a player on a golf course must exercise reasonable care in playing the game to prevent injury to others. The court held that an employer and its employees are deemed to be jointly liable and jointly suable for the employee's wrongful act.

Employee Negligence

Course operators may also be held responsible for injuries resulting from the acts of their employees. One court held an owner liable for the actions of a starter he hired to speed up play. The starter improperly directed a golfer to tee off while the plaintiff was only 125 yards away. Other cases have found operators liable for allowing courses to become overcrowded where such a situation resulted in injury.[34] Likewise, in *Tango*,[35] action was brought against a city and four city employees to recover for injuries which arose out of a tobogganing accident on a golf course. The courts ruled that where a municipality, through its agent or employee acts in the performance of a governmental duty, the municipality has limited immunity from liability. However, when the action complained of is a ministerial action, the municipality is responsible for its negligent execution. As was mentioned earlier, producing a risk free golf course environment is almost impossible, but controlling risks is not only possible, it must be a full time concern of everyone on the golf course, including the golfers themselves.[36]

There have been a handful of additional cases that have centered on the issue of alcohol. In *Ocotillowest*,[37] the surviving family members of the deceased brought a wrongful death suit against the golf course alleging that the sale of al-

32. *Morrison v. Sudduth*, 546 F.2d. 1231 (1977).

33. *Thurston Metals and Supply Company Inc. v. Taylor & Taylor v. Thurston Metals and Supply Company Inc.*, 339 S.E.2d. 538 (1986).

34. See Hurzan at 8.

35. *Tango v. The City of New Haven*, 377 A. 2d. 284 (1977).

36. See Hurzan at 8.

37. *Octotillowest v. Superior Court*, 844 P.2d. 653 (1993).

cohol was the cause of the fatal automobile accident. Two men were out playing a round of golf. Upon their return to the clubhouse, the employees of the golf course noticed that one of the two men was visibly intoxicated and proceeded to take his car keys from him. When the second man, who was clearly sober, intervened and offered to drive his partner home the employees returned the keys to the second individual. When the two men reached the parking lot, the second individual returned the keys back to his golfing partner and allowed him to drive home. On his way home, the intoxicated golfer was killed in a one-car accident. The court ruled that the second golfer had assumed the duty of a good Samaritan to use reasonable care for his drunk partner by offering to drive him home, and then placing him in a worse position by giving him his keys back and allowing him to drive away. The courts determined that the golf course was not liable, and that the second golfer could be a nonparty at fault.

Strategies for Reducing Risk

Injuries caused by golf balls or clubs are numerous and are often quite serious. The most common injuries are fractured skulls or the loss of eyes, but other serious injuries can occur. Golf balls leave the club head at a speed greater than the muzzle velocity of a 22 caliber rifle. It is easy to see, therefore, why they can do such great damage.

Golf is a recreational pursuit, and as such, many people are relaxed and visiting while they are engaged in the game. This adds to the likelihood of serious injury from golf balls or clubs. Those involved in golf need to make every effort to see that proper instruction is given to anyone, even a small child, in whose hands a golf club is placed. Golf course personnel also need to be constantly on the alert for dangerous situations.

For those of us who have played the game for years, we take certain acts of safety such as calling "fore" prior to striking the ball for granted. Those just beginning the game may not be aware of these customs nor of the danger from a swinging club or driven ball. A high priority of risk management must be prevention of injuries from golf balls or clubs.

As a general rule suits on behalf of persons injured from being struck by a golf ball or golf club on or near the golf course whether against another golfer, a course owner, a superintendent or a golf course architect, or even the parent of a minor have not been successful. The courts though often requested to do so by persons injured, have failed to find that golf is a nuisance and that an injury caused by a golf ball or club is a result of negligence on the part of the ball striker simply because another person is injured. They have also failed to find that golf course owners, operators or architects are strictly liable for injuries sustained on or near the golf course.

In fact, courts all across the United States have held all of these legal theories inapplicable to golf course injuries. Under certain fact situations, however, recovery has been allowed where the defendant was negligent in some manner.

Golf Carts

The courts have considered a golf cart in light of its relationship to the automobile. Operation of automobiles is controlled and regulated by statutes. In some instances, operation of golf carts is also regulated by state statutes, but these occur in a much less systematic manner and far less often than rules related to automobiles.

Golf carts can be sources of high-risk exposure unless thoughtful risk management practices are implemented. Some sources of risk concerning golf carts include: (1) improper design, construction, and/or maintenance of golf cart paths, bridges or tunnels, (2) inadequate maintenance or record keeping of periodic or specialized maintenance on the golf carts such as brakes, steering, tires, back-up buzzers, and drive trains, and (3) inappropriately renting a motor vehicle to an unlicensed driver, minor, or drinking driver or those untrained in cart operation.[38] Typically, in any litigation that surrounds golf carts, courts turn to the law as it pertains to automobiles. On the golf course, golf carts are considered automobiles and therefore are generally subject to the same laws that govern actual automobiles on public streets.

Negligence suits involving golf carts usually occur in one of three ways: (1) someone is injured when they are struck by a rolling or moving golf cart, (2) someone is injured when they fall-out of or tip-over in a rolling or moving golf cart, and (3) someone is injured when there is a collision between two or more golf carts. In *Utz*,[39] the plaintiff brought suit against a fellow employee to recover for damages for injuries which he sustained when he was struck by a motorized golf cart which was being driven by the defendant. Initially the two individuals were out playing a round of golf with a representative from one of their clients. During the course of the game, a golf cart that was being driven by the fellow employee struck the other individual. Due to the injuries, the employee had to file a claim under worker's compensation. After this was denied because it was not considered a work-related injury, the injured party brought suit against the employee who was driving the golf cart to recover for lost wages. The court ruled that where there was issue as to whether a negligence action could be maintained against a fellow employee or was barred by applicable statute. Subsequently it found in favor of the defendant. Further, in *Holst*,[40] a golfer filed a negligence action against a golf course for injuries he sustained when a golf cart fell on him from an upper level of the clubhouse and struck him in the head. The court once again found in favor of the defendant. The court determined that the golf cart was an instrumentality that caused the injury and not the entire clubhouse premises. Furthermore, the court felt that the plaintiff failed to identify the golf cart and thus failed to establish that the operator of the clubhouse had exclusive control and management of the golf cart.

While in *Monroe v. Grider* (1994), a golfer who was hit by a golf cart sued the driver for negligence, as well as the cart owner for negligent entrustment. The court rendered the second claim against the cart owner groundless for several reasons. The court indicated that in order to establish negligent entrustment, the plaintiff must show that the vehicle was entrusted by the owner to the incompetent driver and that the owner knew or should have known that the driver was unlicensed, incompetent or reckless, that the driver was negligent on the occasion in question, and that the driver's negligence proximately caused the accident. There must be knowledge of incompetence when giving consent to the use of a vehicle in order for there to be guilt of negligent entrustment. Finally, the cart owner's knowledge that the driver had been involved in other collisions did not

38. See Hurzan at 10.
39. *Utz v. Powell*, 288 S.E. 2d. 601 (1982).
40. *Holst v. Countryside Enterprises, Inc.*, 14 F.3d. 1319 (1994).

create an inference or conclusion of incompetence, particularly where the record showed that the drivers previous collision occurred in an intentional attempt to prevent another cart from rolling over. For these reasons, the court ruled the second claim as groundless; however, with respect to the first part of the claim, the court ruled in part in favor for the plaintiff. Almost every golf course has some area not safe for the use of golf carts.[41] Things such as insufficient signage and directions, poor traveling surfaces for the carts, inadequate pathways, and landscape in general terms of hills and valleys that all pose subtle risks for golfers. With this is mind, another manner in which a golf cart creates a risk for owners and operators of golf courses is when a person is injured when he/she falls out of a cart. In *American Golf Corporation,*[42] a golf course patron and his wife sued a golf course operator for injuries they sustained when the golf cart they were riding in crashed at a hairpin turn on the cart path. The path of the golf cart proceeded down a steep hill and then made a sharp turn in a hairpin fashion. The turn was not marked and the plaintiff could not see the turn from the cart and cart pathway. Prior to this accident, there were two prior accidents at the same location and were extremely similar to the plaintiff's accidents. Based on this, the court found that the operator had superior knowledge of the dangerous condition at the accident site and was negligent in failing to warn invitees about it. The court reasoned that since there were in fact two prior accidents at the same location on the golf course, the operator should have been alerted to the dangerous condition of the path and taken adequate measures to bring attention to the risk. Further, in *Ryan,*[43] a golf cart driver brought a negligence suit action against the owner of a golf course to recover for injuries he sustained when the golf cart he was riding in over turned. The court found in favor of the plaintiff stating that there were no guardrails or warning signs to advise cart users of the uneven nature of the golf cart path.

There are problems with accidents and collisions between golf carts on the golf course. In *Del E. Webb Cactus Development,*[44] a passenger in a golf cart was injured and brought action against the driver of the golf cart and the owner and operator of the golf course. The golf course on which the plaintiff was playing required that all persons playing golf use a golf cart and therefore included a fee for the golf cart, in the greens fee that was charged to all players. On the course the golf carts were required to cross a public highway in order to get from one part of the course to the other. In deciding the verdict, the court ruled that the rented vehicle liability insurance statute applied to golf carts operated on a golf course traversed by a public highway, and that noncompliance with the statute imposed joint and several liability upon the owner of the course. Under this section of law, the owner of the motor vehicle who rents it to another party without having procured public liability insurance is jointly and severally liable, with the renter, for damage caused by the renter's negligence in operating the motor vehicle.

Course owner and operators also need to make sure that golf carts are properly kept and maintained to ensure safe operation. Inadequate maintenance or record

41. See Hurzan at 10.

42. *American Golf Corporation v. Manly v American Golf Corporation*, 473 S.E.2d. 161 (1996).

43. *Ryan v .Mill River Country Club, Inc.*, 510 A.2d. 462 (1986).

44. *Del E. Webb Cactus Development v. Jessup*, 863 P.2d. 260 (1993).

keeping of periodic or specialized maintenance of such items as brakes, steering, tires, back-up buzzers or drive trains can create risks for the owner or operator of a golf course. For example, in *Montes,*[45] a patron of a public golf course was allegedly injured by a negligently maintained golf cart and subsequently brought action against the parks and recreation district which owned and operated the golf course. It was ruled that the golf cart was not a "facility" within the meaning of the statute waiving immunity conferred by Governmental Immunity Act in actions for injuries resulting from a dangerous condition of public facility located in a recreation area maintained by a public entity.

Manufacturers and lessors of motorized golf carts have also found themselves in court dealing with negligence suits. In *Cavers,*[46] an action was brought against the manufacturer and lessor of a motorized golf cart when someone was injured while riding in the cart. It was ultimately found that the defendants failed to warn the plaintiff of the cart's propensity to tip while turning, and that the absence of such a warning rendered the product substantially dangerous to the user. In deciding this case the court determined that an otherwise faultlessly made article may be deemed defective if the manufacturer/lessor fails to warn users of dangerous propensities which in absence of adequate warning render the article dangerous.

Injuries to the Non-Golfer

The rules with regard to injuries caused to members of the general public (non-golfer) as opposed to other golfers, caddies, employees, and spectators are slightly different. Other golfers, caddies, employees, and spectators are saddled with the responsibility of knowing the rules of golf and the inherent dangers of participating in the sport. Members of the public generally are not. Persons on a golf course can be divided into four categories: A business invitee, a member or paying customer, who is owed the greatest level of duty for the golf organization; an invitee, a person who is invited to the facility but not required to pay, is owed a high level of duty but not as high as the business invitee; the licensee is a party who has leased the facility for a period of time, the golf organization needs to make sure the facility is safe and the leasee has appropriate and adequate insurance; and a trespasser to whom there is theoretically no duty of care, except the organization needs to protect its facilities from children since golf courses and swimming pools are considered "attractive nuisances."

45. *Montes v. Hyland Hills Park*, 849 P.2d. 852 (1993).
46. *Cavers v. Cushman Motor Sales, Inc.*, 157 Cal.Rptr. 142 (1979).

A Final Word . . .

According to Tonner, et al.,[47] the following is a listing of risk management tips developed based on the case law found over the past 25 years (1973-98) regarding negligence and golf litigation:

> "Golfers are viewed as having "assumed the risks" inherent in golf, which includes the risk of being hit by an errant ball.
>
> The rules and customs of golf must be followed (e.g., yelling the customary "fore" when another golfer is in the line of flight of the shot).
>
> Courts have held that a golfer has no duty to issue an audible warning upon striking the ball, nor protect a partner from injuries that might result from injuries that might result from the ordinary and ever present risks of golf.
>
> Further, the courts have established the following as a general rule: a golfer is only required to exercise ordinary care for the safety of persons reasonably within the range of danger of being struck by the ball.
>
> However, a bad shot may constitute negligence in a situation where a golfer has the propensity to shank his/her golf shot.
>
> Yet, courts have established another general rule of thumb that indicates a player cannot be held liable for anything more than a bad shot when the ball deviated from the intended line of flight.
>
> There is generally no duty to warn persons not in the intended line of flight of the shot on another tee or fairway.
>
> Golfers are only required to exercise reasonable care for the safety of persons reasonably within the range of danger of being struck by the ball.
>
> Golf course management is required to use ordinary care to ensure that the premises are in reasonably safe conditions for the spectator (business invitee), guarding the invitee against all reasonably foreseeable dangers in the light of the totality of the circumstances.
>
> Golf course operators have a duty to discover dangerous conditions existing on the premises and to give sufficient warning to invitees to enable them to avoid harm.
>
> Courts have found that the only duty owed to a spectator at a golf tournament is to provide reasonable opportunity to view the participants from a safe area.
>
> Negligence is often determined by what kind of relationship existed between the plaintiff and the defendant. The business relationship that exists between a golf facility and the people on or around the premises imposes a legal obligation on the part of the facility operator to do whatever is appropriate to provide for a reasonably safe environment. It is not required that

---

47. See Tonner at 6, 136.

every conceivable preventive measure or precaution be taken. It is only what the reasonable businessperson would do under similar circumstances that dictates what is required. What are the other golf courses doing in the area?

The courts, as a general rule, suggest that if the golf course operator chooses to utilize a particular safety feature, the operator owes a duty of reasonable care to patrons to use it correctly (e.g., if the operator decides to construct shelters for players to seek refuge from inclement weather, he/she must build lightning proof shelters; if the operator has an evacuation plan, he/she must post where members can see and understand the plan.

Golf course operators need to understand the risks that golf carts pose including: (1) improper design, construction, and/or maintenance of golf cart paths, bridges or tunnels, (2) inadequate maintenance or record keeping of periodic or specialized maintenance on the golf carts such as brakes, steering, tires, back-up buzzers, and drive trains, and (3) inappropriately renting a motor vehicle to an unlicensed driver, minor, or drinking driver or those untrained in cart operation. Typically, in any litigation that surrounds golf carts, courts turn to the law as it pertains to automobiles. On the golf course, golf carts are considered automobiles and therefore are generally subject to the same laws that govern actual automobiles on public streets.

Negligence suits involving golf carts usually occur in one of three ways: (1) someone is injured when they are struck by a rolling or moving golf cart, (2) someone is injured when they fall-out of or tip-over in a rolling or moving golf cart, and (3) someone is injured when there is a collision between two or more golf carts.

Almost every golf course has some area not safe for the use of golf carts. Things such as insufficient signage and directions, poor traveling surfaces for the carts, inadequate pathways, and the landscape in general in terms of hills and valleys all pose subtle risks for golfers. With this is mind, another manner in which a golf cart creates a risk for owners and operators of golf courses is when a person is injured when they fall out of a cart.

The courts have held that the owner of the motor vehicle (i.e., a golf cart) who rents it to another party without having procured public liability insurance is jointly and severally liable, with the renter, for damage cause by the renter's negligence in operating the motor vehicle.

Course owner and operators also need to make sure that golf carts are properly kept and maintained to ensure safe operation. Inadequate maintenance or record keeping of periodic or specialized maintenance of such items as brakes, steering, tires, back-up buzzers or drive trains can create risks for the owner or operator of a golf course.

Courts have reasoned that a public entity might be found to have been engaged in willful and wanton conduct, so as to be liable for injuries resulting from a dangerous condition on recreational property. This is the case only, if the district has been informed of the dangerous condition, knows others who have been injured because of the condition, or intentionally removes a safety device or feature from the property.

Generally, the courts have ruled, that the owner is only responsible for dangers of which only the owner is aware. The operator need not protect players from dangers that are either known to the players or are so obvious that the players should have been aware of and protected themselves from them. Producing a risk free golf course environment is almost impossible. One area that should be of a concern for owners, deals with slip, fall and trip accidents, which accounts for nearly 75% of all accidents occurring on a golf course." (136)

There are two specific types of rights by which golf balls can become a nuisance—public and private. When there is interference of a public right such things as public highways, sidewalks or other public thoroughfares are affected. Private rights refer to private homes and properties.

"When the interference of the golf course affects a public right such as danger to the highway, sidewalk or other public thoroughfare, it is often dealt with as a public nuisance. A large number of cases have involved dangers to an adjacent public highway. Once the highway or roadway has been established, the public's right of passage carries with it an obligation upon the occupiers of abutting land to use reasonable care to see that the roadway remains safe. Golf course operators will likely be found liable for any unreasonable risk to people who are on the public thoroughfare lawfully and must exercise due care for their safety.

Do motorists who deliberately decide to drive on a public highway or thoroughfare adjoining a golf course accept the occasional, concomitant annoyances such as an errant shot which may shatter windshields and possibly injure the driver or passenger? The courts have held that the golfer owed no duty to warn the person of the impending tee shot. Even if a duty was owed, their failure to warn the individual was not the proximate cause of the person's injuries as a matter of law. There would be only a remote possibility that the person would have heard or been able to respond to the warning had one been given.

The situation involving homeowners or residents adjoining a golf course is somewhat different. Decisions of the courts in the past have upheld the defense of "assumption of risk" where the adjacent property owner built or purchased his home subsequent to the construction of the golf course. If the golf course was there first, it should have been known that errant golf balls could accidentally land on the property. If however, homeowners around a course have the use and enjoyment of their land impaired by flying golf balls, they would probably have to rely on a theory of nuisance to recover . This would be the case if the problem was acute and the frequency of golf balls landing in the yard of the property owner was frequent enough to cause material annoyance or discomfort . Depending on the circumstances, if the adjacent property is an apartment building or condominium, liability may be divided between the owner of the course and the owner of the property.

Sometimes the courts will give consideration to the problem of "coming to a nuisance." This is when a plaintiff builds or buys a home near an existing golf course. It would seem that if he is allowed to recover for damages then the court would be giving the plaintiff a windfall gain at the expense of the defendant. If the course were already in existence then the plaintiff made a conscious choice to build in that location after taking into account the possibility of errant golf balls landing on his property during the course of play. He should not be allowed to purchase the property with an eye to also buy a cause of action against his neighbors . If however a natural barrier that was in place to act as a buffer zone between the two properties was for some reason removed (e.g., storm or diseased trees) the frequency and risk of injury from golf balls is increased dramatically the courts look at this situation differently. If this were the case, the courts would not prevent the person from recovering for damages since the annoyance has been increased by reason of change . Regardless of the situation, it is essential that the interests of adjoining property owners or occupiers and users be taken into account. Owners and operators of golf courses must become and remain conscious of this problem and take effective risk management steps to avoid litigious situations concerning adjacent property owners.

Golf course operators need to clearly understand contracts—the laws that support a contract, remedies for breach of contract, and how to develop a contract. No contract should be entered into unless first reviewed by an attorney.[48]" (137)

48. Id, 137.

Chapter 1

The Foundations of Law

Blackstone, the English jurist whose famous Commentaries influenced the development of the Anglo-American law, firmly believed that "a competent knowledge of the laws of one's country is the proper accomplishment of every gentleman and scholar, and is almost an essential part of a liberal education." However, two hundred years later finds the average American, who is knowledgeable in many areas, generally uninformed in regard to the legal system which profoundly affects her or his everyday life.

The legal system interacts with and influences the political, economic and social system of every civilized society. When society operates peacefully, efficiently and prosperously, its legal system is a primary cause. When a society appears to break down, it may be the result of the abuse, corruption or malfunction of its legal system requiring change or improvement, but the fact remains that every civilized society is founded upon law and none has ever survived without law or without an efficient legal system. Hence, the beginning of all progress and improvement in any society must be based upon a thorough and complete knowledge of its law and the system which the totality of its laws comprises.

The Law

Western civilization developed two systems of law under which most of the civilized world now lives. The Roman or Civil Law system is the older of the two and is found in all of the Continental European countries and in those areas which were colonized or controlled by the nations of Continental Europe. The younger system is the English or Common Law system which is followed by all of the English-speaking countries of the world and by the countries colonized or controlled by them. The American legal system has functionally developed from the English common law, which, in turn, has roots in Roman law.

Law is "that which is laid down, ordained, or established....in its generic sense, law is a body of rules of action or conduct prescribed by controlling authority, and having binding legal force. That which must be obeyed and followed by citizens subject to sanctions or legal consequences is a law. Law is a solemn expression of the will of the supreme power of the State."[1]

1. Black's Law Dictionary, 1990, 884.

Civil Law

This is a legislative system based on written codes or statutes coming down through generations from the compilation of Justinian and his successors comprising the Institutes, Code, Digest and Novels, and collectively denominated the "Corpus Juris Civilis". The rules change, but the fundamental legal principles remain fairly continuous. There is little lawmaking for judges in this system. Their main function is to apply the proper code provision to the factual situation has come before the court. This is a system of "written law" as compared to law made by court decisions.

Common Law

The common law originated in England's feudal society. The history of the common law of England is the history of the expansion of royal justice, administered by courts of the king, at the expense of the local judicial bodies, the manorial courts which had adjudicated controversies. This transition was encouraged and abetted by the advantages that litigants had in the king's court, including trial by jury.

This was judge-made law or case law. It is referred to as the "unwritten law" although voluminously recorded and in great part published in statutory or code form in subsequent years. In order to provide continuity to this system, the judges imposed on themselves an unwritten rule called "*star decisis*", which means to stand by decided cases. For example, a case would be tried before a judge involving a legal problem which had never been decided upon before. The judge's decision was called a "precedent" or an original rule of law. In later cases involving the same problem, other judges would follow the same rule whether or not they agreed with it. The result was that the precedent became the law. It was called the common law since it was applied to all persons and was, therefore, a law common to all people. The doctrine of "*stare decisis*" is not, however, completely rigid. There are certain elements of elasticity that keep the common law changing. For example, the reason for the original decision may have changed so that the judge would not be bound to follow the decision. The factual situation before the judge might be different than the one in the original case so that the judge would not follow have to follow the same rule. Finally, the later judge might feel that the original decision was wrong and so he refuses to follow it. The result of these later decisions is the making of new and conflicting law which creates a certain amount of confusion until a higher court decides which ruling is better and hence "the law".

The common law developed in three basic areas: (1) crimes, wrongs committed against the state or against society as a whole; (2) torts, wrongs committed against an individual's inherent interests which the state protects against infringement by any other person; and (3) contracts, individual rights created by agreement and consent of the contracting parties.

Equity

The common law judges had limited authority to grant relief. They could only award money damages or restoration of property. If a person wanted to enjoin another from doing a certain act, such as a nuisance, or he wanted the other party to contract specifically to perform that contract, he had to go to the king for relief. The king, of course, had the power to grant specific performance or enjoin a nuisance. This relief was known as a dispensation of equity or equitable relief. However, the king did not have time to handle all of the cases presented to him so he appointed a high churchman as his agent to conduct these cases. This man was called a Chancellor, and the court he presided over was called the Court of Chancery. Soon the cases became so numerous that there rose from the Court of Chancery the courts of equity to handle all cases where the relief in the common law courts was inadequate. Thus there grew up, side by side, the two systems, the common law courts and the courts of equity. The common law courts gave relief in the form of money or restoration of property, and the equity courts gave relief in the areas of specific performance, injunction, rescission, and relief from forfeiture. In most states in the United States, however, the distinction between law and equity courts has been abolished which means that one court can administer both types of relief.

Sources of Law

The sources which contribute to the development of a legal system, and particularly to the American legal system, are formalized in three principal ways and appear as the immediate sources of law, namely, Federal and state constitutional law, legislation or statutory law or ordinances of countless local municipal governments and the rules and regulations of Federal and state administrative agencies, and an increasing volume of reported court decisions or case law and precedents established by prior decisions of courts.

Constitutional Law

Underlying all the law in the United States, whether case law or statutory law, is the Federal constitution, which is the supreme law of the land. No law, Federal or state, is valid if it violates the Federal constitution. The final arbiter as the constitutionality is the Supreme Court of the United States.

The first ten amendments of the constitution is the "Bill of Rights." The Bill of Rights is not a grant of privileges handed down to them by the government, but rather it is a curb and a restriction laid upon the government by the people. The first eight amendments described the specific individual freedoms which government cannot infringe. The ninth and tenth amendments provide further checks. These two amendments retained for the people of the States jurisdiction over those matters not specifically granted to the Federal government by the Constitution nor restricted by it to the States.

First Amendment. This amendment declares that Congress shall make no law respecting an establishment of religion, or prohibiting its free exercise, or abridging the freedom of speech, or of the press, or the right of the people peaceably to assemble, and to petition the government for a redress of grievances.

Second Amendment. It affirms the right of people to bear arms, stating that this right shall not be infringed.

Third Amendment. It provides that no soldier shall, in time of peace be quartered in any house, without the owner's consent, nor in time of war except in a manner prescribed by law.

Fourth Amendment. It guarantees the right of the people to be secure in their persons, houses, papers, and effects, against unreasonable searches and seizures, and that no warrants shall issue, except upon probable cause, supported by oath, and particularly describing the place to be searched, and the persons or things to be seized. It is only unreasonable searches and seizures that are proscribed.

Fifth Amendment. No person, the fifth amendment ordains, shall be held to answer for a capital or otherwise infamous crime, unless on a presentment or indictment of a grand jury. Further, it provides no person shall be subject for the same offense to be twice put in jeopardy of life or limb; nor shall be compelled in any criminal case to be a witness against himself, nor be deprived of life, liberty, or property, without due process of law; nor shall private property be taken for public use, without just compensation.

Sixth Amendment. It guarantees that in all criminal prosecutions, the accused shall enjoy the right to a speedy trial, by an impartial jury of the State and district wherein the crime shall have been committed, and be informed of the nature and cause of the accusation. Further, it provides that the accused shall enjoy the right to be confronted with the witnesses against him or her, and to have the assistance of counsel for his defense.

Seventh Amendment. It provides that in actions at common law, where the value in controversy is in excess of twenty dollars, the right of trial by jury shall be preserved, and that no fact tried by a jury shall be otherwise re-examined in any court of the United States than according to the rules of the common law.

Eighth Amendment. It prescribes that excessive bail shall not be required, nor excessive fines imposed, nor cruel and unusual punishment inflicted.

Finally, the Constitution states "The judicial power shall extend to all cases, in law and equity, arising under this Constitution, the laws of the United States, and treaties made, or which shall be made, under their authority."

Legislation

Whereas case law evolves from the judicial determination of particular controversies, statutory law is the product of a legislative body and, in general, operates only prospectively. The legislative body can be either Federal, state, county, or city. And finally, the many rules and regulations developed to administer statutes by Federal and state administrative agencies.

Classification of Law

There are five classifications of law—substantive law and procedural law, public law and private law, tort law, criminal law, and administrative law.

Substantive Law and Procedural Law. Substantive law includes laws which create, define and regulate legal rights and obligations. For example, the rule in contracts that an offer must be communicated to the offeree is a statement of substantive law. Procedural law or adjective law, also called remedial law, prescribes the methods of enforcing rights which exist by reason of the substantive law. Remedial law is found in codes of procedure to ascertain the method by which he is to obtain redress in court. In law school substantive law courses focus on contracts, torts, property, and agency; whereas adjective courses deal with civil, criminal, and administrative procedure and evidence.

Public Law and Private Law. Public law is that branch of law which deals with the rights and powers of the state, in its political or sovereign capacity and its relations to individuals or groups. It comprises constitutional, administrative, and criminal law. Private law is that which governs private individuals in their relations with one another, or law which is administered between citizen and citizen. Business law is primarily private law.

Tort Law. A tort is a wrong consisting of the violation of a right not created by contract for which the courts will provide a remedy. It is infringement by one person of an inherent right that another person enjoys as against the entire world.

Criminal Law. A crime is any act or omission prohibited by public law in the interest of protection of the public and made punishable by the state in a judicial proceeding brought by it. Crimes are prohibited and punished upon the ground of public policy, which may include the protection and safeguarding of government (as in treason), human life (as in murder), private property (as in larceny), or institutions and interests.

Crimes are classified as felony, misdemeanor, or petty crime. Felonies are arson, rape, robbery (stealing from a person by force or intimidation), burglary (entering any building for the purpose of committing a felony), mayhem (disfigurement), grand larceny (theft of goods above certain stated value), and inexcusable homicides (murder, voluntary manslaughter, involuntary manslaughter). Misdemeanors include assault, battery, false imprisonment, and criminal libel. Finally, petty crimes are theft of goods below a stated value.

Administrative Law. This branch of public law deals with various functions and activities of the government in its executive capacity as performed, supervised, and regulated by public officials, departments, and boards and commissions, and with controversies arising in connection between individuals and such public officials and agencies. Administrative functions and activities concern such important matters of national safety, welfare, and convenience, as the establishment and maintenance of military forces, police, citizenship and naturalization, coinage of money, highways and watercourses, elections, environmental protection, and public health, safety, and welfare.

Court Systems

The judicial system is composed of Federal and state courts.

The Federal Courts

The Constitution created the Supreme Court and authorized such inferior courts as Congress may from time to time establish. Congress, pursuant to this authority, has established eleven United States Courts of Appeal, the United States

Chart 1.1
Federal Court System

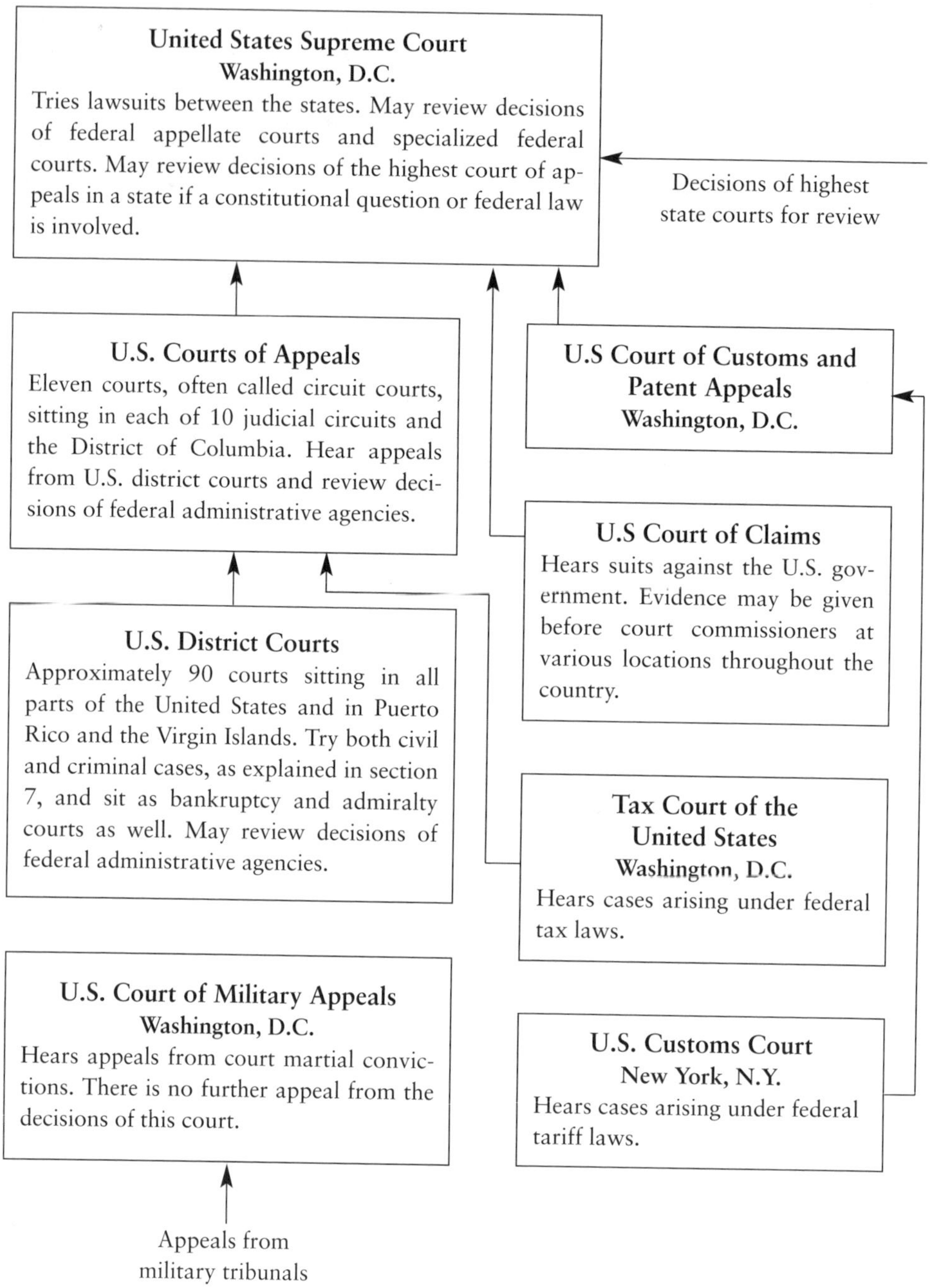

Source: ______ (1997). You and the Law. Pleasantville, NY: Reader's Digest, 31.

District Courts of which there is at least one in each state, and others such as the Court of Tax Appeals, the Court of Customs and Patents Appeals, and the Court of Claims (See Chart 1.1).

District courts are courts of original jurisdiction or tail courts. The Court of Appeals are review courts and are courts to which an appeal may be taken from the District Courts. A Court of Appeal will review the case tried in the District Court and will either affirm, reverse, or modify the judgement of the trial court. From the Courts of Appeal, the case may then be appealed to the United States Supreme Court which has the final word on the legal problems involved.

The State Courts

Most states follow the basic federal system and have trial courts of original jurisdiction, intermediate appellate courts and the highest court of the state as the one of final appeal (see Chart 1.2). At the lowest level is a series of courts with very limited jurisdiction or power. Their names differ, the name usually conveying a good idea of the specific function of the court.

Arbitration

Arbitration is a procedure by which a dispute is brought before one or more arbitrators who make a decision which the parties may agree to accept as final. It is encouraged as a means of avoiding expensive and timely litigation, and relieving congestion and delay in the courts. Generally speaking, virtually every state has some kind of arbitration statute. Information regarding the rules of arbitration and wording of arbitration clauses to be used in a contract can be obtained from the American Arbitration Association which is a private, non-profit organization founded in 1926 to foster the study of arbitration and to perfect the techniques of this method of settling disputes.

Standing to Sue Doctrine

Standing to sue means that a party or parties have sufficient stake in an otherwise justiciable controversy to obtain judicial resolution of that controversy. Standing is a concept utilized to determine if a party or parties is sufficiently affected so as to insure that a justiciable controversy is presented to the court. It is the right to take the initial step that frames legal issues for ultimate adjudication by court or jury. The requirement of "standing" is satisfied if it can be said that the plaintiff has a legally protectible and tangible interest at stake in the litigation. Standing is jurisdictional issue which concerns power of federal courts to hear and decide cases and does not concern ultimate merits of substantive claims involved in the action.

Burden of Proof

In the law of evidence, the necessity or duty of affirmatively proving a fact or facts in dispute on an issue raised between the parties in a cause. The obligation

Chart 1.2
State Court System

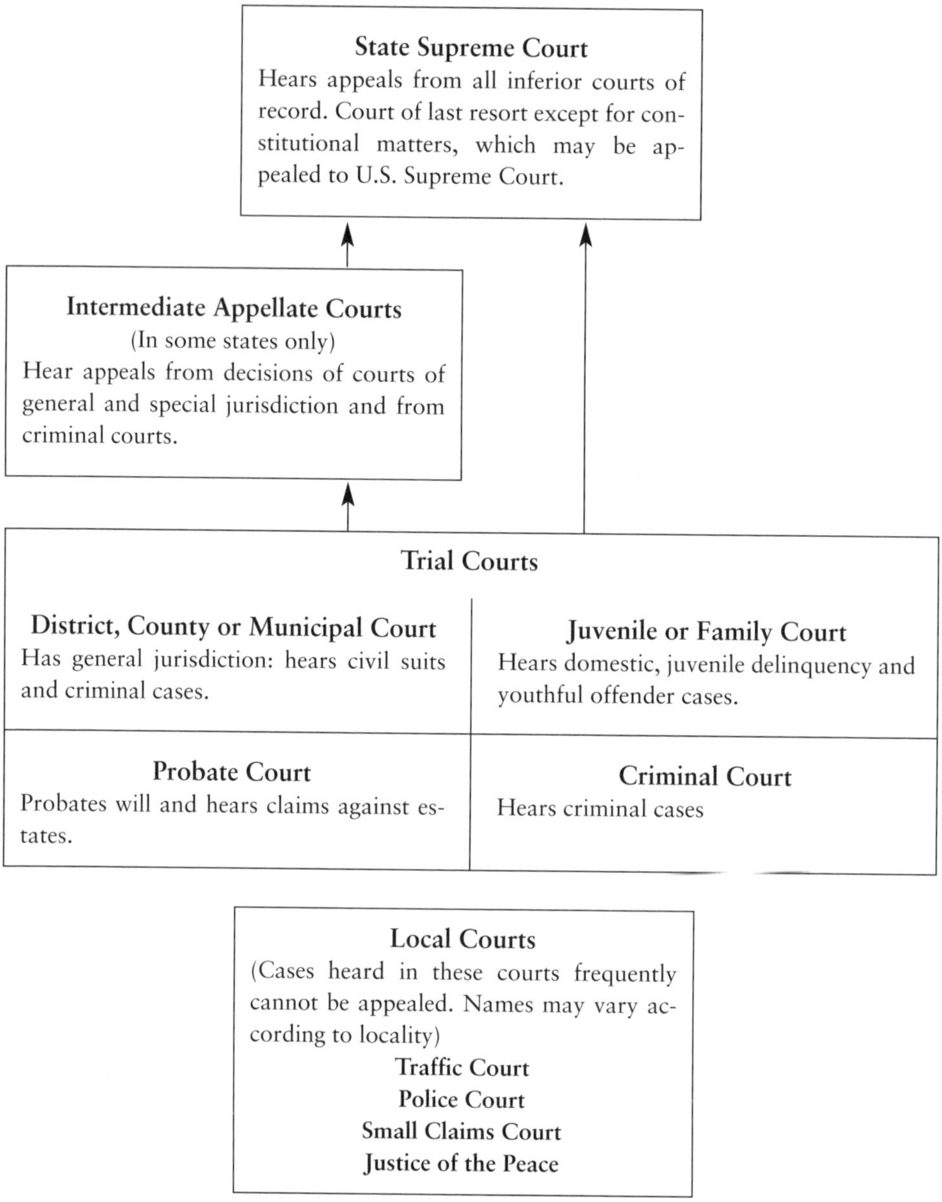

Source: ______ (1997). You and the Law. Pleasantville, NY: Reader's Digest, 33.

of a party to establish by evidence a requisite degree of belief concerning a fact in the mind of the court. The burden of proof is a term which describes two different concepts—burden of persuasion (never shifts from one party to the other at any stage of the proceeding), and burden of going forward with the evidence (which may shift back and forth between the parties as the trial progresses).

The burden of proof may require a party to raise a reasonable doubt concerning the existence, or nonexistence of a fact or that he establish the existence or nonexistence of a fact by a preponderance of the evidence, by clear and convincing proof, or by proof beyond a reasonable doubt.

A Final Word . . .

The American Legal system has been designed over the years to treat everyone fairly and equally before the bar. Laws are designed to protect the citizenry as well as those who provide services to the citizens. We all need to know what our rights are as well as how important those rights are to us and society as a whole. The golf manager needs to understand the various laws that protect the participants, employees, and spectators. The more the golf manager knows about the law and the rights of others the better he/she will be able to protect the golf industry as a whole. Knowledge is power. The more knowledge one has the greater the power base. Legal knowledge in the 21st century will become increasingly important for golf managers and their overall success.

Chapter 2

The Lawyer

Throughout this book a discussion will focus on many of the points of law you may encounter in the management of a golf course. In many cases it will be pointed out that the advice and assistance of a lawyer are either desirable or necessary. This chapter will describe a little about lawyers.

Unfortunately, for reasons discussed below, some people are vaguely distrustful of lawyers and are reluctant to seek out legal advice when they need it. This is unfortunate, because a lawyer can be a real friend in need. S/he is a specially trained person whose purpose in life is to serve her or his clients and the community in which s/he lives and to give you the best advice s/he can about some of the most complex problems of modern life. By describing what the lawyer does, it is hoped to make it easier for you to see her or him as a human being whom you can confide in and trust and who may be of enormous help to you in ordinary transactions and in time of trouble.

Historical Role of the Lawyer

Lawyers are involved in so many vital aspects of modern American life that it is easy to forget that they once were very much on the outside. The early colonists, especially in New England, were strongly opposed to lawyers. The colonists believed each man should be able to assert and protect his individual rights, and because all the early settlers were—or thought they were—like-minded, having left England for the same reasons, they did not expect any conflicts to arise among themselves or between them and the colonial governments that would require the help of lawyers to resolve.

Human nature being what it is, however, the colonists soon learned that they had to establish a method of handling disputes between individuals as well as a method of reviewing and prescribing punishment for the commission of crime and violations of governmental orders. Courts were established in the colonies well before there were lawyers to appear before them.

The conscious effort to conduct a system of courts without lawyers was unsuccessful. The judges found that issues were not being clearly framed, that the people appearing before them were unable to assert their rights effectively. It was not long, therefore, before individual courts began authorizing men well read in government and law to appear in the courts to represent other persons not so well educated. In the middle Atlantic and southern colonies sons of wealthier colonists went to England, studied law in the English Inns of Court (which compare loosely to our law schools) and returned to America to become lawyers and practice law.

Because the very nature of their legal studies (even the informal sort that long prevailed in New England gave the lawyers an understanding of governmental operations and society in general that most of the colonists lacked, the lawyers moved into positions of influence in the colonial governments and took prominent parts in the movements and organizations that led to the establishment of a new nation—the United States. Thomas Jefferson made an observation that is perhaps even more apt today than it was at the end of the eighteenth century: the legal profession is the "nursery of the legislature."

So, by the time of the adoption of the United States Constitution, lawyers had become an essential part of the government of our country. It took somewhat longer for them to win acceptance in the states, such as Massachusetts, which had traditionally distrusted them. But during the early 1800s the legal profession took shape pretty much as it is today. Lawyers are called different things in different parts of the country, but the verbal distinctions mean little.

Kinds of Lawyers

Attorney-at-law is perhaps the most common term for a lawyer. As distinguished from an attorney-in-fact, who is authorized to act for another person in a specific situation (for example, the person to whom you give a power of attorney to sign a contract in your absence), an attorney-at-law represents you in lawsuits and other legal matters. Counselor-at-law means the same thing as attorney-at-law: a person trained and qualified to give you counsel or advice on legal matters (see Figure 2.1).

A trial lawyer is a lawyer who tries cases in court. In the United States, all lawyers are presumed qualified to try cases in court and before various administrative agencies. But in England a trial lawyer, called a barrister, is sharply distinguished from a lawyer called a solicitor, who may not appear in court. The British barrister is prohibited from seeking or even having his own clients; all his cases are referred to him by a solicitor. The solicitor "briefs" the barrister on what the case is all about, frequently just a short time before the case comes up in court. The barrister handles all aspects of the court proceeding, including the appeal if one is indicated, and then bows out while the solicitor takes over again.

This British line between barrister and solicitor exists in fact in parts of the American legal profession: Hundreds of our lawyers, perhaps the most influential ones, seldom if ever appear in court. They regard their role as counseling, and they are most likely to counsel that every effort be made to keep their clients from the risks of unnecessary litigation. If they conclude that litigation is unavoidable, or even desirable, they may in a big or complicated case turn to an outstanding trial lawyer, just as the British solicitor turns to the barrister.

The criminal lawyer is a legal specialist of great importance to our society, because everyone accused of a crime has a right to representation in the courts. Criminal laws are complex and vary considerably from state to state, and the average "family lawyer" or general adviser is seldom familiar with them in enough detail to make the best possible defense of a person charged with a crime. If anyone in your family is ever charged with a serious crime, your lawyer will probably recommend that the case be handled by a specialist in criminal law.

Figure 2.1 Three Kinds of Lawyers

Lawyers fill many roles. Some are primarily advisers to private individuals managing their personal affairs; others develop expertise in specialized fields; still others concentrate on trial work. Three of the most familiar kinds of lawyers are described below.

The Family Lawyer

The so-call family lawyer is a generalist in much the same sense as the old family doctor. Usually active in the affairs of his community, he advises his clients on matters such as leases, contracts, wills, estate planning, the purchase and sale of real estate, divorce and separation proceedings, adoption and hundreds of other problems that arise in an ordinary lifetime. He is a friend and a counselor in time of trouble. One of his most important functions is to keep you out of litigation unless it is clearly necessary.

The Trial Lawyer

Although some successful lawyers never appear in court, many individuals and firms make a specialty of representing parties in litigation. The trial lawyer does not necessarily limit himself to courtroom work, but his greater experience in it makes him alert to procedural points and nuances in the presentation of evidence that might escape a competent attorney whose major interests lie elsewhere. Some courtroom experience is valuable to any lawyer, regardless of his special field of competence.

The Corporation Lawyer

The corporation lawyer is a salaried employee of a company for which he has gone to work either right after passing his bar examination or, more likely, after a period of employment with a large law firm. He specializes in whatever fields of law are of particular importance to his company. A lawyer in a publishing company, for example, might be particularly strong in areas such as copyright law, libel, plagiarism and the interpretation of royalty contracts. He may or may not be involved in courtroom work.

Source: You and the Law. 1997. Pleasantville, NY: Reader's Digest.

Another specialty in U.S. Legal practice should be mentioned: the patent lawyer, who spends his entire professional life advising about patent matters. Most American lawyers' early education is in the social sciences or humanities. Consequently, these lawyers carefully avoid patent matters because they involve technical and scientific areas of knowledge of which the average lawyer is usually ignorant. The patent lawyers, who are trained in engineering or some other scientific specialty, have the whole patent field to themselves. They are much in demand by patent law firms, corporations and the government.

When Jefferson called law the "nursery of the legislature," he recognized a duality in the U.S. legal profession that remains strikingly true today. American lawyers are both counselors and activists, to an extent unknown in any other country. The reason, perhaps, is the scope of their education, which we will elaborate upon later. But whatever the reason, you as a citizen may look to lawyers either for counseling on your personal problems or for leadership in coping with society's problems. You probably would be unwise to look to one lawyer for both, if only because no lawyer has time to do both well.

A counselor must retain some degree of objectivity to be able to give good advice. Many people believe that a lawyer has no business being an activist, that s/he is abandoning his historical role as advocate for individual clients if s/he becomes too wound up in political and social affairs' that s/he should remain above the battle—or at least a good distance from it. You must decide what kind of service you are after when you consult a lawyer. If you want dispassionate advice on what the law is in the situation confronting you, make sure (as we shall tell you how) to find a lawyer who knows what the law is, not one whose consuming interest is what the law should be. The latter lawyer is necessary to keep the country's policies up to date and to make essential improvements, but the former is the one you want in a personal crisis.

When Should You Consult a Lawyer

There is a difference between when you should and when you must consult a lawyer. However, the line between these situations is not always clear. Some general rules should be helpful in guiding you.

As far as civil actions are concerned—such as damage suits, suits for breach of contract and the like—it is essential that you have a lawyer if you are sued for a substantial amount, and all the more so if the person suing you has a lawyer working for him. You also need a lawyer if you want to sue for more than can be recovered through an action in small claims court (see Figure 2.2). It is more than an untrained person can do to follow the twists and turns of a damage suit or to argue the meaning of a complicated contract before a court. It is also advisable to have a lawyer when a written contract is to be drawn up between you and another person or a business concern.

In criminal cases you must have a lawyer. It would be a folly of trying to represent yourself when charged with the commission of a felony or misdemeanor. The seriousness of the penalties if you are found guilty, in some cases depriving you of basic civil rights; the fact that the criminal courts are so congested you may be held in jail for weeks or even months without a hearing; the risk that bail may be set at a figure you cannot afford to pay; the intricacies of criminal procedure—all argue the wisdom of consulting a lawyer at once should you run afoul of the police or the public prosecutor in your area.

Federal law now requires that you have the benefit of legal counsel. State laws differ, but the United States Supreme Court recently ruled that the states must require legal counsel for persons accused of the more serious offenses. You should do everything possible to avoid a "criminal record"—particularly in these days when your credit is so important in making essential contracts, and so many governmental and private agencies are keeping files on all of us. Doing everything possible means finding a lawyer to represent you.

Figure 2.2 Small Claims Court

A cheap and effective way of getting fast justice without the help of a lawyer is by using one of the many small claims courts that exist in most urban areas. The general procedures are outlined below.

If you want to make a claim for an amount below the statutory limit—usually from $200 to $500—you may be able to handle the case yourself through a local small claims court. The normal steps in such a proceeding are these:

1. You go to the clerk of court in the defendant's borough or county and tell him your story—briefly. He will give you forms to fill out, including a formal complaint, and will charge you a modest filing fee. The clerk may assist you in drawing up the legal papers.

2. The clerk will assign a date for the hearing of your case and will arrange for the delivery of your complaint to the defendant, usually by mailing it to his legal address.

3. Either you or the defendant may request a postponement of the hearing if the date is inconvenient or does not give you enough time to prepare your case.

4. On the appointed day you both appear before the magistrate for an informal recital of the facts in your case. Failure to appear will result in a judgment against you. Bring with you any evidence or any witnesses you need to prove your side of the story. Hearings are often held in an ordinary office before a judge dressed simply in a business suit. Concentrate on making your case clear to him, not on arguing with the other party.

5. After listening to the testimony for both sides and examining whatever evidence is presented, the judge will frequently render a decision on the spot. If you are successful, the will then issue an order that the defendant pay your claim or a sum that the court considers fair.

Source: You and the Law. 1997. Pleasantville, NY: Reader's Digest.

Situations Where You Clearly Should Consult a Lawyer

Situations where you clearly should get a lawyer are probably obvious: (a) when you are negotiating a contract; (b) when you receive notice, called a citation, that you have been named as a legatee in the will of a recently deceased member of the golf club and a contest seems to be developing over the validity of the will; (c) when your staff are involved in an automobile accident and are sued for an amount of money larger than the organization's insurance protection; and (d) when someone with whom you do business has broken his contract with you, causing substantial damages. In all such cases and a host of others you need the services of a lawyer to be as certain as possible that your interests will be fully protected. In the last analysis, common sense should be your guide.

How to Find a Lawyer

There is no reason why you cannot find a lawyer if you use common sense and make the most of your associations in whatever circumstances you live. This statement can be made with assurance even though in an absolute sense there are not enough lawyers in the United States at the present time.

If You Cannot Afford a Lawyer

Even if your income is very modest, you should not hesitate to look for legal help, because today, more than ever in the country's history, legal services are being made available to persons of limited means, or of no means at all.

If you find yourself in jail, charged with a serious offense, and have no money, the court will assign you a lawyer who will represent you free of charge. The system varies from state to state and is different in federal and state courts. In some metropolitan areas there are legal aid societies, staffed by lawyers with varying degrees of experience: some are permanent members of the society's staff, whereas others are young lawyers associated with large law firms in the area and loaned to the society for six months to a year. In other areas there are newly formed groups of public defenders: lawyers who handle criminal cases for persons having little or no funds of their own—all with the approval of local bar associations and of the local criminal court judges.

If your legal troubles are civil rather than criminal, lawyers can be found, although not by assignment by the court. Neighborhood legal offices are being established in city after city, staffed by young men and women lawyers eager to obtain the experience of dealing directly with clients like you, for a variety of reasons. First, in the larger law offices such face-to-face contact with the client may not come for two to three years. Second, these young lawyers believe strongly that you should have legal advice whether or not you can pay for it. Third, they are eager to correct social ills—as epitomized by landlords who demand excessive rents and furnish inferior services—by representing you with all their enthusiasm and newly acquired skills and compelling others to behave decently and responsibly toward you.

These neighborhood legal offices take many forms. Some are financed by grants from the U.S. government; there are hundreds of these across the country. Others are both financed and staffed by law firms who assign partners and associates to them for varying periods of time. More and more frequently these firms are also taking on as regular clients persons with real legal complaints, however small may be the amount of money involved and however little the client can afford to pay. Suffice it to say that if you will look and ask around you, you can get a lawyer for both civil and criminal matters that you may face from time to time.

Finding a Lawyer Sources of Information

What has happened in many parts of American life is that persons on the middle-income level are finding services of all kinds increasingly hard to finance. Legal services are no exception. We have already described what services are available to the poor. The rich are sure to associate with lawyers either in making or preserving their money. The rest of this discussion will therefore be directed toward the millions of Americans whose income is well above the poverty level but who have had no firsthand contact with members of the legal profession.

Let us assume you are faced with one of the many situations described throughout this book in which you must or should obtain a lawyer. Analyzing your problem is the first step toward selecting one. If you need to make or revise a will or if you receive legal papers in connection with a probate proceeding, several possibilities come to mind. An official of the bank where you keep a checking account, or which holds the mortgage on your home, is sure to know several lawyers in your area. S/he will give you their names and outline their experience in the field of estates. The clerk of the local court with jurisdiction over wills and trusts, usually called the probate court, knows all the local lawyers who come before his court and will give you guidance among them.

If you have questions about the language in a contract for sale that you have been given to sign when you are about to buy a house, you would again get help in locating a lawyer from your bank, or from the real estate agent who is negotiating the sale of the house to you.

Apart from these obvious sources of information about lawyers, you should consult your friends, your insurance salesman or your accountant. Another place to turn, especially in a small community, is to the librarian. Chances are s/he knows the various lawyers in town or can easily find out for you. Nor should you forget that you can get suggestions from the fraternal or benevolent association you may belong to, or from your doctor, because as a professional person s/he has his own lawyer or, if s/he does not, her or his local medical association has one.

If none of these sources is available to you, there are two other places to go. One is the local bar association, which exists both to serve the interests of the lawyers in your community and, where necessary, to discipline them. Many bar associations throughout the United States now maintain lawyers' referral services. They were created for the very purpose you have in mind: to give you an opportunity, at a minimum fee, to explain your legal problem and get advice as to how to handle it.

Lastly, bear in mind that American political life is dominated by lawyers. If you belong to a political party and have done any work for it, you have a claim on your party's local leadership for help in finding you a lawyer suited to your needs. You should take as much care making up your mind about the referrals you get from the political leader as about the referrals you get from others. But his referrals are likely to be extremely helpful and well adapted to your ability to pay.

Choosing a Lawyer

If you have followed any one of these suggested methods of finding a lawyer, you have probably received several names. Your problem now becomes one of selection, and again your only guide is your common sense. You should not hesitate to request an interview with one or more of the persons on the list. You are, hopefully, entering into a longtime association with the lawyer you select—unless you want advice in a highly specialized area and are unlikely to need it again. You should feel that your lawyer is someone with whom you can easily discuss any problem you may confront. You should not settle on someone you do not like or trust.

Lawyers Who Are Specialists

There is considerable specialization within the practice of law. It is clearly impossible for any lawyer to become or remain an authority on all fields of law. If there were a great need for such an authority, the lawyer in greatest demand would he the recent law school graduate who has just successfully passed an examination for admission to the bar of his state after a thorough review of all or a great part of the laws in his state. But s/he cannot use any of that knowledge unless s/he has a chance to put it to work for a client. At that point, his future is decided for her or him. If s/he goes to work by her/himself or with a few other lawyers in a small office, the chances are s/he will continue to have a very general practice. If s/he goes to work for the government, a corporation or a large metropolitan law firm, s/he will inevitably spend much of his time in one or a few areas of law. As s/he becomes known as an expert, and if her or his areas are broad ones, such as corporation law in all its aspects, clients are likely to consult her or him as a wise man. He is then in a position to broaden out again and spend his career as a generalist, referring specific matters to specialists. The fields of law that occupy most American lawyers are: corporate law; real estate or property (including zoning); condemnation; patent; copyright and trademark; negligence or torts; taxation; wills, trusts and estates; labor law; and criminal law.

A Final Word . . .

For the average reader of this book, it is suggested that you look for a lawyer who shares her or his workload with a few partners and associates, whose time is spent on a variety of matters and who therefore will be able to direct you to, or her/himself take up your problem with, a specialist as seems necessary. Things may work out differently for you, however. You may go to a condemnation expert because the state is about to condemn for a ridiculously low price the small house that you bought with your life's savings—and the condemnation lawyer may so win your confidence that from then on you go to her or him first for help with a host of other problems. If so, s/he is your legal general practitioner and only proves the point being made. Find a lawyer you trust and let her or him guide you through any legal wilderness you may encounter.

Chapter 3

Golf Course Manager's Guide to Negligence and Standard of Care

Golf course managers are faced with many different situations that could be caused by an employee's or patron's negligence. Managers need to understand how the courts define negligence. Further, they need to understand what is met by standard of care and how a standard of care is established in a legal sense. This chapter will outline for the professional golf manager how negligence and standard of care are established in court.

Negligence

Negligence for a golf manager would focus on two key issues: (1) failure to do something that a reasonable golf manager would have done in similar circumstances (a wrong action attributable to omission) or (2) doing something that a reasonable golf manager would not have done in similar circumstances (a wrong action attributable to commission). The court considers negligence as the failure to use appropriate care as a reasonable and prudent golf professional would use under similar circumstances. Carelessness on the part of a golf manager, for whatever reason, can and does cause accidents and injuries. A wrong action or carelessness, whether it be by commission or omission, can and is the basis for claims of negligence.

The argument presented in court will be that golf manager "A" failed to use appropriate care to protect the employee, golfer, or spectator as compared to golf manager "B" in a similar circumstance. For example, golf manager "A" allows a youthful golfer under 12 to operate a golf cart without supervision and the youthful golfer loses control of the golf cart running into a tree breaking a leg. However, golf manager "B" does not allow a youthful golfer under 16 to operate a golf cart without supervision. Based on this comparison the court might determine that golf manager "A" was negligent because a reasonable and prudent golf manager would not have allowed a youthful golfer under 12 to operate a golf cart without supervision.

Components of Negligence

There are four components that need to be established in order for a negligence claim to be successful in court. The plaintiff's lawyer must first show that *damage* is present and that the damage was caused by the defendant's carelessness. If damage is present then the next step is to establish that the golf manager had a *duty* to the plaintiff and was in fact careless. Once duty is established then it must be proved that the golf manager *breached the duty*. Finally, the lawyer must show there is a direct proximate casual link between the breach of duty and the injury the plaintiff sustained. This is known as *proximate cause*. Once this final link can be made, it is not difficult to show that the golf manager's carelessness in fact caused the damage.

What Is Duty?

A duty is an obligation that a person has either by law or contract. The obligation to conform to a legal standard of reasonable care in light of the apparent risk. In negligence cases, duty is frequently defined as an obligation to which law will give recognition and effect to conform to a particular standard of care toward another. Finally, the word "duty" is used to denote the fact that the actor (golf manager) is required to conduct her/himself in a particular manner at the risk. If s/he does not do so, s/he becomes subject to liability to another to whom the duty is owed for any injury sustained by which that actor's conduct is a legal cause.

Every golf course manager should consider the following as their legal duties as established by years of litigation focusing on negligence on the golf course or its management:

- provide adequate supervision for employees, players, and spectators;
- develop a supervision plan for course management and safety;
- warn employees, players, and spectators of inherent risks in the activity and on the course;
- furnish safe facilities for employees, players, and spectators;
- provide adequate training for all employees in first aid and CPR;
- render immediate and temporary care for all injured employees, players, or spectators;
- provide for adequate and proper equipment for employees and players;
- establish rules and regulations for safety of employees, players, and spectators that comply with policy and statutory requirements; and
- provide for regular inspection and remedy for dangerous conditions on the course and with equipment.

Levels of Negligent Behavior

Negligence is any conduct which falls below the standard established by case law and professional associations for the protection of others against unreasonable risk of harm. There are seven levels of negligence that the golf professional needs to understand:

1. *Malfeasance* or a commission of an unlawful act. For example, you employ grounds keepers and do not have them certified to work with the chemicals applied to the golf course.
2. *Misfeasance* or an improper performance of some lawful act. For example, the grounds keepers have been certified to use the chemicals that are applied to the golf course but they improperly apply the chemicals.

3. *Nonfeasance* or failure of a person to act. For example, all personnel are certified in Cardio Pulmonary Resuscitation (CPR) but one employee in the restaurant area fails to perform an anti-choking technique on a choking victim.
4. *Reckless Misconduct* or intent to commit an act but with no intention to harm anyone. For example, a golfer tees off thinking that the party in front of her/him is out of range but accidently hits one of the players.
5. *Wilful/Wanton Conduct* or intentional act of an unreasonable character in total disregard for human safety. For example, a golfer tees off from a tee box close to a public roadway intentionally aiming at cars passing by the golf course.
6. *Gross Negligence* or failure to use even slight care or the omission to use ordinary care and diligence to avoid a discovered or apparent danger. For example, you have purchased new golf carts and in the manufacturer's warranty information was a section regarding regular systematic inspection and maintenance procedures including a maintenance reporting form that could be duplicated for future use. You totally and wilfully ignore the manufacturer's suggestions and fail to inspect regularly or provide necessary maintenance for the equipment. A few months later a client is injured on the new equipment due to faulty equipment maintenance.
7. *Slight (ordinary) Negligence* or the failure to exercise great care or an absence of that degree of care and vigilance to which persons of extraordinary prudence and foresight are accustomed. For example, using the equipment example above, the owner decides to modify the manufacturer's suggested maintenance procedure and allows for a longer period of time between inspections and actual performance of necessary maintenance. A golfer is injured when the brakes fail on the golf cart and the maintenance procedures established by the golf manager are found to be inappropriate.

Care

Care can be defined as caution, concern, custody, prudence, regard, security, vigilance, or watchful attention. It can also be defined as the opposite of carelessness. However, in negligence cases, it is the amount of care demanded by the standard of reasonable conduct in proportion to the apparent risk. As the risk escalates, the amount of care required becomes greater.

There are three degrees of care that correspond inversely to the three degrees of negligence—slight care, ordinary care, and greater care. *Slight care* is the degree of care which a person exercises about his own concerns though he may be a person of less than common prudence. *Ordinary care* is that degree of care which may reasonably be expected from a person in the person's circumstances. *Great care* is that degree of care usually bestowed upon the matter in hand by the most competent, prudent, and careful person having to do with the particular activity.

Reasonable Person Doctrine or Standard

The phrase *reasonable care* is commonly defined as care an ordinarily prudent person would exercise under similar conditions existing at the time of the action. It is synonymous with ordinary or due care. This degree of care only requires the care and skill exacted of a person engaged in the same or similar activities.

The *reasonable person doctrine or standard* refers to the standard which one must observe to avoid liability for negligence. The *reasonable person doctrine or standard* applies under all the circumstances surrounding negligence including the foreseeability of harm to a plaintiff. Further, a reasonable person is thought to possess a minimum level of knowledge common to the activity in which the injury occurs. A negligent defendant who possesses superior knowledge (i.e., college degree in golf management), skill (i.e., a PGA or LPGA player's card), or experience (i.e., x number of years practicing in the field) will be held to a greater degree of care. The activity engaged in must conform to that of others with similar knowledge, skills, and experience.

Standard of Conduct (Care)

As a rule of thumb courts in negligence cases define standard of conduct (care) as the degree of care which a reasonably prudent person should exercise in the same or similar circumstance. If the person's conduct falls below the standard, s/he may be liable in damages for injuries or damages resulting from a person's conduct. The plaintiff's lawyer will measure the conduct in each negligent situation against the reasonable person standards established by statute, case law, and/or expert witnesses. It is important to understand that the conduct of the reasonable person is not necessarily perfect conduct, but rather, conduct of a person who is a reasonable and prudent individual in a similar situation. Finally, the professional standard of conduct (care) does not vary on the qualifications of the person in charge, but rather, is determined by the situation—what is the nature of the golf activity, what are the inherent risks involved in the golfing activity, who are the golf participants, what knowledge and skill levels are necessary to participate, and what are the environmental conditions (i.e., thunder and lightning, heavy rain, heavy wind)?

Risk Management Considerations

Legal Theories for Recovery

The following are the common legal theories for recovery by the plaintiff relating to golf course negligence:

- "golf is consider a nuisance and all injuries related to playing golf are a result of negligence,"[1]
- "golf is a dangerous activity and all injuries related to playing golf are a result of negligence,"[2]
- the golf course, equipment, or carts are negligently designed,
- driver of the golf cart was negligent (i.e., excessive speed, moving before passenger is seated, intoxicated, hit another party),[3]
- lessor of golf cart was negligent (i.e., defective cart, failing to warn of defective condition(s), renting cart to a person using alcohol or other impairing substances, failing to maintain golf cart, failing to maintain cart paths),[4]
- failing to warn of defective or unsafe conditions,[5]
- failure to develop and post safety rules,
- failure to enforce safety rules (i.e., speeding in golf cart, failure to wear safety goggles when using a weed eater, failure to wear rubber gloves when working with chemicals),[6]
- failure to post accurate yardage on signage and scorecards,
- failure to erect protective screening to protect players and passing vehicles,[7]
- violation of civil rights,
- violation of OSHA rules and regulations,
- violation of health codes,
- violation of American with Disabilities Act, and
- violation of Child Labor Laws.

Person or Parties Liable

The following is a partial list of the possible persons or parties liable in golf course litigation:

- golfer
- owner/operator of the course[8]
- golf course manager/superintendent
- golf course architect[9]
- golf course contractor
- parent of minor who causes injury[10]
- corporate employer of a party causing injury[11]
- liability insurance carrier[12]

---

1. De Coster, Jules V. (1993). *Risk Management for Golf*. Canton, MO: RIMAGO Company. Chapter 3, 2.
2. Id.
3. See 1, Chapter 4, 2.
4. Id.
5. See 1, Chapter 5, 1.
6. Id.
7. See 1, Chapter 6, 1.
8. See 1.
9. Id.
10. Id.
11. Id.
12. Id.

- independent contractor
- manufacture of equipment (i.e., golf carts, mowers, tractors, weed eaters, etc.)
- golf professional and/or
- lessor renting the golf carts.[13]

Defenses for Negligence

Assumption of Risk

The golf course manager needs to understand how to make sure an employee, player, and/or spectator knows about the dangers and risk involved and chose to act as s/he did. Later in the book, waivers and warnings will be discussed that relate specifically to establishing knowledge of a risk for employees, players, and/or spectators. The doctrine of assumption of risk (*volenti non fit injuria*) means legally that a plaintiff may not recover for an injury received when s/he voluntarily expose her/himself to a known and appreciated danger. The requirements to establish assumption of risks are: (1) the plaintiff has knowledge of facts (i.e., warning or risks inherent in the game of golf such as being hit by a ball or club) constituting a dangerous condition, (2) s/he knows the condition is dangerous (i.e., thunder and lightning), (3) s/he appreciates the nature or extent of the danger, and (4) s/he voluntarily exposes her/himself to the danger.

Assumption of risk is not a defense under state worker's compensation laws and many states have abolished the defense of assumption of risk in motor vehicle cases with the enactment of no-fault insurance acts or comparative negligence acts.

Comparative Negligence

This type of negligence is measured in terms of percentage and any damages allowed shall be diminished in proportion to the amount of negligence attributable to the person for whose injury, damage, or death recovery is sought. This simply means that the fault for the injury is assigned to both parties involved in the incident based on the evidence presented. The amount of fault assigned to the plaintiff will be barred from recovery while the amount of fault assigned to the defendant will be assessed in the final judgement. It should be noted that many states have replaced contributory negligence with comparative negligence.

Contributory Negligence

Under this doctrine if the plaintiff is found to be responsible for any part of her/his injury, s/he will be barred from recovery. This doctrine has been replaced by the comparative negligence doctrine in many states.

---

13. See 3.

Governmental Tort Immunity

Public golf course managers have been judged to be free from liability for torts committed in a number of cases. This has occurred because governmental tort immunity suggests that the federal government and state and local governments are free from liability for torts committed except in cases in which they have consented by statute to be sued. However, most states, either by statute or case law, have abolished or greatly restricted the doctrine of sovereign immunity at both the state and local levels.

Risk Management Considerations

Legal Defenses

The following are the common legal defenses used in golf course litigation:

- assumption of risk in those states that recognize this defense,
- injury was simply an accident,
- contributory negligence in those states that recognize this defense,
- waiver of liability clause signed,[14]
- intervening negligence of a third party,[15]
- strict liability does not apply,[16] and
- accident was not foreseeable.

Doctrine of *Respondeat Superior*

This translated doctrine means let the master answer. In the case of a golf course, the master would be the official governing body (i.e., park commission or board of directors). Under this doctrine the master is responsible for providing personnel and facilities that will protect the players and spectators from injury. The master owes the employees, players, and/or spectators a duty of care while they are on the golf course property. If employees are acting outside the legitimate scope of authority and responsibility, the doctrine of *respondeat superior* is inapplicable.

Standard v. Guideline

There is a simple difference between a standard and a guideline. A standard is a rule or regulation carrying the full authority of the rule of law. It is established only after rigorous formal rule making process which involves drafts, public notice and comment, and re-drafts while a guideline provides best practice informa-

14. See 1 at 3.
15. See 3 at 3.
16. See 7 at 2.

tion only and does not impose any new legal obligation or constraint on employers. More specifically, a standard addresses a specific situation and suggests specific solutions (i.e., handicap access) whereas a guideline simply recommends a solution that maybe chosen voluntarily (i.e., weather sirens should be installed to warn golfers of dangerous weather conditions).

Another way to explain the difference between a standard and guideline is as follows:

- A standard is a goal for the application of certain chemicals on a golf course to control disease and weeds. This standard is measurable and attainable and complies with various Federal and state statutes, regulations (i.e., EPA, OSHA), policies, and directives (manufacturer) applicable.
- A guideline is a management approach, method, and/or practice that is intended to achieve a common best practice. It is developed and applied consistent with the desired condition and within site capability. Finally, the guideline is adjusted overtime to make allowances for changes in common practice and use.

Code of Professional Responsibility

A code is a cannon. A canon is a law, rule, or ordinance in general. It is also considered to be a criterion or standard of judgement or a body of principles, standards, rules, or norms. A code of professional responsibility are statements of axiomatic norms expressing in general terms the standards of professional conduct expected of the specific professional in their relationship with the public and professional's profession. The golf course manager belongs to a profession consisting of golf management professionals. These professionals may belong to a professional organization. Every professional organization has a code of conduct that its members agree to adhere to as professionals in the field. If the golf management professional is unaware of her/his code of conduct (professional responsibility), s/he should immediately become aware of the code.

A Final Word...

All golf management professionals need to know, understand, and appreciate the ramifications of negligence and the common defenses for negligence in the state the golf manager is practicing. They need to understand what is meant by standard of conduct (care) and what other golf managers understand to be the best practices to provide a safe environment for employees, players, and spectators. Finally, standards of conduct (care) are dynamic and change with the times as should the professional golf manager.

Chapter 4

Understanding Warnings and Waivers

In Chapter 3 negligence was discussed and defenses for negligence. One of the defenses discussed was assumption of risk. It indicated that if it could be shown in court that the employee, participant, or spectator had been made aware of the danger or inherent risk and s/he decided to continue her/his activity s/he would have assumed a risk. This chapter has been designed to assist the golf course manager in developing warnings that will warn the employee, participant, and spectator of impending danger, and preparing an appropriate waiver instrument to relieve the manager, her/his employees, and the golf course from liability.

Duty to Warn of Danger

The duty of a golf course manager is to warn the employee, participant, and spectator of potential dangers or hazards in connection with use of the golf facility arises out of the duty of ordinary or reasonable care which is the basis of liability for negligence. The elements of duty have been explained in Chapter 3.

Almost any golf club or cart may be used or misused in a manner which involves danger of physical harm. Being hit by an errant golf ball or golf club may cause a serious injury to another participant or bystander. Failure of the brakes on a golf cart may cause serious bodily injury. The excessive drinking of liquor during play or at the nineteenth hole can be dangerous. Traveling over poorly maintained foot or cart bridges can cause serious injury if the bridge collapses. Driving a golf cart carelessly or under the influence of an intoxicating substance which causes injury is not the manner the golf cart owner or manufacturer intended. The hazards that arise out of the use of the golf cart in this manner or to the extent that it was not intended by the owner or manufacturer to be used are not the fault of the owner or manufacturer; therefore, there is no duty imposed upon the manufacturer or owner to give warning against the possible dangers that might arise from such misuse of the golf cart.

The duty to give a warning arises out of a foreseeable danger of physical harm arising out of the normal use or probable use of the product or facility and the likelihood that unless warned, the user will not ordinarily be aware of such danger or hazard.

What Is the Purpose of a Warning?

The purpose and function of a warning is to apprise a party of the existence of danger which s/he is not aware to enable her/himself against it. In the case where s/he is aware of the danger, the warning will serve no useful purpose and is unnecessary, and there is no duty to warn against risks which are open and obvious. Federal laws and OSHA regulations require warning labels to be affixed to potentially dangerous products, chemicals, tools, and the like.

Before a person can assume a risk, s/he must (1) know the danger or risk exists, (2) understand (comprehend) the magnitude of the danger or risk, and (3) appreciate the danger or risk. For example, a golf course located in Florida which regularly has alligators frequenting its fairways and are found in the waterways near the fairways has the duty to warn players and spectators who are not aware of the wildlife and the danger presented by the presence of such wildlife. The warning alerts the player and spectator of the dangers of alligators so they can comprehend the magnitude of the danger or risk and appreciate what could happen if attacked by an alligator.

What Is Meant by Inherently Dangerous?

An inherently dangerous activity is one that requires special precautions to prevent injury. For example, when a person practices her/his drive s/he generally goes to a driving range. The driving range has been designed to protect the golfer from being hit by golf balls. The golfer hits a basket of balls. S/he does not retrieve the balls. A protected ball retriever collects the balls for others to use periodically. If the golfer walked out after her/his balls, s/he would most definitely get hit by other golfers. Further, each tee area at the driving range is separated so that the golfers will not hit each other with their clubs during their swings.

It is possible for golfers to assume the danger or risk of a sore back from swinging the club too hard or blisters on their hands from squeezing the club too tight, but they should not assume the danger or risk of being bitten by an alligator. However, inherently dangerous situations change depending on the improvement in the golf facilities and equipment. For example, changing the design of a golf course may accidently place golfers in danger or at risk of being hit when one tee box is in range of another. In this scenario the management needs to erect a fence to protect the golfer from the golfers teeing off on the other tee box. The fence needs to be high enough with small mesh to stop the errant balls.

The golf course manager must understand that the employee, golfer, and/or spectator can only assume those dangers or risks which are an inherent part of the activities, and the manager must do whatever is necessary to assure the employee and spectator know, understand, and appreciate the dangers or risks. The inherent dangers or risks for golf course employees include chemical burns, eye injuries, amputations, severe lacerations, broken bones, or being victim sunburn, heat cramps, heat exhaustion, or heat stroke; for golfers include being hit by a ball, a golf club, a golf cart, or lightning, being a victim of sunburn, heat cramps, heat exhaustion, or heat stroke, or falling from a golf cart, in holes, or over stumps, roots, or rocks; and for spectators include being hit by a ball or lightning, bleachers collapsing, or being a victim of sunburn, heat cramps, heat exhaustion, or heat stroke.

Components of a Warning

A warning has the following common components:

- the warning should be in written form in the appropriate languages,
- the specific dangers and risks should be outlined clearly and concisely,
- the wording must be strong and forceful,
- the reasons for the warning must be provided,
- the warning must be displayed graphically,
- the warning must be conspicuous so it catches the user's attention, and
- the warning must reach the foreseeable user.

Beyond the components outlined above the warning should encourage safe performance, emphasis any major standard warning(s), explain any safety rule(s)/protocol(s), outline the manufacturer's recommendations and uses, and solicit and encourage questions. Further, the warning should summarize the know, understand, and appreciate statement(s). Finally, the golf course manager should request that any statement provided the employee, golfer or spectator be signed and dated, and it should be filed for further reference.

Table 4.1 is an example of a golfer's warning that is a common general warning. It is important to understand that specific golf courses will have specific needs that will be added to a general warning.

Table 4.1

Mark Twain Championship Golf Course

A Golfer's Warning

Participating in a friendly round of golf should be relaxing and enjoyable without concern for inherent dangers or risks; but like many other activities today, there are dangers and risks involved in playing golf. The following is a generalized golfer's warning.

All golfers should be cautious of the following inherent risks in the game of golf:

- the golfer should never walk in front of another golfer who is swinging;
- the golfer should not stand closer than two club lengths of any other golfer who is swinging a club;
- the golfer should warn other golfers or errant balls that might accidentally hit another golfer playing on the course;
- the golfer should not use intoxicating substances or beverages and drive a motorized golf cart;
- the golfer driving a motorized cart should not exceed 10 mph;
- the golfer should understand where to go for shelter on the golf course during a lightning storm;

- the golfer should understand where to go during a heavy rain storm that might cause flash flooding; and
- the golfer should avail her or himself to adequate fluids from the water sources provided throughout the course on hot and humid days to avoid heat cramps, heat exhaustion, and heat stroke.

Waivers in Golf: Are They Worthwhile?

A waiver means the voluntary, intentional relinquishment of a known right. It is essentially unilateral. Essential to the waiver is the voluntary consent of the individual. The waiver is considered a contract.

A waiver can be voided for the following reasons: (1) fraud or misrepresentation, (2) one party in a clearly dominant position, (3) the use of force or coercion so that the waiver is signed under duress, (4) ambiguity—both parties should know what they are signing, and this should be conspicuous and the result of open bargaining, (5) the presence of any unreasonable conditions, and, (6) the presence of wanton, intentional, or reckless misconduct.

Key Terms

Liability Waiver is an agreement between the employee, golfer, and/or spectator and the golf course wherein the participants promise not to sue the golf course for any injury s/he might sustain because of the golf course's negligence.
Agreement to Participate is not a contract but a signed statement that the participant understands the dangers inherent in the activity, that s/he know the rules and the importance of following directions, and s/he appreciates the consequences of the risks involved including the possibility of injury or death.

Why Use a Waiver?

Many lawyers suggest strongly that the two main benefits of using a waiver include discouraging an injured party from filing a lawsuit, and enhancing other legal defenses (i.e., assumption of risk). A waiver is also useful in encouraging prudent planning on the part of managers, communicating the possible dangers, reducing litigation, and reducing guilt of personnel when injuries happen.

What Are the Elements of an Effective Waiver?

The golf course manager needs to understand what elements should be included in an effective waiver. The waiver needs to be prepared by an attorney or at least reviewed by an attorney. The following subjects should be addressed (1) name of organization, (2) identify parties, (3) inform participants about the activity, (4) inform participants about the dangers and risks, (5) acknowledge that participants have read the waiver, and (6) provide for participant and witnesses signatures and date. It is important to understand that an enforceable waiver must let the party signing know the terms of the release, be conspicuous, and have resulted from free and open bargaining.

A Final Word . . .

It is necessary for the golf course manager to draft, with the assistance of an attorney, and use warnings. The ensuing guidelines should assist the manager in developing sound warnings which in turn will reduce risk:

- Warn all employees, golfers, and/or spectators of all inherent risks. Be sure the warning enables the reader to know, understand, and appreciate the risks involved.
- Put the warnings in written form and be sure they are carefully read and signed. Retain a copy of this signed form for the files.
- After presenting the warnings, be sure to ask questions, giving and recording thorough and unbiased answers to these questions.
- Attached to the warning is a waiver form to be signed by the participant releasing the organization and its employees from liability.

It is strongly recommended that no warning or waiver form be adopted for any program until it has first been reviewed by an attorney and the medical advisor for the organization. Each form must be written in accordance with prevailing laws and should simply state to the participant the reasons for the procedure, the risks, and benefits, etc. in a manner specific to the program activities for which consent is being considered to be acceptable.

Chapter 5

Contracts and the Golf Course Manager

The golf course manager is faced with entering into numerous contracts as a matter of business. These contracts focus on merchandise, services, concessions, equipment, staff, and clients to name a few. This chapter is designed as a primer for contracts to assist the golf course manager in understanding the basics regarding contracts.

Introduction to Contracts

A contract is most often defined as a promise or set of promises for the breach of which the law gives a remedy, or the performance of which the law in some way recognizes a duty. Contracts may be either oral or written. However, a written contract is easier to enforce.

The following are the ingredients of a valid contract, agreement, or promise:

1. An *offer* is a definite proposal made by one person to another which by its terms is conditional upon an act, forbearance, or return of promise being given in exchange. The person making the proposal is the offeror. The person to whom it is made is the offeree. An offer is always a promise.
2. *Acceptance* is an expression of willingness to accept the offer or proposal. Acceptance of the offer is essential to the creation of a contract. It may not change any of the terms of the offer nor add to, subtract from, or qualify in any way the provisions of the offer. An acceptance must strictly comply with the terms of the offer.
3. *Consideration* is basically what is given in exchange for something else. Consideration is present therefore only when the parties intend an exchange whether it be a promise exchanged for a promise, a promise for an act, or a promise exchanged for a forbearance to act. The central idea is that the parties have bargained with one another.
4. The *legality* ingredient means that the formation or performance of the agreement is not criminal, tortious, or otherwise opposed to public policy. If the agreement is criminal or tortious, the bargain is illegal and unenforceable.
5. *Capacity* defines what persons have the ability or capacity to make a valid contract. Persons commonly exempted from making valid agreements are: minors (i.e., under the age of 18), mentally incapacitated, intoxicated persons, non-citizens, and felons.

Types of Contracts

Contracts have been classified from various standpoints, for example, their method of formation, their content, and their legal effect. In this section the following types of contracts will be defined: formal and informal contracts, express and implied contracts, unilateral and bilateral contracts, void, voidable and unenforceable contracts, and executed and executory contracts.

Formal and Informal Contracts. A formal contract is one under seal (i.e., government seal) or of record (i.e., deeds for property or mortgages). All other contracts are called informal (simple) contracts.

Express and Implied Contracts. A contract in which the parties manifest assent in words is called an express contract. A contract will be implied when a person accepts and retains the beneficial results of another's services which were rendered at her/his own request and which s/he had no reason to suppose were gratuitous.

Unilateral and Bilateral Contracts. A unilateral contract is one-sided and has only one promise outstanding. For example, suppose A says to B, "If you mow my lawn, I will give you five dollars." A contract will be formed when B mows the lawn. The contract is one-sided.

A bilateral contract is two-sided and has two outstanding promises. For example, a car dealer agrees to provide a clear title and the purchaser agrees to pay the asking or negotiated price.

Void, Voidable, and Unenforceable. A void contract is no contract. A voidable contract is a contract but because of the manner or method in which it was brought about, one of the parties is permitted to avoid her/his duties. For example, A through fraud induces B to enter into a contract. The contract induced by fraud is not void but is voidable at the election of the defrauded. Finally, a contract may be unenforceable because of a failure to satisfy the requirements of the Statute of Frauds which require certain types of contracts to be in writing in order to be enforceable.

Executed and Executory Contracts. If a contract has been fully performed on both sides, it is an executed contract. The term executory contract applies to the situations where there are one or more unperformed promises on one side, that is, a contract which is wholly performed on one side, but unperformed or executory on the other side, or unperformed on both sides in whole or in part.

Warranty

A warranty is a promise by the seller concerning some aspect of the sale such as quality of the goods or the title. There are two types of warranties—express and implied. An express warranty is made part of the contract by the words or conduct of the seller. An implied warranty is made part of the contract by operation of the law (i.e., warranty of merchantability and warranty of fitness for a particular purpose).

Warranty of merchantability is a warranty that the goods shall be merchantable is implied in a contract for their sale if the seller is a merchant with respect to goods of that kind. In general, "merchantable" means of average or medium quality.

Warranty of fitness for particular purpose is a warranty where the seller has reason to know the particular purpose for which the goods are required and that the buyer is relying on the seller's skill or judgement to select or furnish the goods. There is an implied warranty that the goods shall be fit for such purpose.

Cases Involving Contracts

Breach of Contract

Breach of contract comprised nearly 15% of golf litigation over the 25-year period (1973–1998).[1] Within this area of litigation, cases could be further broken down into five primary areas. The most common breach of contract are contracts between golf courses and its investors, followed by golf courses and construction firms, golf courses and design-build firms, and contracts dealing with real estate issues. Contracts involving licensees and lessors, and employees round out this area of golf litigation.

Construction and Design

Over the past 25 years, it has become evident that contracts that exist between a golf course and contractors hired for construction or design purposes has been a legal handicap for owners and operators alike. In the *Gundersons*[2] case, a contractor brought action against the owner of the golf course for breach of construction. The court held in favor of the contractor stating that the contractor met the burden of establishing with reasonable certainty the amount of expected net profit as a basis for an award for lost profits. In addition to this, it was found that the owners' breach of contract for the construction of the golf course, in itself, entitled the contractor to at least nominal damages. The amount of expected net profit was used as a basis for an award of lost profits. Furthermore, the contractor was also entitled to the consequential damages for maintenance of long-term leases on equipment that he had leased for the project and was therefore left idle by the breach of contract. Golf courses have also brought breach of contract suits against contractors as well. In the *Breckenridge*[3] case, the Town of Breckenridge filed a breach of contract suit against the designers of a public golf course. As a basis of determining fault in this case the court evaluated the contractual obligations between the two parties regarding the performance and supervision of sampling and testing procedures to determine compliance with the golf association's standards for drainage and percolation conditions. It was clear that the evidence supported that the contract between the town and the designers for the construction of the golf course had been breached. Consequently, the courts found in favor of the town.

1. Tonner, C., Sawyer, T.H., & Hypes, M.G. (1999). Twenty-five years of golf litigation: 1973–1998. *Journal of Legal Aspects of Sport*, 9(3), 125-153.
2. *Gundersons v. Tull*, 678 P.2d. 1061 (1984).
3. *Breckenridge v. Golforce, Inc.*, 851 P.2d 214 (1993).

Real Estate

In the *Oceanside Community Association* case,[4] the homeowners association brought suit against developer and subsequent purchasers of developer's property adjacent to the residential development seeking a mandatory injunction to restrict the subject property for use as a golf course as covenanted by the developer. The superior court denied the mandatory injunction but granted an equitable lien on the property for each month the golf course was not in the process of being renovated or maintained. The association and most recent purchaser of the property cross-appealed. The appeals court ruled that the clauses of the contract restricting the use of the property as a golf course was a burden rather than a benefit to the property and that it was not personal to covenantor developer but, rather, was intended to run with the land to bind the developers successors. Likewise, in *Breen*,[5] action was brought by a member of a corporate golf club following the sale of the club for determination of value of his certificate of ownership and award of damages. The court ruled that the statutory appraisal provisions, which fall under the statute governing corporations established for carrying on business for profit, did not apply to the corporations formed under the statute which governs corporations having civic, educational, charitable, benevolent, religious or state cognate purposes. This also included corporations whose purpose was of fostering, encouraging or engaging in athletic exercises or yachting, and which contains no reference to or adoption of appraisal provisions. Finally, in *McHugh*,[6] a real estate broker brought action to recover for commission from the defendant who is the joint owner of the golf course. The court held that there was sufficient evidence to establish a contract between the plaintiff and defendant, notwithstanding the absence of a written listing. In addition, it was further ruled that the broker who had produced a buyer who was willing and able to buy, on terms that were acceptable to the defendant joint owner of the golf course, with whom he dealt, was entitled to commission as was agreed between the two parties.

Lessor/Lessee/Licensee/Licensor

The agreements between licensee and licensor, and lessor and lessee, are also areas of concerns for the owners and operators of golf courses. Whether the agreement concerns the pro shop or the food concessionaire at the club, managers and operators of golf courses need to be sensitive to the risks that these areas can pose if not carefully managed. For instance, in the *Association Creditors Agency* case,[7] a credit agency as the assignee of the creditors who furnished alcoholic beverages and foodstuffs to concessionaire at the golf club, brought action against the golf club, whose liquor licenses had been used by the concessionaire. The supreme court ruled that the concessionaire merely paid rent to the golf club owners, and therefore was not the agent of the owners. The court reasoned that the agreement that allowed the concessionaire to use the golf clubs liquor license did not establish an agency as a matter of law since the golf club owners who had

4. *Oceanside Community Association v. Oceanside Land Co.*, 195 Cal.Rptr. 14 (1983).
5. *Breen v. Wollaston Golf Club*, 335 N.E. 2d (1975).
6. *McHugh v. Johnson*, 268 N.W. 2d 225 (1978).
7. *The Association Creditors Agency v. Davis*, 530 P.2d 1084 (1975).

leased the restaurant and bar concession to another party never directly undertook to order and pay for the beverages or provisions furnished to the restaurant and bar. However, the use of the license by the concessionaire could, if relied upon by the creditor, have created an ostensible agency. The court ruled that the creditors who had supplied foodstuffs never investigated to whom the on-site liquor license had been issued. They never relied on the credit of the licensees in furnishing foodstuffs and could not recover on theory of ostensible agency. In the *City of Needles* case,[8] the defendant breached a written agreement with the city to operate the golf course that was owned by the city. In the agreement, the City reserved the right to terminate the license for cause upon 180 days notice to the defendant. Within the agreement it was stated that if there should be any sort of disagreement or controversy with regards to the termination, it would be settled by arbitration in accordance with the rules of the American Arbitration Association. As a part of the agreement between the two parties, the defendant was obligated to provide whatever personal property was necessary to equip, operate, maintain and supply inventory for the golf course and its attendant pro shop and restaurant. Upon the termination of the lease, the city used the land and personal property of the defendant for public purpose. Furthermore, the court decided that the city contravened the constitutional limitations in eminent domain power.

In the *Woburn Country Club* case,[9] the former lessee brought action against the city golf and ski authority to recover for goods left on leased premises. The city sought to recover fees collected by the lessee. The superior court initially ruled in favor of the city on its claim for the fees collected and allowed a new trial as to the claim that was presented by the lessee. The court of appeals ruled that the city golf and ski authority was a gratuitous bailee for the use of goods left by the former lessee on the premises for an indefinite term, and as such, had an obligation to confine its use of goods to that contemplated at the creation of the bailment. The court further ruled that there existed a responsibility to exercise care with respect to the goods, and to return the goods to the lessee, or to make them available to be picked up if demanded so. The court also ruled that the former lessees' demand for rent for the goods left on the leased premises was not equivalent of the demand that the city golf and ski authority return such goods. Therefore they did not terminate the authority's rights to use such goods. Even if the city golf and ski authority's right to use the goods left by the former lessee was terminated by the lessees' demand for rent, the authority had no obligation to pay rent. Instead, continued use of the property while denying obligation to pay rent would, in effect, constitute conversion of property entitling lessee to recover fair market value of the goods at the time of conversion with interest to the date of judgment.

In *Kautza*,[10] the co-owners of a miniature golf course brought action against the city and some of its officials alleging a lack of statutory authority for the city to operate the course, unfair competition, and constitutional violations. After being initially dismissed by the district court, the owners appealed. The supreme court ruled that the co-owners contention that the lease agreement was detrimental to them was insufficient to mount a third party challenge to the validity of the lease. It also ruled that the city was not subject to the unfair competition statute

---

8. *City of Needles v. Griswold*, 8 Cal.Rptr. 2d 753 (1992).
9. *Woburn Country Club v. Woburn Golf and Ski Authority*, 486 N.E. 2d 1128 (1984).
10. *Kautza v. City of Cody*, 812 P.2d 143 (1991).

since the city had statutory authority to own and lease the miniature golf course. In it's ruling the court reasoned that the City had the authority to own and lease the miniature golf course, where there was no claim that the lease involved discriminatory or other questionable practices, and it appeared that the ownership and lease was for the benefit of the citizens of Cody.

Investors/Investments/Corporations

In the *Simmons*[11] case, a property owner appealed a summary judgment from the circuit court in which favor was given to the corporation in a postarbitration suit by the property owner alleging a breach of contract, fraud, and personal liability on the part of the president of the corporation. The court of appeals held that the contract included an arbitration clause, which stated that it is mutually agreed that the decision of the arbitrators shall be a condition precedent to any right of legal action that either party may take against the other. Based solely on this, it was reasoned that the corporation was entitled to confirmation of an arbitration award. Similarly, in *Kraus*,[12] investors in the investment corporations golf course project filed a complaint against the golf course corporation, the golf course limited partnership and others alleging breach of contract and fraud. The superior court held favorably for the plaintiffs and determined that only certain defendants held their interest in the golf course for the benefit of the plaintiffs and other investors. The defendants appealed the verdict. The court of appeals held that since the investors in the golf courses' limited partnership made claims in bankruptcy proceedings instituted by the investment corporation, it did not preclude them from asserting claims as third party beneficiaries against the corporation which had agreed to assume the indebtedness to all those who had paid money to it for the development of the golf course. In contrast to this case, in *Buckner*,[13] a former member of a private country club brought action against the private capital stock corporation which operated the club, seeking an injunction ordering his reinstatement as a member of the club. The initial ruling by the superior court was in favor of the defendant with a denial of injunctive relief. The member appealed this decision. The appellate court found that the former member was not entitled to the injunction ordering his reinstatement since he had been expelled by a vote of the club's boards of directors after a hearing before the board at which witnesses were heard. The trial court expressly found that the former member had not suffered irreparable harm and was therefore not entitled to an injunction.

Employee-Related Contracts

Employees and employee-related contracts are also another concern that could give rise to contract law for owners and operators of golf courses. For example, in *Catropa*,[14] a golf professional who received a portion of his compensation from the operation of the pro shop in his employer's clubhouse brought a forcible entry and detainer action against his employer for possession of the pro shop following early

11. *Simmons v. Golf Course Specialist Incorporated*, 310 N.W. 2d (1981).
12. *Kraus v. Willow Park Public Golf Course*, 140 Cal. Rptr. 744 (1977).
13. *Buckner v. Shorehaven Golf Club Incorporated*, 537 A. 2d 532 (1988).
14. *Catropa v. Burgas*, 551 A. 2d 1282 (1988).

termination of his at-will employment. The superior court found that the golf professional paid no rent and therefore could not maintain the forcible entry and detainer action against his employer. The courts reasoned that the golf pro was not a tenant, and whatever right he had to use the pro shop premises were incidental to his at-will employment. Similarly, in *Cole* et al.,[15] a group of professional golfers brought action against the city alleging that the city had breached an oral contract. The contract was said to include provisions that would provide the golfers services on the city's golf courses until each of them reached the age of seventy and to enjoin the city from leasing the golf courses. The court of appeals held that the golfers could not prevail against the city on the claim and recovery based on the theory of quantum meruit. The courts reasoned the decision in two ways. First, a person asserting a contractual claim against a city must clearly show that the contract was authorized, any person dealing with a municipality in a contractual context has a duty to determine that the city has complied with the law limited and prescribing its powers. Second, providers can recover damages on the theory of quantum merit for the value of the services received by the recipient, but not for the cost of their own expenditures.

Practical Uses of Contracts in Golf Management

The golf manager must realize that a business transaction is involved when dealing with outside suppliers. A supplier is any person or organization that contracts for supplies, services, or events. Some of the primary areas of involvement with suppliers are merchandise, services, concessions, medical and emergency medical, agreements with other organizations or schools, joint facilities, and leases. Other contract areas are personnel, independent contractors, architect, contractors, and equipment purchases.

Merchandise Contract

When purchasing merchandise it is important to understand the terms of delivery and payment as contained on the order form or other agreement. When merchandise is delivered it should be carefully examined for defects. Check the terms of payment to see if: (1) discounts for early payment are available, (2) merchandise may be returned, and (3) time limits have been established on returns.

Service Contract

When contracting for services (e.g., custodial, lawn maintenance, towel and uniform cleaning, purified water, etc.) obtain a list of references and check them

---

15. *Cole et al. v. City of Atlanta*, 392 S.E. 2d 283 (1990).

to ascertain if the contractor is capable of adequately performing the task(s). Be careful of service contractors who use standard contracts. Generally, a standard form contract is unfavorable to the purchaser. Remember to inquire whether or not they are insured.

Concessions Contracts

Concessions can be a "cash cow." Concessions are not just food. It is an umbrella term covering other sales including parking, car detailing, clothing (e.g., hats, tee-shirts, sweat shirts, glassware, and much more), magazines and newspapers, audio and video recordings, and much more. It is important to consider the following before deciding what to do about concessions:

- How will the concessions be handled at events?
- Are they provided by the organization or an outside concessionaire?
- Should the outside concessionaire be under contract?
- Who is liable for injuries caused by the concessionaire's personnel or equipment or food poisoning?
- What financial should be entered into with concessionaire?
- Who provides the personnel?
- Who provides the equipment?
- Who secures the alcohol license?
- Who is responsible for the restaurant license?

If it is decided to secure an outside organization to provide concessions, there should be a contract for this service. The contract should contain the following covenants and conditions:

- type of products to be sold,
- financial considerations for both parties,
- proof of liability insurance up to $1 million and indemnification,
- alcohol and restaurant licenses,
- security,
- equipment,
- length of contract,
- option to renew,
- termination, and
- duties and responsibilities of each party.[16]

16. Sawyer, T.H., & Smith, O.R. (1999). *The Management of Clubs, Recreation, and Sport: Concepts and Applications*. Champaign, IL: Sagamore Publishing, 88-90.

Medical and Emergency Care Services Contract

It is extremely important to provide medical and emergency care services for employees, customers, clients, and/or student-athletes. The following questions need to be answered before a contract can be drafted:[17]

- Do you have a doctor present at all of your events or only for major undertakings (e.g., road races, contact sport activities, racquetball or tennis tournament)?
- Are you required by law to have a doctor present at events?
- When should you have a doctor present?
- When do you have an emergency vehicle present?
- Should you contract for these services?

The following are the components that should be in a contract for medical or emergency care services:

- type of doctor desired (e.g., cardiologist, internist, orthopedic),
- retained for what purpose(s) and service(s),
- consult with whom (e.g., management, trainers, coaches, athletes, clients),
- time commitment,
- rate of compensation, and payment schedule,
- physician's recommendations, include prescriptions, prescribing treatment, recommendations for surgery, recommendations for rehabilitation,
- proof of liability insurance (i.e., at least $1 million),
- understanding that the physician or emergency medical service is an independent contractor and is not acting as the organization's agent, employee, or servant,
- option to renew contract, and
- termination clause.

Agreements with Other Organizations

When should you have agreements with other organizations? The following are suggested as contractible:

- activity schedules
- fund raising events (e.g., a non-profit agency requests to use your facilities for a fund raising event that will involve not only your facilities but also clients as well as other people—you had better have a contract to cover liability as well as expenses),
- for services (e.g., cleaning, laundry, food), and
- education (e.g., local college or public schools do not have racquetball facilities and elect to teach the classes at your facility).[18]

17. Id.
18. Id.

Equipment Contract

Golf facilities purchase a variety of equipment from kitchen to maintenance to programming. It is important that the purchaser of the equipment be aware of all guarantees and warranties for the selected equipment. Further, that the purchaser understands what will invalidate the guarantee and warranty (e.g., failure to install equipment properly, failure to assemble equipment properly, failure to maintain equipment as prescribe by the instructions). A wise manager would have the manufacturer or its representative assemble and initially install all equipment. Further, the maintenance supervisor would maintain a record of all manufacturer recommendations for maintenance of equipment, and replace all parts with recommended manufacturer parts.

Contractors Contract

A golf facility has the opportunity to utilize a variety of contractors on a regular basis to maintain the facilities. The type of contractors include electrical (e.g., telephone, audio or video wiring, electrical, or security), mechanical (e.g., plumbers, heating and air conditioning, or ventilation), concrete, masonry, roofing, framing, asphalt, or earthmoving. When negotiating a contract with a contractor consider including the following cost of materials, hourly rate, union or non-union labor, guarantee, warranty, insurance, construction timeline, late fees, bonus for completing early, payment schedule, and inspection requirements.

Architect Contract

When selecting an architect contact the American Institute of Architects (AIA) in Washington, D.C. The AIA will send you a listing of certified architects in your area. The basic considerations for selecting an architect are the following:

- membership in the AIA,
- a state license,
- a good reputation,
- good references,
- examples of work on similar projects,
- close enough proximity to the project to provide weekly visitations,
- ability to work with the "building,"
- ability to recommend reliable and respected contractors and subcontractors, and
- ability to provide strong competent supervision for the project.

Joint Facilities Contract

If you share ownership or use a facility with another organization (i.e., public school or college), do you have a written agreement defining the rights and responsibilities of each owner or user? Does the agreement adequately protect you if an accident occurs while the other party is using the facility? A carefully drafted agreement defining the terms of use, supervision required during use, and the specific responsibilities of each party could be very important in the event of an injury at the jointly operated facility.

Lease Agreement

For *each* facility that you lease for your use, or that you lease to others, you should have a written lease agreement. That lease agreement should have the following components:

- definition of lessor and lessee,
- consideration, and
- terms and conditions, such as (a) commencing and terminating the lease, (b) rights to the facility, rent, insurance (copy of binder to be attached), security, concessions, maintenance, catastrophe, additional facilities, special terms or conditions, construction, option to renew, termination clause, affirmative action clause, signature by appropriate personnel, and notarized if appropriate.

Staff Contracts

It is important for both the employer and employee to enter into an employment contract which describes the responsibilities of both, rate of compensation, fringe benefit package, evaluation, length of contract, option to renew, and a termination clause.

Contracts with Clients, Customers, or Participants

Many golf facilities require members to sign a membership contract. Contracts with users and participants (e.g., membership, fitness/health, scholarships, injuries, club sports) are common. The membership contract obligates the member to pay dues for services rendered.

A Final Word . . .

A major responsibility of a golf professional will be preparing and reviewing contracts. In many organizations an administrator may routinely draft and/or review documents such as service contracts or facility leases. It is suggested that an attorney always review such documents to determine whether they would withstand legal review. At a minimum all standard form contracts should be reviewed at least once annually. In preparing a contract, it is critical for the administrator to provide the attorney drafting the contract with as many pertinent facts as possible so that the attorney can fully protect the organization's rights under the agreement. Since many of the contracts used in golf course management are unique to the industry, the attorney will require significant input from the administrator in order to draw up a proper contract. Administrators should be prepared to provide such data and to review drafts of contracts to check for errors.

Do you need an attorney?

Yes, an attorney is an extremely valuable and necessary member of the management team. Those organizations that do not consult with a lawyer are asking for serious management problems that will lead to large legal expenses in the future.

The attorney you select must understand the needs of the organization, be experienced in dealing with matters the affect the organization's programs (e.g., contracts, bonding, insurance, affirmative action, and much more), and be willing to assist in planning events/programs and other transactions. You should develop a list of legal needs before you try to select an attorney. The attorney's expertise must parallel the needs of the organization. You should enter into a contract for the legal services. Do not select the least expensive but rather the most experienced. Further, use the attorney in the planning stages of a proposed event or transaction. Frequently, the attorney's advice at the planning or negotiation levels may lead to better results, and he can make suggestions which may be beneficial to both parties and save the organization money in the long run.

Finally, do not attempt to be a lawyer. Do not assume that because a situation was handled one way last year, that a similar situation will be handled exactly the same this year. If the law has changed, or if the circumstances are not exactly the same, then last year's solution will not work. Never simply retype an agreement which you have previously used and substitute names and dates.

Chapter 6

Planning, Planning, Planning

An important duty is to plan properly, and planning, or the lack of it, is usually a component in the breach of other duties. Behind every instance of negligence there is usually an element of poor planning. Whether it be faulty design of a building or piece of equipment, or improperly teaching a golf class, or maintaining the golf course or motorized golf carts planning is an essential element. Realtors are taught that the most important aspect to a successful business is location, location, location. The most important aspect to managing an organization successfully is planning, planning, planning.

Good prior planning should help a professional for after-the-fact reviews of his/her professional behavior. While poor prior planning, or the absence of a plan will not.

Planning is the process of determining the organization's goals and objectives and selecting a course of action to accomplish them within the organization as well as outside. Its primary purpose is to offset future uncertainties by reducing the risk surrounding the organization's operations. It requires the organization to review its internal accomplishments (strengths) and challenges (weaknesses), and external opportunities and threats. During this process the organization will develop a strengths (accomplishments), weaknesses (challenges), opportunity, and threat (SWOT) chart (i.e., the depiction of internal strengths and weakness, and external opportunities and threats of the organization and identify connections within the organization as well as externally that will allow the organization to become strategically competitive in the future (see Figure 6.1). This process is best facilitated by the use of brainstorming.

Brainstorming

Brainstorming, developed by Alexander F. Osborn (1888–1966), involves forming a group of six to eight members who are presented a problem and asked to identify as many potential solutions as possible. The sessions usually last from thirty minutes to an hour. At least two days before a session, group members are given a one-page summary of the problem they are to consider.[1] There are four rules of brainstorming: (1) criticism is prohibited—judgment of ideas must be withheld until all ideas have been generated; (2) "freewheeling" is welcome—the

1. Husey, D.E. (1991). *Introducing Corporate Planning: Guide to Strategic Management*. New York: Pergamon Press.

Figure 6.1
A Connections SWOT Chart

Internal Strengths List (Accomplishments)	Internal Weaknesses List (Challenges)
External Opportunities List	External Threats List

wilder and further out the idea the better, it is easier to "tame down" than to "think up" ideas; (3) quantity is wanted—the greater the number of ideas, the greater the likelihood of an outstanding solution; and (4) combination and improvement are sought—in addition to contributing ideas of their own, members are encouraged to suggest how the ideas of others can be improved, or how two or more ideas can be combined into still another idea.

The Steps in the Planning Process

There are five steps in the planning process including establishing objectives, developing premises, decision-making, implementing a course of action, and evaluating the results.[2]

Step 1: Identifying Internal and External Connections and Relationships

The initial step in the planning process is identifying internal strengths (accomplishments) and weaknesses (challenges), and external opportunities and threats (concerns). This information is placed into a SWOT analysis chart which will assist in the identification of connections and relationships relating to the internal organizational environment and external environment.

Step 2: Establishing Objectives

The next step in the planning process is the establishment of organization objectives. Objectives are an essential starting point since they provide direction for all other managerial activities. Objectives are generally based on perceived opportunities that exist in an organization's surrounding environment.

2. Wright, P.L., Pringle, C.D., Kroll, M.J., & Parnell, J.A. (1994). *Strategic Management: Text and Case*. Boston: Allyn and Bacon.

Step 3: Developing Premises

Once organizational objectives have been established, developing premises about the future environment in which they are to be accomplished is essential. This basically involves forecasting events or conditions likely to influence objective attainment.

Step 4: Decision-Making

After establishing objectives and developing premises the next step is selecting the best course of action for accomplishing stated objectives from the possible alternatives. There are three phases of decision-making: (1) available alternatives must be identified; (2) each alternative must be evaluated in light of the premises about the future and the external environment; and (3) the alternative with the highest estimated probability of success should be selected.

Step 5: Implementing a Course of Action

Once a plan of action has been adopted, it must be implemented. Plans alone are no guarantee of success. Managers must initiate activities that will translate the plans into action.

Step 6: Evaluating the Plan

Plans and their implementation must be constantly monitored and evaluated. All managers are responsible for the evaluation of planning outcomes. Comparison of actual results with those projected is necessary, as well as to refine plans."

Classification of Plans

Plans can be viewed from a number of different perspectives. From the viewpoint of application, plans can be classified in terms of functional areas (e.g., marketing plans, production plans, human resource management plans, financial plans). Plans may also be classified according to the period of time over which they are projected (e.g., short- or long-range) or with respect to their frequency of use (standing versus single-use). The nature of functional plans is evident. However, further explanation is needed for period of time and frequency of use plans.

Short- and long-range plans are the most popular classification of plans. In practice, however, the terms short-range and long-range have no precise meaning, but rather express relative periods of time. These plans are interrelated in at least two respects. First, they compete for the allocation of resources. Consequently, there can be a dangerous tendency to sacrifice long-term results for short-term gains. Second, short-range plans should be compatible with long-range plans. It is usually difficult, if not impossible, for long-range plans to succeed unless short-range plans are accomplished. Thus, both are important in achieving an organization's objectives.

The term short-range is often titled Operational in many organizations, and long-term has been changed to Applied Strategic. These terms will be used interchangeably throughout the remainder of the chapter.

There are three criteria most often used in determining the length of a plan: (1) how far into the future an organization's commitments extend; (2) how much uncertainty is associated with the future; and (3) how much lead time is required to ready a good or service for sale.[3]

Planning by most effective organizations is often done on a "rolling" basis. This simply means those organizations that develop applied strategic plans for a five year period and two year operational plans are updating both plans on an annual basis. As the current year of a five year plan closes, it is extended or rolled forward to include a new fifth year. This procedure allows an organization to revise its plans on the basis of new information and to maintain a degree of flexibility in its commitments. A general guideline is to refrain from formalizing plans until a final commitment is absolutely necessary.[4]

Standing plans are used again and again, focus on managerial situations that recur repeatedly. Standing plans include policies, procedures, and rules.

Policies are general statements that serve to guide decision-making. They are plans in that they prescribe parameters within which certain decisions are to be made. Policies set limits but they are subject to interpretation because they are broad guidelines. Figure 6.2 provides examples of policies. Notice that each example is purposefully broad and only provides a general guideline subject to managerial discretion. However, each statement does prescribe parameters for decision-making and, thus, sets limits to the actions of organization members.

A *procedure* is a series of related steps that are to be followed in an established order to achieve a given purpose. Procedures prescribe exactly what actions are to be taken in a specific situation. Procedures are similar to policies in that both are intended to influence certain decisions. They are different in that policies address themselves to single decisions, while procedures address themselves to a sequence of related decisions. Table 6.1 shows how an organization might write procedures for processing a golf membership.

---

3. Paley, N. (1991). *The Strategic Marketing Planner*. New York: AMACOM.
4. Fogg, D.C. (1991). *Team-based Strategic Planning: A Complete Guide to Structuring, Facilitating, and Implementing the Process*. New York: American Management Association.

Figure 6.2

Examples of Policies

Customer Service:	It is the policy of this organization to provide customers with the finest service possible within limits of sound financial principles. [Interpretation = What are the limits of sound finance?]
Employee Benefits:	It is the policy of this organization to provide employees with acceptable working conditions and an adequate living wage. [Interpretation = What is acceptable and adequate?]
Promotion from Within:	It is the policy of this organization to promote qualified employees from within the organizations' ranks whenever possible. [Interpretation = What is meant by qualified or feasible?]
Gifts from Suppliers or Vendors	It is the policy of this organization that no employee shall accept any gift from any supplier or vendor unless it is of nominal value. [Interpretation = What is nominal?]

Source: Adapted from Sawyer, T.H. (2001) Employee Services Management: A Key Component of Human Resource Management. Champaign, IL: Sagamore Publishing.

Rules and *regulations* are different from policies and procedures in that they specify what personal conduct is required of an individual. Stated differently, rules are standing plans that either prescribe or prohibit action by specifying what an individual may or may not do in a given situation. Therefore, the statements, "eye goggles must be worn," "no swimming alone," "no smoking," "no drinking on premises" are all examples of rules. Rules are usually accompanied by specifically stated penalties that vary according to seriousness of the offense and number of previous violations. Unlike policies that guide, but do not eliminate discretion, rules leave little room for interpretation. The only element of choice associated with a rule is whether it applies in a given situation. Of the three forms of standing plans discussed, rules are the simplest and most straightforward. They are without question the narrowest in scope and application.

Single-use plans are specifically developed to implement courses of action that are relatively unique and are unlikely to be repeated. Three principal forms of single-use plans are budgets, programs, and projects.

A *budget* is a plan that deals with the future allocation and utilization of various resources to different activities over a given time period. Budgets are perhaps most frequently thought of in financial terms. However, they also are used to plan allocation and utilization of labor, raw materials, floor space, machine hours, and so on. A budget simply is a tool that managers use to translate future plans into numerical terms. Further, they are a method for controlling organization operations.

Programs are typically intended to accomplish a specific objective within a fixed time. Table 6.2 offers six guidelines for effective program development.

Table 6.1

Procedure for Processing a Golf Membership

Step 1:	Prior to recording, all noncash sales will be forwarded to the credit department for approval.
Step 2:	Following the necessary credit approval, all memberships (renewal or new) will be presented to membership department for issuance of a membership card.
Step 3:	Subsequent to issuance of the membership card, all memberships will be delivered to the accounting department where they will be recorded.
Step 4:	Pursuant to their processing in the accounting department, all memberships will be filed with the club house supervisor within 24 hours.

Source: Adapted from Sawyer, T.H. (2001) Employee Services Management: A Key Component of Human Resource Management. Champaign, IL: Sagamore Publishing.

Projects are usually a subset or component part of a specific program. Accordingly, projects often share some of the same characteristics as the overall programs of which they are a part. Projects are less complex than their supporting programs and, are, by definition narrower in scope. Table 6.3 summaries the various standing and single-use plans.

Table 6.2

Guidelines for Effective Project/Program Development

1. Divide the project/program into parts, each with a clearly defined purpose.
2. Study the necessary sequence and relationship between the resulting parts.
3. Assign appropriate responsibility for each part to carefully selected individuals or groups.
4. Determine and allocate the resources necessary for the completion of each part.
5. Estimate the completion time required for each part.
6. Establish target dates for the completion of each part.

Source: Adapted from Sawyer, T.H. (2001) Employee Services Management: A Key Component of Human Resource Management. Champaign, IL: Sagamore Publishing.

Strategic Planning

Strategic planning, unlike operational planning which focuses on more direct aspects of operating an organization, focuses on an organization's long-term relationship to its environment. The strategic plan should be developed through participatory involvement by all members of the organization and its clients. By focusing on an organization as a total system, strategic planning recognizes that all organizations face many uncontrollable elements within the environment. Competitors' actions, economic conditions, regulatory groups, labor unions, and changing customer preferences represent factors over which an organization achieves its objectives. Therefore, strategic planning concerns itself with shaping an organization so it can accomplish its goals. A strategic plan attempts to answer such questions as:[5]

- What is the organization's business and what should it be?
- What business should the organization be in five years from now? 10 years?
- Who are the organization's customers and who should they be?
- Should the organization try to grow in this business or grow primarily in other businesses?

Table 6.3

Summary of Standing and Single-Use Plans

Type	Definition	Example
Standing Plans		
Policy	A general statement that guides decision making.	Preference will be given to hiring the handicapped.
Procedure	A series of related steps that are followed in an established order to achieve a given purpose.	Filing for travel expenses reimbursement.
Rule	A statement that either prescribes or prohibits action by specifying what an individual may or may not do in a specific situation.	No eating at work stations.
Single-use Plans		
Budget	A plan that deals with the future allocations and utilization of various resources to different enterprise activities over a given time.	Allocation and utilization of machine hours.
Program	A plan typically intended to accomplish a specific objective within fixed time.	Membership recruitment program.
Project	A subset or component part of a specific program.	Telemarketing project.

Source: Adapted from Sawyer, T.H. (2001) Employee Services Management: A Key Component of Human Resource Management. Champaign, IL: Sagamore Publishing.

5. Antoniou, P.H. (1994). *Competitiveness Through Strategic Success*. Oxford, OH: Planning Forum.

Objectives

Objectives are those ends that an organization seeks to achieve by its existence and operation. There are two essential characteristics of an objective: (1) objectives are predetermined, and (2) objectives describe future desired results toward which present efforts are directed. There are eight key result areas in which all organizations should establish objectives according to Peter F. Drucker—market share, innovation, productivity, physical and financial resources, profitability, manager performance and development, worker performance and attitude, and social responsibilities.

There are two ways to establish objectives. The first is the entrepreneurial method. According to this method, objectives are established by an entrepreneur (top management or stockholders). An organization's objectives are defined as the entrepreneur's objectives. The entrepreneur insures that employees' actions are consistent with these objectives by paying them—salaries, bonuses, or pensions—to support the goals.

The second method is the consensual method. In this method, the objectives of an organization are established by the general consent of those concerned. Organization members share in setting the objectives and conflict is eliminated by identifying common or consensual goals.

The Planning Premise

Once enterprise objectives have been established, developing planning premises about the future environment in which they are to be accomplished is essential.[6] Unfolding environmental conditions almost invariably influence enterprise objectives, forcing modifications in both current and anticipated activities. Premises, which attempt to describe what the future will be like, provide a framework for identifying, evaluating, and selecting a course of action for accomplishing enterprise objectives.

The Components of Applied Strategic and Operational Plans

The applied strategic plan is composed of a situational analysis, highlights, introduction, vision statement(s), value(s), mission statement, internal environment, external environment, connections, major action plans, action priorities, monitoring and evaluating, and review, approval, and commitment.[7] The *situational analysis* has five sections including a description of the geographical location and pertinent demographics (e.g., population, economic indicators, industry, average income, etc.), a description of the organization, a SWOT summary, an overview of major strategies and plans, and organization progress since last review.

---

6. Hamel, G., & Prahalad, C.K. (1994). *Competing for the Future*. Boston: Harvard Business School Press; Hoffman, A.N., & O'Neill, H.M. (1993). *The Strategic Management Casebook and Skill Builder*. Minneapolis/St.Paul: West Publishing.

7. Goodstein, L.D., Nolan, T.M., & Pfeiffer, W.J. (1993). *Applied Strategic Planning: A Comprehensive Guide*. New York: McGraw-Hill.

The *highlight* section describes major challenges, customer/client needs, and major accomplishments. The *introduction* provides the reader with a brief description of the planning process and the people involved in the process. The *vision statement* describes the dream of the future for the organization. The *values* section describes that which is desirable or worthy of esteem by the organization (e.g., fostering a we care image with our clients). The *mission statement* is a statement outlining the purpose and mission of the organization. The *internal environment* is composed of a description of the organization's strengths (accomplishments) and weaknesses (challenges), and the *external environment* consists of a description of the organization's external opportunities and threats (concerns). After the internal and external environments have been analyzed a series of *connections* are established based on the relationships found in the analysis. From the connections a series of *major action plans* are established. The actions plans are then translated into *major action priorities*. These major action priorities are the foundation for the one- or two-year operational plan. The applied strategic plan must have established *monitoring and evaluating* procedures in place to assure the proper implementation of the plan. Finally, there must be *review, approval, and commitment* steps established for the final acceptance of the plan.

The operational plan includes the following components major action priorities, problem, project summary, priority issue(s), background, vision of success, goals and objectives of the plan, and action plans (strategies, objectives, baseline data, and action steps).

Each major action priority will have a specific *problem(s)* that will be resolved at the completion of the project. The *project summary* describes briefly the project that will be undertaken by the organization. Each project will have one or more *priority issues* to be tackled during the project. Each major action priority will have a section that outlines the historical significance of the issue(s) relating to the action priority. This section is called *background*. The authors of the operational plan will describe a *vision of success* for each major action priority. Each major action priority will have one or more *goals* and a series of *objectives* for each goal.

Each major action priority has an *action plan*. The action plan can have one or more *strategies* which can have one or more *objectives*. Each action plan has *baseline data* to be used to compare what was with what is. This comparison over the years will establish progress. For each action plan their will be a series of *action steps*. Each action step will outline the *resources* to be used to complete the step, whose *responsible* for the completion of each step, when the project will *start* and *complete*.

What Are the Pitfalls of Planning?

Strategic planning is a process requiring great skill. It can be as frustrating and require a great deal of time. An inability to predict the future can create anxiety and feelings of inadequacy. The ten biggest pitfalls to successful planning are:[8]

8. Nolan, T. (1993). *Plan or Die: 10 Keys to Organizational Success*. San Diego: Pfeiffer & Co.; Piorier, C.C. (1996). *Avoiding Pitfalls of Total Quality*. Milwaukee, WI: ASQC Quality Press.

- Top management assumes that it can delegate its planning function and, thus, not become directly involved.
- Top management becomes so involved in current problems that it spends insufficient time on planning. As a consequence, planning becomes discredited at lower levels.
- Failure to clearly defines and develop enterprise goals as a basis for formulating long-range goals.
- Failure to adequately involve major line managers in the planning process.
- Failure to actually use plans as a standard for assessing managerial performance.
- Failure to create a congenial and supportive climate for planning.
- Assuming that comprehensive planning is something separate from other aspects of the management process.
- Creating a planning program that lacks flexibility and simplicity and fails to encourage creativity.
- Top management fails to review and evaluate long-range plans that have been developed by department and division heads.
- Top management makes intuitive decisions that conflict with formal plans.

Tips for Writing Plans

The following are a few tips that may assist the organization planner in preparing the applied strategic and/or operation plans:

- Include a table of contents describing the overall content and organization of the plan, including page numbers;
- Provide an executive summary describing the plan;
- Format the plan consistently, using the same style for sections, subsections, headings, and subheadings, etc., with a consistent use of numbers or letters for headings;
- Number all pages consecutively;
- Spell out and define all acronyms so that readers unfamiliar with the organization's programs and operations will understand the plan;
- Write clearly and concisely, with short declarative sentences and active verbs;
- Order the plan elements, provide cross-references when necessary, and develop a topic or subject index so that a reader can follow major ideas, themes, throughout the document;
- Make all references to other documents, plans or reports clear and specific enough to allow a reader to easily find the item or section referenced;
- Include in an appendix any information that is not critical to understanding the plan, but which provides useful background or context;
- Structure the plan in a way that will permit sections to be excerpted and distributed to specific audiences, and which will permit changes, edits, or updates without revising the whole plan;
- Test the understandability of the document by having it reviewed by individuals who were not directly involved in its development; and

- On each section, type its computer file name (to speed retrieval in the future). In addition, during the draft process, include date/time code (to keep track of the most recent up-to-date revision). During the draft process, it helps to also hand write the draft (revision) number in the corner as each revision is printed or establishing a watermark (Draft Document 1).

A Final Word . . .

The need for planning stems from the fact that virtually all enterprises operate in a changing environment. The uncertainty resulting from environmental change makes planning a necessity in all but the simplest circumstances. This chapter has identified the phases of the planning process, commented on the importance of planning, examined the scope and application of different types of enterprise plans, introduced the concept of strategic planning and discussed pitfalls in planning.

Chapter 7

Lightning and Golf Course Liability

Golfers injured by lightning while playing golf is a dangerous situation. The following are a few actual accounts of injuries from the National Weather Service files:

- On April 12, 1993, four people were struck by lightning, two injured seriously, at a golf course in a Long Island Community. The four had been playing golf when it began raining and they were standing under a tree at the number 5 green.
- On May 25, 1994, a 26 year old male took refuge under a tree on a golf course in Henrico County, Virginia. The tree was struck and the lightning killed the man.
- On June 14, 1994, a bolt of lightning struck and critically injured a 50 year old woman and a 38 year old man playing in a golf tournament at Greenbrier Country Club in Norfolk. Both received severe burns.
- On April 4, 1999, on a golf course in Culpeper County Virginia around 4pm, a 37 year man was struck and killed under a tree. The rest of his group had already safely retreated to the club house when the incident occurred.

Since 1959, lightning has been the leading cause of weather-related deaths in the U.S., yet people continue to recreate in dangerous circumstances. Curran & Holle[1] indicate that lightning has caused over 9,800 injuries and nearly 3,300 deaths since 1959.

The lightning season is typically late spring through early autumn. Lightning occurs most often in the southeastern U.S., and strikes between mid-afternoon and early evening.[2] Combining the seasonal propensities for lightning, the time of day it occurs, and the tendency for striking open fields; lightning can be a dangerous threat for recreational participants. It is critical for employee services providers to understand lightning and its potential danger as well as have a supervision plan for action in the event of a lightning storm[3] (see Chart 7.1 for strategies to reduce liability in the event of lightning).

---

1. Curran, E., & Holle, R. (1996). *Lightning Fatalities, Injuries, and Damage Reports in the United States from 1950–1994*. Fort Worth, TX: National Oceanic and Atmospheric Administration.
2. Cooper, M.A. (1994). Electric and lightning injuries. *Emergency Medical Clinics of North America, 14*(2), 489-501.
3. McChesney, J.C., & Cooper, N. (1998). Risk management: The key to safe fitness programs and facilities. *Employee Services Management, 41*(10), 9-11.

Chart 7.1

Strategies to Reduce Liability in the Event of Lightning

Prepare the staff
- Review with the staff the Emergency Action Plan
- Require the staff be currently certified in CPR and First Aid
- Review the written lightning safety policy and procedures to be followed
- Require the staff to utilize updated weather information from the National Weather Service
- Have the staff explain to the participants the dangers of lightning and the procedures to be followed in the event of lightning.

Provide safe shelter
- The shelter must meet the qualifications of a safe shelter (see Chart 7.2)
- The shelters must be in close proximity to the outdoor venues
- The shelter must be easily accessible to all participants.

Warn all participants

Use written reports

Post warnings—on large signs

Tell participants of the warnings

Educate participants of what warning signs indicate

Source: McChesney & Cooper, 11.

Appenzeller and Baron "indicated a 16-year-old high school student in Dallas, Texas, died four days after he was struck by lightning during football practice. The boy suffered burns and cardiac arrest after lightning struck his helmet."[4]

"Ten football players from Pahokee High School in Florida were injured by lightning as they headed off the practice field to the locker room. The boys sued the Palm Beach School Board alleging that the coaches knew the storm was impending, but refused to safeguard the students by canceling practice. According to the lawsuits, the coaches waited too late to move the players to the gymnasium to prevent injury from the thunderstorm."[5]

Robert Rennell, assistant golf professional at Richland Country Club in Nashville, Tennessee, reported that an appeals court in Tennessee recently held a club liable when a player was struck by lightning. The court held that the club was negligent for:

- failure to post signs warning of the hazards of lightning;
- failure to provide lightning proof shelters; and
- lack of a policy to clear the course during thunderstorms.

Airborne Research Associates, a meteorological research firm warned that "half of the people killed or injured by lightning each year in the United States are

4. Appenzeller, H., & Baron, R. (1996). *From The Gym to the Jury*, 7(2).
5. Appenzeller, H., & Baron, R. (1997). *From The Gym to the Jury*, 8(4).

on golf courses." The report noted that "most are not struck directly, but are in the immediate vicinity since lightning can induce currents in nearly grounded objects." This poses a very real threat and impacts the liability factor of golf courses.[6]

The National Summary of Lightning reported that 85 were killed in 1995 in the United States by lightning while 510 were injured in the same year.[7] The report lists the places of occurrence as follows:[8]

- "golf courses,
- open fields, ball fields, etc.,
- under trees,
- boating, fishing, and water-related activities,
- near tractors, heavy road equipment,
- at telephones, and
- various other unknown locations."

Enlightening Facts about Lightning

The following are a few interesting facts about lightning:

- average lightning stroke is 6 miles long,
- average thunderstorm is 6–10 miles wide,
- average thunderstorm travels at a rate of 25 miles per hour,
- once the leading edge of a thunderstorm approaches to within 10 miles, you are at immediate risk due to the possibility of lightning strokes coming from the overhanging anvil cloud. Because of this, many lightning deaths and injuries occur with clear skies directly overhead,
- on average, thunder can only be heard over a distance of 3–4 miles, depending on humidity, terrain, and other factors,
- approximately 100,000 thunderstorms occur in the United States each year. Approximately 10% of all thunderstorms are severe enough to produce high winds, flash floods, and tornadoes, and
- thunderstorms cause an average of 200 deaths and 700 injuries in the alone each year.

Source: McChesney & Cooper, 11.

Procedure for Severe Weather Detection

"Thunderstorms constitute the major source of severe weather," according to researchers at Airborne Research Associates in Weston, Massachusetts. Other disturbances include "accompanying strong wind gusts, microbursts, tornadoes, hail, heavy rainfall (flooding) as well as lightning."

6. Airborne Research Association. (1995). Weston: MA.
7. *Angel v. Hison* (1995).
8. Id.

"The National Weather Service advises that when thunder is heard, lightning is present—despite not being visible to the human eye. Therefore, the National Weather Service advises reasonable procedures that would dictate a policy that people seek shelter as soon as thunder is heard and not wait for the appearance of lightning."[9]

In an effort to prevent injuries from severe weather, the University of Oklahoma developed "severe weather procedures" through its Department of Public Safety. The Athletic Department purchased a Lightning Detector to "determine when outdoor practice and/or competition should be suspended." The detector would alert school officials when "severe weather or lightning is detected within 30 miles of Norman." A watch condition would follow and campus police would notify athletic department personnel who would then notify coaches staff and student-athletes of the threatening conditions.[10]

If lightning is detected within eight miles of the campus, a warning is declared and all outdoor activities such as intramurals, athletic practice or competition, and other campus activities will cease until lightning has cleared the area. The weather detector was purchased for less than $200 and offers protection to the participants at the university.

Many Professional Golfers Association (PGA) Tournaments now utilize the weather detector to alert its patrons and golfers of approaching severe weather. Lights are activated on the leader boards to warn spectators of severe weather. Spectators must be instructed where to go or how to respond.

Lightning Safety Tips

According to Appenzeller and Baron, the National Lightning Safety Institute as a public service, recommends lightning safety tips that include the following:

- "When you first hear thunder, begin to plan your lightning defense. Can you get to a car or building quickly? These offer the best protection. Can you get 100 yards away from all metal objects? Lightning often precedes rain, so don't wait for the rain before suspending activities. Typically, the distance from Strike A to Strike B to Strike C can be .5–2.5 miles. Plan in advance your evacuation and safety measures."[11]

If Outdoors

- "Avoid water.
- Avoid all metal objects including electric wires, fences, golf clubs, machinery, motors, power tools, etc.
- Unsafe places include golf carts, tents, open-sided rain shelters, small boats, or underneath isolated trees. Avoid high ground and open spaces.

---

9. Appenzeller, H., & Baron, R. (1997). *From The Gym to the Jury*, *8*(4).
10. Webb, J. (1995). *Policies and Procedures for Severe Weather*. Norman, OK: University of Oklahoma, Athletic Department.
11. Appenzeller, H., & Baron, R. (1997). *From the Gym to the Jury*, 8(4).

Where possible, find shelter in a building or in a fully enclosed vehicle such as a car, truck, or van with the windows completely shut.

- If no shelter is available and lightning is striking nearby, you should:
- Avoid direct contact with other people.
- Remove all metal objects from your person.
- Crouch down, with feet together and hands on knees."[12]

If Indoors

- "Avoid water.
- Stay away from open doors and windows.
- Hang up the telephone and take off headsets.
- Lightning may strike electric and phone lines and induce shocks.
- Turn off and stay away from appliances, computers, power tools, TV sets, etc.
- Remain inside until the storm has passed.
- If a nearby person is injured from lightning, give first aid procedures if you are qualified to do so. An injured person does not carry an electrical charge and can be handled safely. Call 911 or send for help immediately."[13]

Warning of Inherent Dangers of Lightning

The National Lightning Safety Institute promotes a "Flash-to-Bang" method of measuring the distance between lightning and a person. This practice measures the interval between the time lightning is seen (flash) to hearing thunder (bang). Each five-second count represents one mile between lightning and the person counting. Although it is documented that lightning can strike from as far away as 10 miles, the Institute urges people to take immediate defensive action at a count of no less than 15 seconds or three miles. The National Federation of State High School Associations in its rule books tells officials to suspend the game and clear the field at the first sight of lightning. The National Severe Storms Laboratory in Norman, OK has more cautious standards than the National Lightning Safety Institute. It recommends seeking shelter at a count of 30 seconds (six miles). Therefore, the employee services provider, armed with the knowledge that a storm is less than three miles away, and understanding lightning can strike from a distance of 10 miles, would order participants to seek safe shelter immediately. Finally, all three organizations favor a 30-minute waiting period after the last lightning flash before returning to the field to continue play.

McChesney and Cooper[14] suggest that a clear and rehearsed warning signal is vital to ensure safe and expeditious retreat from a potentially dangerous lightning situa-

12. Id.
13. Id.
14. See McChesney & Cooper at 3, 9.

tion. Further, each recreational venue should have a recognized warning signal (e.g., three blasts on a horn or whistle every few seconds) that indicates danger is imminent, and the field or course should be cleared immediately. Pre-event meetings with staff, officials, coaches, and participants should provide instructions of what to do if such a warning sounds. This information should provide detailed directions on how to, as well as basic personal safety plans if lightning is about to strike. Finally, the event packet that is provided to everyone, including officials, should include an agreement to participate form, a waiver form, and a handout describing the dangers of lightning, defining a safe shelter, names of locations of such shelters, description of the warning signal, and suggesting to the participants how long to wait in the shelter prior to returning the outside. The participant should sign and date the bottom of the handout stating that he/she has read and understands the lightning policy. This should be maintained in the official as an official record.

A Safe Shelter

According to McChesney and Cooper,[15] a safe shelter is defined as a building that people occupy (e.g., office building, club house, classroom, gymnasium, or garage). If caught in the open, away from any buildings or cars, a person can take shelter in a grouping of similar-size (height) trees or bushes. However, retreating to a lone tall tree is not safe, since single tall objects have an affinity for lightning. If a person feels the hair on his/her body raise or tingle, a lightning strike is imminent, and he should immediately crouch on the balls of his/her feet and make him/herself as small as possible. The forewarning of hair raising indicates that lightning is about to strike, and it is too late to seek safety in a shelter. The employee services provider in areas where lightning strikes often should provide safe shelters that are easily accessible to participants.

Areas that are clearly unsafe are open fields, bodies of water (even puddles), hilltops, near overhead wires, and tall trees. It is wise to avoid these areas/structures at all times if caught in a lightning storm. It is wise to pay heed to the flash-to-bang method of determining how far one is from lightning, so that there will be time to safely find appropriate shelter.

Chart 7.2

Classifications of Shelters[16]

"*Safe Shelters*

- office buildings
- schools
- clubhouse
- gymnasium
- garages

15. Id.
16. Id.

Emergency Shelters

- enclosed car with metal roof
- dense cluster of similar height trees/bushes
- depressed areas

Unsafe Shelters

- convertible car
- golf cart
- storage or maintenance shed
- picnic shelter
- portable toilet
- single tall object (e.g., tree)
- umbrella
- open fields
- bodies of water (even puddles)
- tops of hills"

Lightning and Wrongful Death

Golf is an outdoor game. It is open-air experience that attracts more than 12 million Americans. Consequently, golfers and golf facilities are often exposed to inclement and sometimes dangerous weather conditions.[17] Facility managers must anticipate the effects of adverse weather and take the necessary steps to protect their patrons. Failure to do so may result in property damage, personal injury and sometimes death and will more than likely result in legal liability. All of these could have been avoided by practicing preventative risk management techniques to protect not only the owner and operator of the golf course, but the patron as well.[18]

Lightning claims more lives than any other weather phenomenon—including tornadoes. There are more than 200 people killed and about twice that many are injured by lightning each year in the U.S. and approximately 30% of all lightning victims are engaged in some sort of outdoor recreational activity at the time they are struck.[19] Athletic contests such as baseball, water sports, golf, and camping were the top four pursuits ranked among outdoor recreational activities which resulted in lightning fatalities. Every year approximately 40 people who are either participating in or viewing an athletic event are struck by lightning.[20]

Despite the relatively high number of instances where people have been injured or killed by lightning strikes, there have been only a select few cases where

17. Crist, G.M. (1996). When lightning strikes. *Golf Course Management*, *23*(4).
18. Id.
19. Fucini, M. (1995). Lightning—Don't take a chance. *Referee*, *5*(5).
20. Id.

litigation has resulted. It is the belief of these authors that this is primarily due to the fact that the occurrence of lightning is often regarded as an Act of God. "An Act of God is an unusual, extraordinary and unexpected manifestation of the forces of nature, or a misfortune or accident arising from inevitable necessity which cannot be prevented by reasonable human foresight and care. As a result of this type of classification, few people believe that they can recover for injuries and damages. However, when the negligence of a defendant coincides with an Act of God, a plaintiff can usually recover from a defendant."[21] As is well-known, negligence is often determined by what kind of relationship existed between the plaintiff and the defendant and therefore plays an important role in determining accountability.

Last-Second Safety Measures

All right you still managed to get caught. What can you do? Kozlowski suggests the following steps be taken:

- "If you are on an open fairway try to get to a heavily wooded area, if you can quickly and safely. Take shelter under the shorter trees.
- If you cannot avoid being out in the open, find a low spot away from fences, poles, and isolated trees. Better to get wet than smacked.
- If you feel your skin tingle or your hair stand on end, lightning may be about to strike you. (Consider yourself lucky if you even get this advance warning—many do not.) Squat low to the ground on the balls of your feet. Do not lie flat. If lightning strikes beside you, the current will have an easier time flowing through your body (not a good thing) if you are lying flat on the ground. As you squat, place your hands on your knees with your head between them. The goal is to make a small target get as low as possible and minimize contact with the ground.
- If you are in the middle of a pond looking for your ball, leave it—even if it's your lucky logo ball.
- People struck by lightning should be attended to immediately. They carry no electrical charge."[22]

Administering CPR can revive many victims. Waste no time. Contact your local American Red Cross or Heart Association for information on CPR and first aid.

IDWSP

Inform, Detect, Warn, Shelter, and Protect (IDWSP) golfers and employees from lightning. These five actions will save lives. INFORM—do not assume that

21. Kozlowski, J.C. (1992). No duty to warn of obvious risk of golfing in lightning storm. *Parks and Recreation*, 27(12).

22. Kozlowski, J.C. (1997). Chosen lightning protection on golf course must be properly utilized. *Parks and Recreation*, 32(7).

everyone knows about the dangers of lightning. Display warning signs around the golf course, swimming pool, and clubhouse. DETECT—heed local weather reports or use an electronic detection device to determine if lightning is in the area. WARN—let golfers and employees know that lightning threatens by means of audible and/or visible signals that will be heard and/or seen anywhere on the course. Make sure lifeguards evacuate everyone from the pool area. SHELTER—provide adequate weather shelters (i.e., one shelter for each nine holes). Existing structures such as a halfway house, the maintenance building, clubhouse or rest rooms if equipped with approved lightning rods may be designated as lightning shelters. PROTECT—the clubhouse, cart barn, equipment storage buildings, and maintenance buildings are important to a golf operation and should be protected with approved lightning rod systems. Other vital equipment in need of protection from lightning strikes and surges consist of irrigation systems, alarm systems, electronic data processing equipment, cash registers, etc. This equipment should be protected by surge protectors.

Staying Safe on a Golf Course during a Thunderstorm

The Golf Course Superintendents Association of America knows that golf courses are dangerous places during a thunderstorm. They suggest the following warning to be provided to employees, golfers, and/or spectators:

Mark Twain Championship Golf Course
Thunderstorm Warning

"Golf courses are dangerous places during thunderstorms. If you are caught on the course during a thunderstorm, here are a few tips for your safety:

- When and if the course warning system sounds, seek shelter as quickly as possible.
- Be alert to the signs of changing weather such as darkening skies, a sudden windshift, or drop in temperature.
- Plan your evacuation and safety measures in advance.
- The best place to go when the storm hits is off the course or to a designated lightning shelter.
- Never stand under a lone tree (i.e., deaths caused by lightning over the past 35 years five percent have been golfers standing under single trees). Move away from any tree a distance that is twice the height of the tree.
- Stay away from water.
- Avoid anything that contains metal, including golf clubs, golf bag, golf cart, umbrella, electric wires or fences.
- Remove shoes with metal spikes.
- If stranded in the open seek a low place (i.e., a ravine or valley).
- Avoid high ground.
- Use the 30-30 rule: at the very least, seek safety when thunder and lightning are separated by 30 seconds (when the storm will be 5–6 miles away), and do

not resume activities for 30 minutes after the last observed lightning or thunder (when the storm has passed 10–15 miles away).
- If lightning is striking nearby when you are outside, you should: (a) Crouch down with your feet together. Do not lie down. Place your hands over ears to minimize hearing damage from thunder. (b) Avoid proximity to other people—keep at least 15 feet apart."[23]

Lightning Protection for Shelters

A lightning protection system is designed to intercept lightning and safely direct its current to the ground. For an ordinary shelter, the system includes three elements: air terminals, down conductors, and ground terminals. Golf managers should consider eliminating small shelters without lightning protection from the golf course. Finally, shelters should be located in low areas preferably surrounded by a large number of trees of approximately the same height.

Weather Monitoring

It is important that all golf course employees are taught how to monitor the weather. The following is a list of some of the most popular weather-related Web sites:

- WeatherNet—http://cirrus.sprl.umich.edu/wxnt/
- http://www.weather.com
- National Weather Service—http://www.nws.noaa.gov
- Interactive Weather Information Network—http://iwin.nws.noaa.gov/iwin
- COLA/IGES Weather & Climate Images—http://grads.iges.org/pix/head.html
- The Weather Page—http://www.esdim.noaa.gove/weatherpage
- Weather Map—http://www.mit.edu:8001/usa.html
- The Weather Channel—http://www.weather.com
- CNN Weather—http://www.cnn.com/WEATHER/indes/html
- Weather Online!—http://www2.cybercomm.net, http://www.weatheronline.com/wxtool.html

Many golf courses have purchased a weather station to assist in the task of constantly monitoring weather. Peter Levy of Weather Metrics in Shawnee Mission, Kansas suggests the following are questions that should be asked by the golf course manager prior to purchasing a weather station:

"– Which weather parameters are to be monitored?
  - Temperature
  - Wind speed
  - Wind direction
  - Barometric pressure
  - Rainfall
  - Humidity

23. Golf Course Superintendents' Association of America, Thunderstorm Warning, 1996.

  - Solar
- Is the software user-friendly?
- Does the weather station software operate in the windows environment?
- Is the data presented on the screen in "real-time" as it is occurring?
- Does the information update multiple times per second?
- Can the data be stored for future analysis?
- How often is the data recorded?
- Can evapotranspiration be calculated for user-defined mowing heights, different grass types, and user-defined time frames?
- How many evapotranspiration rates are calculated?
- Can alarms be set to allow the user to define own disease models?
- Can the data be accessed from a home computer?
- How much storage space will one year of data require on my computer?
- Can I add sensors to the system?
- Does the system require a dedicated computer or can the course's existing computer handle it?
- Does the system calculate degree days?
- Does the software calculate rain date, wind chill, heat index, dew point, wet bulb, and leaf wetness?"[24]

Preventive Measures and Safety Tips

Crist outlines the following preventive measures that can be taken to make employees, participants, and spectators more aware of the golf course dangers and risks associated with adverse weather:

"- Post warnings and informational signs,
- Ensure that at least the clubhouse is lightning-safe,
- Establish course evacuation plans and procedures,
- Erect on course lightning-safe shelters,
- Install a weather system,
- Subscribe to a thunderstorm warning service or at least monitor regularly weather monitoring Web sites,
- Equip employees with appropriate clothing and equipment,
- Install a weather warning system for the golf course, and
- Purchase appropriate liability and property insurance coverage."[25]

24. Levy, P. (1997). Purchasing a Weather Station. Shawnee Mission, KA: Weather Metrics.

25. Crist, see at 16.

Strategies for Reducing Risks

The golf manager needs to develop a number of strategies to reduce risk of litigation regarding lightning strikes and damage to facilities and equipment as well as people.

A Final Word...

Planning for emergency situations, like a player being struck by lightning, is an essential part of an effective risk management program that is overlooked by many golf courses. Only through training and practice can staff members be expected to react appropriately when faced with a real emergency situation. You can never prepare too well when people's health and safety is at stake.

Finally, there are some actions that can be taken to make patrons and employees more aware of the golf course risks associated with adverse weather particularly lightning: (a) post warnings and informational signs, such as the ones available from the USGA at a nominal cost, displaying the following: DO go directly to designated lightning shelters, the clubhouse, maintenance buildings, other on-course buildings, automobiles with metal tops and bodies and, as a last resort, dense woods or lowly areas. DO NOT go near open areas, water, metal, wire fences, power lines, isolated trees, elevated ground, maintenance machinery and golf carts. DO NOT raise golf clubs or umbrellas over head when lightning is near; (b) ensure that at least the clubhouse is lightning-safe; (c) establish course evacuation plans and procedures; (d) provide on-course shelters and note their locations on scorecards; (e) install lightning prediction equipment; (f) subscribe to a thunderstorm warning service; (g) equip employees with appropriate clothing and equipment; and (h) purchase appropriate liability and property insurance coverage.

Chapter 8

Employment Issues and the Golf Course Manager

Legal issues permeate almost all aspects of employee relations, from the initial recruitment selection of applicants to their discharge, retirement, or layoff. Because the impact of legal issues is so pervasive and complex, golf course managers who face legal issues on a daily basis, often mourn, "You have to be a lawyer to understand all this stuff!" Although sometimes the help of an attorney is needed, many legal matters can be resolved independently by the manager or supervisor. Thus, these individuals must clearly understand the various legal issues in the workplace.

Employee laws address a variety of issues. Some pertain to specific employment practices, such as the administration of polygraph tests or the need to offer medical family-based leaves. Others deal with broader issues, such as employment discrimination, safety, privacy, and employees' rights to due process.

Equal Employment Opportunity

As part of John F. Kennedy's and Lyndon Johnson's attempt in the 1960s to create the "Great Society," Congress passed an avalanche of legislation aimed at ensuring equal employment opportunity (EEO) in the workplace. These laws were specifically designed to eradicate certain types of employment discrimination that had been all common-discrimination based on race, color, sex, religion, national origin, age, and disability. These categories are referred to as protected classifications because they are protected from discrimination by EEO laws. Subcategories of people within each protected classification are referred to as protected groups. For example, "male" and "female" are the protected groups within the protected classification of "sex."

EEO legislation affords protection to all protected groups within a protected classification, not just the minority groups. Thus, discrimination aimed at a man is just as unlawful as that aimed at a woman. The lone exception to this rule is the use of affirmative action programs, which, under certain circumstances, allow employers to treat members of certain protected groups preferentially.

EEO Laws

The major EEO laws are summarized in Figure 8.1. Each prohibits discrimination based on an individual's protected classification. These laws differ from one to another primarily in terms of the specific protected classifications covered.

Figure 8.1

Major EEO Laws

CIVIL. RIGHTS ACT of 1964 (TITLE II)

Prohibits employment discrimination on the basis of race, color, religion, sex, and national origin. Covets most employers of 15 or more employees.

CIVIL RIGHTS ACT OF 1991

Amendment to the Civil Rights Act of 1964 extending the rights of claimants to receive punitive damages:. It also provides a more detailed description of the evidence needed to prove a discrimination claim.

PREGNANCY DISCRIMINATION ACT OF 1978

An amendment to the 1964 Civil Rights Act, it prohibits discrimination because of a woman pregnancy-related condition.

IMMIGRATION REFORM AND CONTROL ACT OF 1986

Prohibits employers from-knowingly hiring aliens who are not authorized to work in the United States. It also prohibits discrimination based on national origin or citizenship.

AGE DISCRIMINATION IN EMPLOYMENT ACT OF 1967

Prohibits discrimination based on age: It protects workers 40 years of age and older and covers most employers of 20 or more employees.

AMERICANS WITH DISABILITIES ACT OF 1990

Prohibits discrimination based on an employee's disability. The law covers most organizations employing at least 15 people.

CIVIL RIGHTS ACT OF 1964 (TITLE VII)

Title VII of the Civil Rights Act (CRA) of 1964 covers organizations that employ 15 or more workers for at least 20 weeks during the year. This law prohibits discrimination that is based on the protected classifications of race, color, religion, national origin, and sex. Specifically, the law states that:

- It shall be an unlawful employment practice for an employer to fail or refuse to hire or discharge any individual, or otherwise to discriminate against any individual with respect to his compensation, terms, conditions, or privileges of employment, because of such individual's race, color, religion, sex, or national origin.
- The CRA of 1964 is probably the most valuable tool employees have for remedying workplace discrimination because it covers the greatest number of protected classifications. If a court determines that discrimination has occurred, this law entitles the victim to relief in the form of legal costs and back pay (i.e., the salary the person would have been receiving had no discrimination occurred). For instance, let's say that a woman sues a company for rejecting her application for a $25,000 per year construction job because the company unlawfully excludes women from this job. The litigation process takes two years and, ultimately, the court rules in the applicant's favor. To remedy this discrimination, the court would require the company to pay her legal fees and grant her $50,000 in back pay (two years' salary).
- The Civil Rights Act of 1964 has had an enormous impact on the human resource management practices of many companies. For instance, it has forced them to take a close look at the way they hire, promote, award pay raises, and discipline their employees. As a result of this self-scrutiny, many firms have

changed their practices, making them more systematic and objective. For instance, most firms now require their supervisors to provide detailed documentation to justify the fairness of their disciplinary actions, and many firms are now more cautious with regard to their use of employment tests that restrict the employment opportunities for certain protected groups.

Civil Rights Act of 1991

As the 1990s approached, the impact of the Civil Rights Act (CRA) of 1964 began to fade. A number of Supreme Court decisions in the mid- to late 1980s made discrimination claims more difficult for employees to substantiate. To put more "teeth" into the law, the Congress amended it by enacting the Civil Rights Act of 1991.

This 1991 amendment expands the list of remedies that may be awarded in a discrimination case-the employer now has more to lose if found guilty of discrimination. In addition to legal fees and back pay, an employer may now be charged with punitive and compensatory damages (for future financial losses, emotional pain, suffering, inconvenience, mental anguish, and loss of enjoyment of life). The "cap" for these damages ranges from $50,000 to $300,000 depending on the size of the company. Employees are entitled to such damages in cases where discrimination practices are engaged in with malice or reckless indifference to the legal rights of the aggrieved individual (e.g., the employer is aware that serious violations are occurring, but does nothing to rectify them).

Moreover, the CRA of 1991 adds additional bite to the 1964 law by providing a more detailed description of the evidence needed to prove a discrimination claim, making such claims easier to prove. This provision is discussed in more detail later in the chapter.

The CRA of 1991 also differs from the 1964 law by addressing the issue of mixed-motives cases. This type of case is one in which an employment decision, such as hiring or promotion, is based partly on a "legitimate" motive and partly on a discriminatory one. For instance, a company rejects the application of a woman because she behaves in an unlady-like manner—she is too aggressive for a woman, wears no makeup, and swears like a man. The company is concerned that she would offend its customers. The employer's motives are thus mixed: Its concern about offending customers is a legitimate motive; its stereotyped view of how a "lady" should behave is a discriminatory one.

The CRA of 1991 states that mixed-motive decisions are unlawful. That is, the hiring practice is illegal when a candidate's protected group membership is a fact affecting an employment decision, even if other, more legitimate factors are considered. Thus, if the "unlady-like" applicant can prove to a court that the decision was based, at least in part, on the employer's stereotyped view of how woman should behave, she would win the case.

Pregnancy Discrimination Act of 1978

The Pregnancy Discrimination Act (PDA) of 1978 amends the CRA of 1964 by specifically including discrimination against women based on pregnancy, childbirth, or related medical condition. It states that employees who are unable to perform their jobs because of a pregnancy-related condition must be treated in the same manner as employees who are temporarily disabled for other reasons.

Immigration Reform and Control Act of 1986

The Immigration Reform Control Act (IRCA) of 1986 prohibits discrimination based on national origin citizenship. Specifically, the law states that employers of four or more employees cannot discriminate against any individual (other than an illegal alien) because; that of person's national origin or citizenship status.

In addition to being an anti-discrimination law, this act makes it unlawful to knowingly hire an unauthorized alien. At the time of hiring, an employer must require proof that the person offered the job is not an illegal alien.

Age Discrimination in Employment Act of 1967

The Age Discrimination Employment Act (ADEA) of 1967 is intended to protect "older workers" (i.e., 40 and above) from age discrimination. The ADEA, which applies to nearly all employers of 20 or more employees, promotes the employment of older persons, on their ability, rather than age. The ADEA protects only "older" individuals from discrimination, people under 40 are not protected. The act also prohibits employers from giving preference to individuals within the 40 or older group. For instance, an employer does not discriminate against a 50-year-old by giving preference to a 40-year-old.

Americans with Disabilities Act of 1990 (Title 1)

The Americans Disabilities Act (ADA) of 1990 "provides a clear and comprehensive national mandate for the elimination of discrimination against individuals with disabilities." The employment implications of the act, which are delineated in Titles I (private sector) and II (public sector) of the ADA, affect nearly all organizations employing 15 or more workers. According to the act, an individual is considered disabled if she has a physical or mental impairment that substantially limits one or most of the individual's major life activities, such as walking, seeing, hearing, breathing, learning, as well as the ability to secure or retain employment.

In order to win a complaint, an individual who has been denied employment because; a disability, must establish that, with accommodation (if necessary), he or she qualified to perform the essential functions of the job in question. To defend successfully against such a suit, the employer must demonstrate that, even with reasonable accommodation, the candidate could not perform the job satisfactorily and must demonstrate that the accommodation would impose an undue hardship. The ADA defines "undue hardship" as those accommodations that require significant difficulty to effect or significant expense on the part of the employer.

An example of an ADA case would be one in which an employee is fired because of frequent absences caused by a particular disability. The employee may argue that the employer failed to offer a reasonable accommodation, such as a transfer to a part-time position. The employer, on the other hand, may argue that such an action would pose an undue hardship in that the creation of such a position would be too costly.

What Are the Pitfalls to Avoid with the ADA?

Bartlett and Rabinoff[1] in an article under the legal section of Employee Services Management, outline the following pitfalls to avoid in administering the ADA:

- "Each person must be treated as an individual and must not be treated based upon some general stereotype or concept concerning type of apparent disability.
- An employer cannot avoid responsibility by contracting or otherwise have a third party provide a service. (For example, if an employer contracts with a golf management company to supervise and operate a golf course and its programs, the same restrictions apply against the employer; and the employer may well be held liable for any actions by the golf club in violation of the ADA.)
- A person with disabilities does not need to prove intentional discrimination. An honest, unintentional mistake that is discriminatory and prohibited by the ADA can result in sanctions provided by the law.
- The ADA generally prohibits preemployment medical examinations as well as questions about disabilities but specifically permits voluntary medical examinations in wellness programs.
- Any information gathered through voluntary medical examinations must be confidential and the medical examination requirements must apply to all employees.
- The ADA does not supersede or preempt any other federal or state law. Therefore, it is theoretically possible for an employer to subject herself to liability under another law or laws.
- The greatest pitfall of all would be to do nothing."

Whom to Contact

For more specific information about ADA requirements affecting public services and public accommodations contact and of the following:

U.S. Department of Justice, Civil Rights Division
Office on the Americans with Disabilities Act
P.O. Box 66118
Washington, D.C. 20035-6118
202/514-0301 (Voice)
202/514-0381 (TDD)

Equal Employment Opportunity Commission
1801 L. Street NW
Washington, D.C. 20507
202/663-4900 (Voice)
800/800-3302 (TDD)

Department of Transportation
400 Seventh Street NW

1. Pitfalls to Avoid with the ADA. *Athletic Management*, 34 (8), 26-30.

Washington, D.C. 20590
202/366-9305 (Voice)
202/755-7687 (TDD)

Architectural and Transportation Barriers Compliance Board
1111 18th Street NW Suite 501
Washington, D.C. 20036
800/use-able (Voice)
800/usa-able (TDD)

Federal Communications Commission
1919 M. Street NW
Washington, D.C. 20554
202/632-7620 (Voice)
202/632-6999 (TDD)

Key Provisions of the Americans with Disabilities Act

1. Protected individuals:
   - Have a physical or mental impairment that substantially limits one or more major life activities
   - Have a record of such an impairment
   - Are regarded as having such an impairment

2. Who must comply?
   - Any company with 15 or more employees
   - Private companies and local, state, and federal government agencies

To avoid possible discrimination charges, the employer must develop complete job descriptions for each position in each department or area.

- Current physical and mental requirements
- Essential job functions

Essential job functions vs. marginal functions

There are three characteristics of an essential job function:

- It is a function that, if removed, would alter the job.
- It is a function that cannot be performed by another employee (e.g., an employee on a graveyard shift who works alone being required to walk long distances).
- It is a function that is specialized (e.g., a job requirement for an orderly in a nursing home to be physically able to lift a patient).

Marginal functions are those job duties that an employee may perform but which are not essential to the position (e.g., a job requirement for an orderly in a nursing home to be able to read daily instructions).

3. Reasonable accommodations

A reasonable accommodation is a change in the work environment that allows a qualified disabled individual to perform essential functions of a job that the person would otherwise not be able to do.

There are three types of accommodations according to the ADA accommodations that:

- ensure equal opportunity in the job search
- ensure employees to perform the essential functions of their jobs safely
- enable employees to enjoy equal benefits of employment

Consider these factors when trying to decide if reasonable accommodations are required:

- Is the applicant qualified for the position?
- Does the applicant have a long-term qualifying disability?
- Can the applicant perform the essential functions of the job with or without the disability?

4. Undue hardships

Undue hardship is defined in the ADA as an action requiring significant difficulty or expense. An employer is not required to provide accommodations if doing so would impose an undue hardship.

To evaluate whether or not an accommodation is an undue hardship, consider:

- the nature and cost of the accommodation
- the overall financial resources of the facility or facilities
- the size of the organization and the number, type, and locations of its other facilities
- the type of business the organization is in, the company's composition and structure and functions of its employees

5. Steps an employer can take to protect against ADA litigation:

- Know and understand the rights provided to persons with disabilities by the ADA.
- Treat all employees with the same fairness and provide opportunities equally to all persons, including those with disabilities.
- Consult legal counsel or an ADA specialist before making any personnel decisions regarding persons with disabilities.
- Document legitimate business reasons for any personnel actions taken against or for any employee.

Employment Discrimination

Now for a discussion of discrimination in the day-to-day treatment of employees. Specifically, the discussion will focus on sexual harassment, pregnancy discrimination, family and medical leave, discharge, layoffs, and early retirement.

Sexual Harassment

Sexual harassment at the workplace is a long-standing problem, affecting a large percentage of working women. Sexual harassment came to light during the mid 1970s and has since gained a great deal of national attention, especially in light of the Clarence Thomas Supreme Court justice confirmation hearings, the 1991 "Tail hook" convention, at which several women were severely harassed by naval pilots and the charges of sexual harassment lodged against U.S. President Bill Clinton by Paula Jones.

Sexual harassment is a form of sex discrimination and therefore violates Title VI of the Civil Rights Act (CRA). The number of sexual harassment complaints filed with the EEOC has increased at an alarming rate-it has risen from 6,127 in 1990 to 15,342 in 1997. About 90 percent of the complaints filed each year were filed by women.

Forms of Sexual Harassment

Sexual harassment can fall into one of two categories: quid pro quo and hostile environment. The term quid pro quo is Latin for "this for that" (e.g., "If you do this for me, I'll do that for you."). In the context of sexual harassment, the term refers to a situation in which an employee or applicant must provide sexual favors in order to be hired, promoted, granted a pay raise, or allowed to keep a job.

Hostile environments are those in which employees are subjected to unwelcome, intimidating working conditions. The *Harris*[2] case involving the issue of hostile environment came before the Supreme Court in 1993. Ms. Harris claimed that her boss made her work in an environment hostile and intimidating by:

- Asking her to retrieve objects from his pocket.
- Making derogatory statements, such as "You're a woman, what do you know?"
- Suggesting that she accompany him to a hotel to negotiate her raise.
- Telling other employees that she promised sexual favors to secure an account.

The lower courts ruled against Harris's claim of hostile environment because the boss's behavior did not seriously affect her psychological well-being. The Supreme Court reversed the lower courts' decisions, however, stating the hostile behavior need not cause the victim psychological harm. An environment is hostile if a reasonable person would judge it so, so long as the environment would reasonably be perceived, and is perceived, as hostile and abusive, there is no need to be psychologically injurious.

Concerned that the "reasonable person standard" might be too vague (e.g., a reasonable man may perceive things differently than a reasonable woman), the EEOC issued a 1991 policy statement stating that the standard should be changed to reasonable victim.

Another instance of hostile environment is illustrated in a court case in which an employer was found guilty of sexual harassment for these reasons:[3]

- Pictures of nude women appeared throughout the workplace.
- Male workers frequently made sexual comments.
- Coarse jokes, abusive graffiti, and offensive touching were commonplace.

2. 510 U.S. 17, 11 S.Ct. 367, 126 L.Ed. 2d 295 (1993).

3. *Meritor Savings Bank, FBS v. Michele Vinson*, United States Supreme Court, Docket No. 84-1979, June 19.

Figure 8.2 depicts one other type of sexual harassment, called "reverse sexual harassment." This type occurs when a person is denied an employment opportunity that was given to someone who complied with requests for sexual favors. This form of harassment was found to occur in a court case in which a nurse was denied a promotion, even though she was more qualified than the employee who got the position. The nurse who was promoted was having a sexual relationship with the doctor who made the promotion decision. The action was ruled discriminatory because their relationship played a substantial role in the selection.

Figure 8.2

Types of Sexual Harassment

- Quid Pro Quo
- Hostile Environment
- Reverse Sexual Harassment

How Should Employers Deal with Sexual Harassment?

Kleiman suggests, "an employer should take the following steps:

- Establish a written sexual harassment policy. The policy should specify grievance procedures by which employees can bring claims of harassment to management's attention. These procedures should provide employees with opportunities to by pass their supervisor if the supervisor is the one being accused.
- Provide supervisory training that focuses on the legal definition of sexual harassment. In addition to holding formal training sessions, top management should also meet with employees to stress management's strong commitment to keep the workplace free of harassment.
- Establish investigatory guidelines that maintain employee confidentiality.
- Establish a committee composed of both men and women to investigate sexual harassment claims. Committee members should receive training on how to investigate harassment claims.
- Establish a means of detecting unreported instances of sexual harassment within the company. Attitude surveys and exit interviews may identify such instances."[4]

Pregnancy Discrimination

Many women will become pregnant during their careers. Firms should attempt to accommodate the special needs of these individuals. Competitive advantage can be enhanced by such accommodation, as illustrated by the findings of a two-year national study. The study compared the work-related attitudes and behaviors of women working in "accommodating firms" to those working in "non-accommodating firms." The findings indicated that women working in accommodating

4. See Kleiman at 24, 318.

firms were more productive, took fewer sick days, worked later into their pregnancies, and were more likely to return to work after childbirth.[5]

Pregnancy Discrimination and the Law

Employer behaviors are subject to the 1978 Pregnancy Discrimination Act (PDA). This law specifies that pregnancy discrimination is a form of sex discrimination and is therefore illegal.

According to the PDA, firms may not discriminate against employees on the basis of pregnancy, childbirth, or related medical conditions. EEOC guidelines on pregnancy discrimination state that employees who are temporarily unable to perform their jobs adequately because of a pregnancy-related condition must be treated in the same manner as employees who are temporarily disabled for other reasons.

Family and Medical Leave

The Family and Medical Leave Act (FMLA) of 1993 requires all employers of 50 or more employees to grant workers up to 12 weeks of unpaid leave per year for the care of a newborn child, an ill family member, or their own illness. Employees may take the leave all at once or in increments.

Although it helps employees, the FMLA can be quite costly to employers when they must replace workers on leave. Because women are more likely to use these leaves, companies that employ a majority of women will be especially hard hit.

Discharge and Discrimination

Employers discharge workers all the time in this country. Unfortunately, many individuals lose their jobs unfairly under situations that could lead to charges of employment discrimination.[6] A decision to discharge an employee is discriminatory if it is influenced by the employee's protected group membership.

The evidence needed to justify the legal fairness of discharge decisions varies, depending on the reason for the decision. We will now explore the two most common reasons: employee misconduct and poor performance.

Employee Misconduct

Misconduct occurs when an employee commits an infraction of workplace rules. Although organizations may legally establish rules that serve their purposes,

---

5. Pregnancy: Nine to five (1989). *Executive Female*, May-June, 13.

6. Schreiber, N.E. (1983). Wrongful termination of at-will employees. *Massachusetts Law Review*, *68*(6), 22-35.

firms must also implement discipline and discharge policies for ensuring fair enforcement of those rules.

Discipline and discharge policies spell out the procedures the firm should follow if an employee violates the organization's code of conduct. In the absence of such a policy, managers may make discipline and discharge decisions unfairly or inconsistently, and thus leave the firm open to charges of discrimination or wrongful termination.

Effective policies encompass the notions of just cause and due process. Just cause means that the cause of action should be a fair one (e.g., a violation of reasonable rules). Due process means that employees should be informed of the "charges" against them and be given an opportunity to defend themselves.

Most organizations adopt a progressive discipline system, one in which discipline is enforced in increasingly severe steps. The first step in a progressive discipline system is to give the employee an oral warning in which he or she is informed of the incorrect behavior and how to correct it.

If an oral warning fails to correct the behavior, discipline progresses to increasingly more severe levels: written warning, probation, suspension, and, ultimately, termination. Firms generally bypass the progressive discipline system when the violation in question is a major one, such as theft, drug use, or sabotage. In these instances, most companies recommend immediate discharge.

Workplace Rules

Organizations often impose rules to restrict certain types of employee behaviors such as theft, insubordination, drug use, or horseplay. Although such rules do, by their very nature, restrict workers' personal freedoms, most employees understand why companies need these rules and readily accept them.

Courts also recognize the need for workplace rules and usually allow companies to set any rules they feel are necessary, as long as those rules are enforced in a nondiscriminatory manner.

Employers' rule-making authority is not unlimited, however. Rules are likely to be challenged if they restrict employee freedoms in areas that workers have traditionally viewed as highly private.

Employee Misconduct Outside the Workplace

Many employers impose rules that forbid employees from engaging in unlawful activities outside the workplace. For instance, some companies will suspend or discharge employees who have been arrested, jailed, and/or convicted of a crime.

Does an employer have a legal right to regulate employee behavior outside the workplace? Yes-to some extent. If an employer discharges an employee for misconduct outside the workplace, it must be prepared to prove that (1) there is some relationship between the misconduct and the job (e.g., a bank teller is convicted of theft), or (2) the continued employment of the "guilty" individual would have a disruptive impact on the workforce (e.g., subordinates refuse to work for a manager who has been convicted of child molestation).

Wrongful Termination and Employment-at-Will

An employer's legal right to discharge an employee is governed by a doctrine called employment-at-will. According to this doctrine, employers are free to discharge their employees for any reason, even an unfair one, unless the discharge is limited by contract or by federal or state statutes.

Statutes Prohibiting Wrongful Termination

Several statutes (see Figure 8.3) prohibit certain types of unfair or wrongful termination. In addition, union employees are protected from wrongful termination if their collective bargaining agreement specifies that discharges may be made only if there is "just cause."

The protections described earlier are not all-encompassing, however. Some apply only to certain employees: The Fifth and Fourteenth Amendments protect only government workers, and the collective bargaining agreements protect only those workers covered by the agreement. The remaining statutes listed in Figure 8.3 apply to the great majority of workers, but cover only certain types of unfair discharges, such as those stemming from discrimination or retaliation.

Figure 8.3

Federal Statutes Prohibiting Wrongful Termination

1. Anti-discrimination laws prohibit discharge, based on protected group membership.
2. Employee Retirement Income Security Act prohibits discharge designed to– deprive employees of benefits.
3. Fair Labor Standards Act prohibits discharge of employees who report a violation of this act.
4. OSHA prohibits discharge for reporting violations of the act.
S. National Labor Relations Act prohibits discharges that are intended to discourage union activity.
6. Consumer Credit Protection Act prohibits discharge for garnishment or indebtedness.
7. Whistle Blower's Protection Act prohibits the federal government froze discharging an individual for whistle-blowing.
8. The Fifth and Fourteenth Amendments to the Constitution prohibit federal, state, and local governments from discharging workers without giving them due process.

In fact, the United States is the only industrialized nation in the world that does not fully protect all workers from wrongful termination! Consequently, it is not unlawful in this country for a nonunionized, private-sector firm to discharge someone for seemingly ridiculous or unfair reasons, such as putting too much cream in the boss's coffee! Although reprehensible, such actions are often lawful.

Conducting a Disciplinary Investigation

When discipline problems arise, managers must investigate. If you become aware of a possible violation of company rules, you should proceed as follows:

"– *Get the facts.* Gossip, rumors, and hearsay evidence often prove inaccurate. You want to be certain that the employee has engaged in the suspected behavior before taking any action. You should base corrective action on facts that you have personally verified.
- *Review applicable rules.* Ask yourself: "What workplace rule applies to this situation?" and "Did the employee know the rule and understand its application?" If not, the most appropriate action would be to talk to the employee, explain what the rule is, and why it exists.
- *Meet with the employee.* Get the employee's side of the story. If the employee offers mitigating circumstances, check them out. Decide if these circumstances should influence your final decision.
- *Decide what kind of discipline, if any, to recommend.* It is extremely important that a correct decision be made here. The decision will affect all members of the work group, not just the person in question. For instance, it may serve to make others in the work group aware of expected performance levels, which could result in improved group performance. Moreover, management response to the problem sends other employees messages regarding:
  - What constitutes a violation of this rule?
  - Does the rule really mean what it says?
  - What is the organization's attitude toward violators of the rule?
  - Can our manager handle the problem?
  - What will happen to future violators of the rule?

  As you decide on the appropriate corrective action, consider the following factors:
  - "The circumstances surrounding the violation
  - The seriousness of the offense
  - The offender's past record
  - The offender's intent
- The disciplinary action taken in similar situations in the past."
- *Provide proper documentation.* Proper documentation is vital to justify the fairness of your decision, in the event that the decision is later challenged. Document the incident as soon as possible."[7]

Conducting a Disciplinary Conference

A disciplinary conference typically represents the first step in a progressive discipline system-the oral warning. The conference is supposed to correct, rather than punish, behavior. The conference should be conducted in a way that lessens the employee's tendency to become defensive. The key is to ensure that the employee understands (1) what he or she has done wrong, (2) why the behavior must be corrected, and (3) how the employee can correct the behavior. Furthermore, the offender must promise you that the inappropriate behavior will stop. The following steps should be followed in conducting a disciplinary conference:

"– *Get the facts.* Make sure you have conducted a proper investigation prior to this meeting.

---

7. Supervisors' Handbook. Indiana State University, Human Resources. 2001.

- Arrange for the interview. Select a private place and choose a time during which neither party will be interrupted.
- *Put the employee at ease.* Inform the employee of your purpose and give assurances that you are willing to listen and will consider what the individual has to say.
- *State the facts of the case.* Do not pass judgment or lecture the individual. Merely state the facts, as you understand them.
  - "Several people have informed me that you were smoking in a no-smoking area yesterday afternoon."
  - "Yesterday I saw you leaving work with several of your work tools."
- *Ask for reasons.* Ask the employee to explain why he or she engaged in such behavior. Remain objective; don't pass judgment.
- *State the company policy that has been violated.* For example, "The company rule is that no employees are to take their work tools home without prior approval from their supervisor."
- *State the reason for the policy and the possible harm caused by the employee's violation.*

  This step is designed to help the employee to understand the importance of the rule and why it should be followed. For example, you may state: "If workers take home tools without proper authorization, the company could be held liable if someone were to have an accident at home while using the tool. The company is also concerned about theft-without a record of loaned tools, there is no assurance that all tools will be returned."
- *Get the worker to agree on the problem.* This is probably the most important step. Many workers will become defensive and argue that they had a good reason for doing what they dId. For instance, a worker might argue that he sought to get the manager's permission to borrow the tools just before leaving work, but the manager was unavailable at the time. He may further argue that it's "no big deal, anyway"; he has worked for the company for 15 years and has had an exemplary record-he has certainly never stolen anything. He may also assure the manager that he knows how to use the tools, and the chances of an accident are nil.

  As a manager, you should not become embroiled in an argument at this point. Rather,, your goal is to get the worker to agree that he or she has broken a rule that the company believes is fair, and that future instances of this behavior will not be tolerated.
- *If disciplinary action is needed, state the action and the reasons for it.* State what action you will take now and what future action you will take if the problem goes unresolved.
- *Involve the employee in a problem-solving discussion.* The purpose of this step is to find a solution to the problem. What must the employee do to prevent this problem from recurring? The employee should participate in seeking a solution; because people commit more to solutions that they have formulated. Managers should simply steer them in the proper direction.
- *Have the employee summarize the problem and the agreed-on solution.* This step ensures a common understanding of the problem; it serves as a

check to see whether both parties agree on what has transpired during this meeting.

- *Agree on a follow-up date.* Arrange for a subsequent meeting (to be held after a reasonable length of time, say, two weeks) to discuss whether the worker has made satisfactory progress in resolving the problem.
- *End the discussion on a positive note.* Ideally, employees should leave the conference with a positive attitude and not feel "brow-beaten." Your goal is to demonstrate your confidence in them and to let them know that you are there to help. You should remind employees that their dependability and loyalty are highly regarded by the company and that you have every confidence in their ability to do the job correctly."[8]

Child Labor Laws

Many golf facilities turn to young workers as seasonal help during the summer season. Prior to hiring youth for the summer, child labor laws must be reviewed. Child labor laws have been passed by both the Federal government and all states. The Fair Labors Standards Act of 1938 as amended is the applicable federal legislation. Consult the state department of labor for specific laws applicable. Where a question is covered by a federal law and state law, the more rigorous standard will be imposed. For purposes of child labor laws, the applicable age of majority is eighteen.

Different rules apply to child ages 13 and younger, ages 14 and 15 and ages 16 and 17. Generally, children 13 years of age or younger may not be employed by golf facilities. Children 14 and 15 years of age must be employed under strict guidelines. These children may not work more than 3 hours per day on a school day or 8 hours per day on non-school days. In addition, they may not work more than 40 hours in a non-school week. Their hours of employment may not begin before 7 a.m. or end after 7 p.m. except between June 1st and Labor Day when they may work until 9 p.m. Children aged 14 and 15 may be employed as part of the sales force, for delivery work, cleanup work, office work, food and service jobs which do not involve operating equipment and ground maintenance work which does not involve power driven equipment.

Children 14 and 15 years old may not operate power mowers, chain saws, cutters, trimmers and similar equipment. In fact, children 14 and 15 years old are not allowed to operate most power driven equipment. Children 16 and 17 years old are subject to fewer restrictions. They may work anytime for any number of hours at all jobs, not defined as hazardous by the United State Secretary of Labor. The most hazardous occupations on a golf course would be operating power driven machines including maintenance equipment, saws and motor vehicles; applying chemicals to the greens, fairways, and roughs; and adding chemicals to the swimming pool. However, there is an exception that children ages 16 and 17 may operate motor vehicles with gross vehicle weights under 6,000 pounds during daylight hours.

8. Supervisors' Handbook. Indiana State University, Human Resources. 2001.

Finally, make sure that children (1) are not allowed to apply chemicals or dispose of chemical containers or use substances for which certification or licenses are necessary, and (2) are properly supervised whatever job they are performing.

Employee vs. Independent Contractor

The major difference between an independent contractor and an employee is the amount of control you have over the person.

Employee	Independent Contractor
1. Follows employer's instructions	1. Agrees on job specifications
2. Trains within the company	2. Obtains own training
3. Is hired, supervised and paid by the employer	3. Hires, supervises and pays own staff
4. Works for the employer	4. Services are available to the general public
5. Employer sets work schedule	5. Develops own work schedule within limits
6. Employer furnishes materials	6. Furnishes own materials
7. Business expenses paid by the employer	7. Pays own business expenses
8. Personally performs the work	8. May subcontract work
9. Is an integral part of the company	9. Provides peripheral services
10. Works on a regular basis	10. Works at irregular intervals
11. Usually works 40 hours weekly	11. Usually works part-time
12. Is paid by the hour, week or month	12. Is paid by the job
13. Usually doesn't invest in the company	13.Has investment in the business
14. Works at the employer's place of business	14. Works anywhere
15. Works in the order set by the employer	15. Sets own work order
16. Regularly submits reports to the employer	16. Reports work progress as goals are met
17. Receives wages whether or not the company is making money	17. May or may not get paid depending on profit and loss
18. Works for one company	18. Provides services for several companies
19. Can usually quit at any time	19. Works under contract
20. Can usually be fired at any time	20. Works under contract

A Final Word . . .

Golf course managers should communicate workplace policies and procedures to their employees, create work environments that foster adherence to policies and procedures, and take appropriate action when possible policy violations arise.

Chapter 9

Insurance Transfers Risk

Are you worried that bad weather will cancel the event you have spent days planning for, or that the star athlete will suffer a career-ending injury, or a patron will slip on a spilled soft drink or ice on the sidewalk and break a leg? Today's litigious environment and tight budgets mean managers and owners must take a closer look at insurance and risk-management strategies. In the past 10 years, there has been a dramatic increase in the number of companies specializing in insurance for the fitness, physical activity, recreation, and sport industries.

The golf manager should be prepared to cover injuries arising from other areas of possible liability including: (1) building (e.g., fire, lightning, explosion, windstorm or hail, smoke, aircraft or vehicles striking the property, riot or civil commotion, vandalism, sprinkler leakage, sinkhole collapse [i.e., Florida, Montana, elsewhere], volcanic action, flood, mud slides [i.e., California], and tornado or hurricane) and premises, (2) motor vehicles (e.g., medical expenses for driver and passengers, lost income and services for driver and passengers, damage to automobile(s), additional property damaged [nearby structures, telephone poles, guard rails, road signage, etc.], ambulance expense, funeral expense, investigation expense, legal expense, and overhead of automobile insurers], (3) activities (i.e., from incidents due to the nature of the activity engaged in), (4) employee conduct (e.g., negligent acts of employees, employee dishonesty, forgery, theft, computer fraud, and extortion), (5) business general liability caused by employees, users, or spectators (e.g., direct liability [premises and operations, and products liability], vicarious liability [i.e., indirect liability], and contractual liability, (6) bonds for performance and financial security (i.e., surety bonds guarantee performance, and fidelity bonds protect employers from loss caused by dishonest acts of employees), and (7) fringes for employees covered by federal law (e.g., Social Security Act, Employee Retirement Income Security Act of 1974 [ERISA], Internal Revenue Code [IRC], The Civil Rights Act of 1964 [as amended in 1970, 1972, 1978], Age Discrimination in Employment ACT of 1967 [as amended in 1986], Retirement Equity Act of 1984 [REA], Consolidated Omnibus Budget Reconciliation Act of 1986 [COBRA], Tax Reform Act of 1986, Health Maintenance Organization ACT [HMO], and the Civil Rights Restoration Act of 1987 [1988]) (See chapter 15 for a discussion of these laws and others).

Each day a golf course or other golf facility is open for operation and a golfer plays a round of golf or even hits a bucket of balls at a driving range, potential liabilities are staggering. If anyone pondered all the possibilities of liability or dwelled on them at great length, it is doubtful that they would pursue a career in golf or at the very least, fewer rounds of golf would be played. While golf is a game with inherent risks which can never be totally eliminated or controlled, there are a great many steps all golf course personnel can take which will result in reducing the likelihood that injuries will occur and hence reduce the likelihood of lawsuits. Unfortunately, like individuals, a great many golf facilities have no formal plan for risk management. Insurance companies want their clients to develop sound risk management plans and they reward those who do with lower premiums.

It is important to review once again the steps in developing a sound risk management plan. The first step in risk management is to identify the risks. The first broad area of potential risks are personal injuries and property damage to persons not having an ownership interest in the golf operation. These potential liabilities include injuries to golfers or others using the course or driving range, cart users, employees, persons on or owning adjacent property or on adjacent roadways and spectators or officials at golf tournaments.

The second broad area of potential risks are losses from damage to real property including buildings or equipment and losses from theft, embezzlement and vandalism. As with steps which can be taken to reduce the likelihood that injuries and property damage to others will occur, there are many steps that facilities can take to reduce the likelihood of financial loss from damage to property of the facility, theft and embezzlement.

Taking these risk reducing steps along with a sound program of property and liability insurance is what risk management is all about. The important consideration here is that risk management consists of a great deal more than simply buying one or more insurance policies. For a great many, if not most golf facilities and golf course personnel the simple approach of buying insurance policies has been their total risk management program.

As stated, any program of risk management must begin with an analysis of the risks which the entire golf facility or the concerned personnel face in connection with the golf operation. In identifying the risk factors, one must also analyze the assets against which these risks pose a threat. Once all risks and assets have been identified, a risk management plan can be formulated and put into operation. At one end of the spectrum are golf operations which rely on insurance as their sole form of risk management. At the opposite end. are those facilities with so few assets, or those whose debts exceed their assets, that they have no insurance at all. They do not worry about risk. Either of these approaches can obviously be quite costly. No insurance could result in the loss of not only the facility assets, but personal assets of the owner and any other personnel deemed liable. Relying solely on insurance can result in excessive insurance premiums, unnecessary lawsuits and losses from liability not covered by the policy or policies employed. While any person wants to be in position to win a lawsuit if one is forthcoming, being involved in a lawsuit will in all likelihood be financially distressing even if successful. The period of time after an injury or other incident resulting in potential liability before a lawsuit is even filed can be several years. During this initial period of time, acquisition of attorney's investigation, lining up expert testimony and attempts at settlement through insurance companies or otherwise will be forthcoming.

Once a lawsuit is filed it may involve several parties and various theories of recovery. In most instances, where an insurance policy is in force, an insurance company will provide legal representation for the parties covered. However, the various persons sued may have conflicting interests and usually each will need his or her own attorney. It is unlikely that a party in any lawsuit will be able to recover his or her attorney fees whatever the result. The formal discovery phase of a lawsuit after it is filed, may take several more years before the case is finally tried to determine the outcome of the claim. Once the case is tried, the case may be appealed which can then take additional years and some cases may be appealed more than once. All of these trials and appeals are costly and time consuming and attorney fees and expenses can be hundreds of thousands of dollars. All of the time and expense involved in a lawsuit points out the great advantage of a risk management system which prevents a lawsuit from happening in the first place as opposed to simply being successful in defending the lawsuit. If the lawsuit is lost, a judgment will be entered, which coupled with the time and expense of the lawsuit, even with insurance, may cause financial ruin and loss of the facility. Having determined that risk management is essential to the facility and personnel involved in a golf operation, you are now ready to embark on a risk management program. The first step in the program is completing a risk inventory. Completion of the risk inventory should be a two step process, the first consisting of a complete inventory of all assets of the facility and the second to include all possible areas of loss liability. It is surprising how few facilities have an inventory of all assets. In addition to the golf course or driving range itself, assets include construction and maintenance equipment, buildings, clubhouse, food items, equipment, inventory, sale items, vehicles, options on land and other assets. In completing an inventory of the assets of your golf operation, first break them into broad classifications. These classifications should include:

- Real property consisting of land and buildings;
- Equipment which should be divided into facility and maintenance equipment and further into major items with a value of five hundred dollars or more and minor items such as small tools and equipment with individual values of less than five hundred dollars;
- Clubhouse including cooking facilities and inventory of service items as well as food items;
- Pro shop including equipment and inventory of items for sale;
- Golf cart shop including golf carts, chargers, repair parts and maintenance equipment and tools;
- Driving or practice range including equipment, balls and clubs;
- Swimming pool and adjacent areas to the pool;
- Locker rooms;
- Tennis court facilities indoor and outdoor; and
- Fitness areas.

In addition to identifying each item (take pictures and store in a safe place and save receipts of purchase), a value or replacement cost should be formulated for each item. The management personnel in charge of each particular area should be involved in the inventory process. Having identified and classified the potential of existing risks, the next step in the risk management program is to match insurance coverage to the risk inventory. Some items may be most economically handled by self insurance. If the premium is too high to include that old greensmower which is seldom used, drop the property coverage. If it is stolen or damaged by fire it can be replaced at a relatively small cost and not having it available will not cause great risk to the facility's operation. Be sure that liability insurance remains in effect when it is being used.

After identifying those items for which insurance coverage is necessary, insurance must be obtained which satisfies those needs. Insurance can be classified into three broad categories: property insurance, liability insurance and employee insurance.

Property insurance insures the owner of real or personal property against loss from fire, wind, theft and the like and is used to protect physical assets. This insurance will reimburse the insured party from loss due to the named perils. Liability insurance is insurance which will cover the insured party against liability for injuries to the person or damages to the property of another. Liability insurance in addition to indemnifying the insured against these losses will provide attorney services in settling or defending liability claims. Employee insurance is in the form of workmen's compensation insurance or employer's liability insurance to protect the owner or employer against liability for compensation or damages for injury or death of an employee while working for the employer. Any insurance plan for a golf facility will probably embody all three forms.

Once a determination is made that the risk must be covered by insurance, the first consideration for most policies will be the limits of the policy and the deductible amount. Satisfy yourself that sufficient maximum policy limits are in effect to protect the operation or personnel. If you have $1,000,000.00 in assets, you need more than $250,000.00 in liability insurance. The amount necessary will depend on the assets of the facilities or persons exposed. Larger maximum policy limits ordinarily do not greatly increase liability premiums. Premiums however, are greatly affected by the size of the deductible. For this reason, a close look should be taken at the financial condition of the operation and its ability to absorb the deductible. If a higher deductible can be absorbed, a significant savings on the premium should result. Consider setting aside, in a separate account, the money saved on premiums from raising the deductible, to cover that deductible in the event of a claim. Be sure to review all policies to verify that coverage is included for all potential claims and that the coverage extends to all persons and assets which you are seeking to cover.

A final consideration is that self-insurance or purchasing an insurance policy are not the only methods of managing risks. A third possibility is transferring the risk to another party. As an example, attempts at transferring liability for damages resulting from the operation of a golf cart to the golf cart user by a clause in the golf cart rental agreement whereby the user agrees not to sue the renter have not met with great success. On the other hand, transfer of risks by course designers or owners to adjacent real estate developers or condominium owners by contract or deed have met with success.

Insurance for Recreation and Sport Programming

The manager should become familiar with some basic insurance jargon before trying to engage an insurance consultant. Further, the manager should know what insurance the organization currently has and its limits. A survey of companies specializing in this type of insurance shows a wide variety of coverages available, including:

- Professional teams, athletes, and events—liability and accident medical cover age, high-limit accidental death and disability insurance, contractual bonus and performance incentive programs;

- Amateur athletes and events (e.g., Olympic Festivals, USOC, National Governing Bodies, Pan American Games, World Games);
- College and high school teams, athletes, athletic associations, club/recreational sport activities, sports camps, facilities—sports liability and accident medical coverage, disability insurance, play-practice coverage, transportation insurance, catastrophic injury coverage;
- Youth/adult recreational teams and leagues—liability and accident coverage;
- Health clubs, fitness centers, and sports clubs—property, accident and liability insurance for participants/members and staff, day-care facilities, tanning beds, diving boards, whirlpools, weight rooms, trampolines, food and liquor services;
- Venues (stadiums, arenas, recreational facilities, water parks)—spectator and participant liability, property insurance, casualty insurance;
- Promotions and special events—event cancellation, sponsorship/prize guarantee, special events liability, weather and nonappearance insurance;
- General public liability—products liability, watercraft liability, saddle animal liability, liquor liability, personal injury liability, independent contractor's liability, advertiser's liability, and adventure and tripping program liability;
- Liability coverage protecting employees, directors and officers;
- Vehicle insurance—bodily injury liability, property damage liability, business auto policy, user of other autos, employers non-owned and hired autos, camp bus coverage, medical payments, comprehensive, and collision insurance; and
- Protection of finances and operations—loss of income, discrimination or civil liberties violations, advertising liability, or contractual liability by endorsement (hold harmless agreement or indemnification).

Insurance Consultant

Insurance consultants can be very helpful to the manager. The consultant can keep the golf facility manager out of trouble and assist in selecting insurance coverages as well as companies. The manager should seek a person with the following characteristics to become the insurance consultant:

- has been an insurance agent,
- understands commercial property insurance,
- has knowledge about general liability insurance,
- understands bonding and crime insurance,
- has a basic knowledge of automobile insurance,
- understand employee benefits and health and disability insurance,
- has a knowledge of insurance contracts,
- understands the insurance regulations in the specific state, and
- has a good reputation as an insurance consultant.

Insurance Coverage

All too often, owners renew their same coverage without considering new improvements in facilities and equipment, additional programming and services, new staff, and revenue increases. The manager should review, with the insurance consultant, annually the coverage of each policy in force to guarantee adequate coverage. Insurance is the most valuable way to protect business assets. A comprehensive insurance program should include:

Property Insurance. This covers facilities, equipment, and personal property. The coverage should include improvements (i.e., facilities and equipment), equipment owned or leased, all inventory (e.g., employee store inventory, office supplies, custodial supplies, and expendable recreational and sport supplies [e.g., balls, bats, climbing equipment, racquets]). The deductible for the policy should be between $1,000 and $5,000, including building ordinance coverage to guarantee reconstruction based on current building codes.

The following should also be covered under property insurance: office equipment and furniture; losses from a flood and/or earthquake, if appropriate; glass and exterior mirrors; losses from fire and smoke; computers; and losses from hurricane or tornado, if appropriate. If you lease equipment and you insure that equipment make sure to have the broker provide a certificate of insurance that names the insurance company as the loss payee/additional insured, since the leasing company most likely will have also insured that equipment through another insurance carrier.

Business Income/Extra Expense. This insurance provides income during reconstruction after a loss by an insured peril (e.g., fire, flood, hurricane, tornado, or earthquake). The coverage should be written on an Agreed Value Basis with a 90-day extended period of indemnity. The insurance limit should cover a minimum of six months of gross receipts, less non-continuing expenses and ordinary payroll (include payroll for owners and managers). If renting or leasing a facility make sure to include rent since most lease agreements require payment in full whether or not the leasee is in operation or not.

Commercial Liability—This includes professional liability, fire legal liability, and medical payments liability. Professional liability should include all part- and full-time employees (not independent contractors, they should be required to have their own prior to contracting with them), and tanning bed liability (make sure there are no cancer exclusions). Fire legal liability is insurance to cover losses while renting or leasing a facility. Finally, medical payments liability, allows the insurer to file a claim for medical bills although there was no negligence on the operators part.

Machinery and equipment insurance refers to replacement of HVAC (heating, ventilation, and air conditioning) equipment, pumps, and other mechanical aspects of the facility.

Employment Practices Liability Insurance (EPLI) covers the organization for wrongful termination, employment-related acts of discrimination (e.g., disability, race, handicap, religion, creed, age, gender, sexual orientation, sexual preference, pregnancy, and national origin), wrongful discipline, defamation, invasion of privacy, misrepresentation, negligent evaluation, equal pay violation, wrongful infliction of emotional distress or retaliation, break of employment contract, negligent evaluation, wrongful deprivation of career opportunity, failure to employ or promote, sexual abuse and molestation, and sexual harassment. In Figure 9.1 are a few questions the golf manager should ask prior to purchasing EPLI.

Figure 9.1

Question to Ask Prior to Purchasing EPLI[1]

- How does the state treat EPL punitive damages?
- Does the policy allow the insured choice of defense counsel?
- Does the coverage extend fully to the entity and its owners, partners, officers, directors, shareholders, and employees?
- Does the policy exclude coverage for "intentional acts," and if so, would coverage still be denied if an intentional act committed by an employee results inn the entity being named in the lawsuit?
- Are defense costs outside the policy limits? If not, a sizable chuck of the policy limit could be used to pay for defense costs, which could be problematic if a sizable awards is determined.
- Does the policy include a participation clause (i.e., requiring the insured to pay a percentage of the settlement)? This could prove to be costly to the entity owner.
- Will the policy respond to EFI lawsuits out of the actions of leased employees?
- Is coverage "retroactive" (i.e., will it respond to lawsuits arising out of "prior acts" allegedly committed but not discovered prior to the policy inception date, assuming another EPLI policy was in place at the time)?
- Does the policy offer an extended reporting provision allowing the owner to report a claim during a redetermined period of time after the policy period, for incidents that occurred while the policy was in force?
- Does the policy compel the insured to accept settlement terms as agreed to by the insurance company as a condition of coverage?
- Does the policy promise to "pay on behalf of" the insured, in which case the insurance company would pay for EPL expenses as they occur; or does the policy promise to "idemnify" the insured, which would require the entity to pay out all EPL expenses up front, and be reimbursed by the insurer.

Special Liability Insurance (e.g., environmental impairment—pollution caused by chemicals waste in waterways or disbursed into the air).

1. Dorfman, M.S. (1994). Introduction to Risk Management Insurance. (15th Ed.) Englewoods Cliff, NJ: Prentice-Hall.

Bonding including surety bonds (guarantee performance), and fidelity bonds (protect the employers from loss caused buy dishonest acts of employees).

Crime insurance, which covers perils such as forgery, theft, destruction, computer fraud, and extortion by employees, and

Insurances most frequently provided as employee benefits in your locale (e.g., unemployment, workers' compensation, group life, health, and disability, and pension plans).

The decision as to what insurance is purchased by the golf establishment comes down to overall cost versus potential risk. The manager and insurance consultant will need to develop a careful analysis of potential risk and those that have the greatest potential of becoming a reality will need to be covered in the blanket policy (insurance contract) developed.

The Insurance Company or Companies

It is important to choose a carrier that has a stable, long-term knowledge of this industry. Investigate the insurance company, because there are companies out there that are not experienced in the fitness/recreation/sport field. The cheapest company is not always the best company. The ideal company will have a reasonable cost, provide risk management assistance and advice, continually review the policies under force, and provide quick user-friendly service when a claim arises.

How Do Insurance Companies Determine Insurability?

What do insurance companies consider before determining if a facility or event is insurable? The insurer reviews information regarding variety of basic areas: (1) security, (2) maintenance, (3) housekeeping, (4) emergency services, (5) parking and traffic control, (6) concessions, (7) staff training and preparedness, (8) fiscal operations, (9) staff supervision, (10) activity planning, (11) equipment used in building and ground maintenance (e.g., buffers, vacuum cleaners, mowers, power weed eaters, tillers, etc.), and recreational and sport equipment (e.g., golf carts, playground equipment), and (12) chemical usage and storage. The company is concerned as to how these areas are managed. Premiums are based on how these areas are managed. The only thing that makes insurance inexpensive is good loss experience, and if year after year a facility or event or team has good loss experience, then all the insurance company needs to collect the premium for is the inevitable "what if?" If the experience is consistently good, the insurance company does not have to build in premiums to pay losses and take care of routine claims.

Cost of Premiums

The cost of premiums can be reduced by opting for higher deductibles or taking the initiative of hiring a risk management expert to survey the facilities and programs for unsafe conditions. Some insurance companies offer on-site safety inspections as a value-added service, which can help facilities develop ongoing risk management strategies.

Insurance remains a confusing entity and may be the reason why so many managers take little time to understand what might be needed beyond the corporation coverage and what might be needed for the not-for-profit employee association/club. It is not uncommon for insurance buyers to go for the cheapest price and not pay attention to coverages, policy limits and conditions. The insurance consultant will indicate that not being adequately covered could cost the employee services provider its business.

A Checklist for Selecting Insurance

The following checklist contains recommendations for managers when securing insurance[1] (see Figure 9.2 for checklist for comparing plans):

- "never assume you are covered;
- always check your insurance coverage;
- check insurance policy at least twice a year for changes and to be sure you still have adequate coverage;
- file a report on an incident as soon as it happens and submit a proper claim to the insurance company;
- anyone involved in an activity outside their job jurisdiction or areas of control may seek to secure more personal liability coverage;
- be aware of potential hazards and report them to the necessary people or group;
- secure a short-term group accident policy to cover special activities when risk is foreseeable;
- analyze the liability aspects of your program or area and ensure adequate coverage in these areas; and
- have release forms; they may solve small liability problems because the participants acknowledge the risk they are assuming and their voluntary participation in the program, but do not rely on them to solve any negligent actions, and have participants in events obtain medicals."[2]

---

2. See Moriarity, D., Holman, M., Brown, R., & Moriarty, M. (1994). *Canadian/American Sport, Fitness, and the Law*. Toronto, CA: Canadian Scholar's Press, Inc., 367.

Figure 9.2

Checklist for Comparing Plans

This checklist is furnished, Moriarity, et al., to guide discussions with an agent/broker.

"1. Evaluating the golf club's needs—
   a. Number of eligible employees
   b. Number of dependents
   c. Gender of employees (# male/female)
   d. Employees/dependents of child bearing age
   e. Age of employees
   f. Employees/dependents with pre-existing medical conditions
   g. Employees with health conditions making them high-risk
   h. Employees insured elsewhere

2. Covered medical services? Yes No
   a. Inpatient hospital services
   b. Outpatient surgery
   c. Psychiatric/mental health care
   d. Drug/alcohol treatment
   e. Skilled nursing care
   f. Home health care visits
   g. Rehabilitation facility care
   h. Hospice care
   i. Dental care
   j. Maternity care
   k. Supplemental accident
   l. Prescription drugs
   m. Vision care
   n. Preventative care & checkups
   o. Chiropractic treatment
   p. Physician visits
   q. Medical tests and X-rays
   r. Mammograms

3. Are there medical service limits, exclusions, or pre-existing conditions that will affect employees?

4. What cost containment and quality assurance procedures are included (i.e., utilization review, precertification, second surgical opinions, etc.)

Price (premium) considerations

5. What is the total cost of the policy?
   a. For the club?
   b. For the employee?
   High Medium Low
   c. Single deduction
   d. Family deduction
   e. Co-insurance
   f. Max out-of-pocket (emp)

g. Max out-of-pocket (fam)

6. How long is the premium guaranteed?
7. What is the policy's lifetime maximum amount of coverage?
8. What has the rate history been for comparable groups over the past five years and how is it calculated?
9. What will happen to premiums if one of our employees has a major claim?

Customer Service

10. How will service needs be handled?
11. Will the agent/broker or a customer service representative be available to meet with employees and dependents?
12. How long will it take to process a claim?
13. How often will the golf club be billed?
14. Is the agent/broker qualified in the small group market (100 lives)?
    Does the agent/broker know about the golf industry? Yes No
    a. Good references
    b. Licensed in the state
    c. Professional qualifications
    d. Experience in the small group market and the golf industry?
    e. Doing business for at least three years?
    f. Member of recognized professional organization
15. Is the insurance company sold? Yes No
    a. Good references
    b. Licensed in my state
    c. Company financial stability/rating

List below other questions/concerns you might have regarding the insurance proposals are evaluating:"[3]

Self-insurance

Moriarity, et al, suggests "this option is not appropriate for small organizations but is quite practical for large and governmental organizations. Self-insurance usually means retaining financial risks to a substantial level through establishing a reserve fund to insure availability of cash when needed. The amount of such a fund and its management may be controlled by state regulations or statutes. Taxable profit-making organizations rarely establish such a reserve because of the tax struc-

3. Id. at 350.

ture and usually the working capital is adequate, at least for larger corporations. Some corporations have established trust funds to maintain such funds."[4]

Questions to Ask a Prospective Insurer

Before you purchase any insurance policy, ask the prospective agent the following questions. The answers can help you sort out what type of coverage is necessary, and which amount is best for the operation in question.

"– How many policies has the agent written with similar organizations?
- What is included in the basic policy?
- What is excluded in the basic policy?
- What types of coverage should be considered beyond the basic policy?
- How much insurance can the organization afford?
- Can the agent provide a list of recent claims and losses (say the last five years)?
- What is the carrier's rating?
- How long does it take for a claim to be processed?
- Can the agent recommend a person or firm to assist in loss control analysis, safety issues, and general risk management?
- How often does the agent recommend policy review and updating?"[5]

Other Coverages Available

The following are other coverages available: recreation and sports programs—sports liability and accident medical insurance, disability insurance, play-practice coverage, transportation insurance, and catastrophic injury coverage; dependent care insurance; food and beverage insurance; spectator liability and medical insurance; automobile insurance; workers' compensation insurance; event cancellation insurance; special events liability; and weather and non-appearance insurance.

The following are a few groups that offer insurance programs for health/fitness, recreation, and sport programs:

Allied Specialty Insurance, Inc.
10451 Gulf Blvd.
Treasure Island, FL 33706
800/237-3355

Bollinger
499 Bloomfield Avenue
Montclair, NJ 07042
800/526-1379

Continental Insurance Co.
One Continental Drive
Cranbury, NJ 08570
609/395-2429

Dexter & Company
5910 N. Central Expwy, Suite 600
Dallas, TX 75206
214/891-6400

Health Special Risk, Inc.
880 Sibley Memorial Hwy., #101

Hughes & Associates, Inc.
Rt 202 & Meadowbrook Lane

4. Id.
5. See Moriarity at 2, 376.

Mendota Heights, MN 55118
800//328-1114

International Accident Facilities
One State Street
Boston, MA 02109
800/272-7488

K & K Insurance Group, Inc
1712 Magnavox Way
Fort Wayne, IN 46804
219/455-3000

Chalfont, PA 18914
215/822-8700

ISU Hoffman Insurance
200 Linden Street
Wellesley, MA 02181
800/277-6052

Rollins Hudig Hall of Utah, Inc.
2180 S 1300 E., Suite 500
Salt Lake, UT 84117
801/488-2550

How Should the Golf Manager Choose the Appropriate Deductible?

Choosing the right deductible requires a thorough analysis by the golf manager. A higher deductible can reduce the premium, but at the same time increase out-of-pocket expenditures for care that doesn't meet the deductible amount. On the other hand, decreasing the cost of coverage can allow for more liquid funds and provide the option of building a reserve if funds can carry over from year to year. The following are a few recommendations that should be considered when choosing a deductible:

"– Access student-athletes' or patrons primary insurance first and once it has been exhausted the organization pays until its deductible is reached, then the secondary insurer, the organization's carrier, pays the remaining amount. This is called a straight-deductible policy.
- Select a higher deductible since it will mandate a more aggressive management of insurance claims. However, if the organization has a large number of student-athletes or patrons who lack primary insurance coverage, a lower deductible should be chosen.
- The manager should base the deductible on the physical activity involved and gender of the participants. For example, lower deductible for contact activities, and higher for non-contact.
- The sport manager should coordinate all medical care through an HMO or a special arrangement with a local hospital. This will assist the sport manager in controlling losses and take advantage of a higher deductible.
- The sport manager should consider placing a physician on a stipend which will reduce overall costs and allow for a higher deductible.

- The sport manager should establish a referral policy to maximize in-house medical services. This will also allow for the selection of a higher deductible."[6]

A Final Word...

If you follow the ensuing steps you should be able to select an appropriate insurance program for the golf facility that you manage:

- Select a competent independent insurance consultant;
- Be aware of the suppliers of insurance and the relative advantages and disadvantages of dealing with each;
- Secure a number of quotes and review each closely;
- Make sure your golf facility has adequate insurance coverage;
- Identify the risks that your golf facility will face and adequately insure them;
- Ask yourself, can our golf facility survive any major losses?
- Insure the correct risks;
- Always try to keep your insurance costs down by preventing or reducing losses;
- Review your insurance needs and your business risks annually;
- Understand the basic policy (i.e., exclusions, etc.); and
- Understand the many types of insurance policies and their coverages.

6. Id. at 360.

Chapter 10

Americans with Disabilities Act Accessibility Guidelines: Golf Facilities

The Americans with Disabilities Act (ADA), public law 101-336, was signed into law on July 26, 1990. It provides broad based non-discrimination protection for individuals with disabilities in employment, public services, public accommodations, and services operated by private institutions, transportation, and telecommunications.

The term *disability* is defined in the act as meaning with respect to an individual "(a) a physical or mental impairment which substantially limits one or more of the major life activities of such individual, (b) a record of such impairment, or (c) being regarded as having such an impairment." Title one of the act provides that no covered entity shall discriminate against a qualified individual with a disability because of the disability in regard to job application procedures, the hiring, advancement, or discharge of employees, employee's compensation, job training, and other terms, conditions and privileges of employment. The same section of the act defines *employer* as a person engaged in an industry affecting commerce which has 15 or more employees. The term *qualified individual* with a disability is defined as "an individual with a disability, who, with or without reasonable accommodations, can perform the essential functions of the employment position that such person holds or desires."

If the person seeking employment is a qualified person under the definition provided in the act and the employer is a qualified employer, there are few exceptions. The employer, at the employer's expense, must provide reasonable accommodations unless such accommodations would impose an undue hardship on operation of the business. If the golf facility suggests that the particular accommodation imposes an undue hardship, the golf facility must devise an alternative plan which would not create a hardship. It is not sufficient to say that the accommodation is too costly. The employer must also consider outside funding from local, state or federal agencies, tax credits, and other offsets against the cost of accommodating the disabled party.

In addition to not discriminating against an individual on the basis of his disability there is an affirmative duty to determine whether the particular available employment can be adapted to the disabled applicant by modifying the requirements or necessary performance.

Once the disabled person is employed, all benefits and privileges which are conferred on other employees must be made available to the disabled employee. If dining facilities, golfing privileges, transportation, outings, insurance and other services are available to other employees these must be available on the same basis to disabled persons. As with other Civil Rights legislation, this act prohibits retaliation against a disabled person who asserts rights provided to him or her by the act.

Architectural and Transportation Barriers Compliance Board (Access Board)

The golf subcommittee of the Architectural and Transportation Barriers Compliance Board (Access Board) developed[1] recommended accessibility guidelines[2] for newly constructed 18 and 9 hole golf courses and for miniature golf courses. In examining 18- and 9-hole golf courses, the golf subcommittee considered all elements of the course and made recommendations that would increase accessibility for persons with disabilities without significantly changing the game of golf. Issues involving the application of Americans with Disabilities Act Accessibility Guidelines (ADAAG) accessible route provisions were important in the golf subcommittee's discussions.

Definitions

This section defines terms used in the proposed rule. Terms and definitions established within the industry have been used to the greatest extent possible. The term "*golf car passage*" is defined as a continuous passage on which a motorized golf car, also known as *golf carts*, can operate. Designers and operators sometimes use the term "golf car path" to identify what the Board is defining as a "golf car passage." Because the term "*golf car path*" may connote a prepared surface, the term was not used. While a golf car passage must be usable by golf cars, it does not necessarily need to be a prepared surface.

The Access Board recognizes that not all golf courses provide golf cars or golf car passages. However, by requiring a course to be designed and constructed to allow for golf car travel between accessible elements and spaces on a course, individuals who bring their own golf car or use those provided at a course, will have the opportunity to play the game of golf. On most courses where golf cars are not provided, paths for maintenance vehicles often exist which could support golf car passages and generally connect many of the elements and spaces required to be accessible.

A "*teeing ground*" is defined as the starting place for a hole to be played. This definition is consistent with the United States Golf Association (USGA) definition,

---

1. 1331 F Street NW., suite 1000, Washington, DC 20004-1111. Fax number (202) 272-5434 extension 18 or (202) 272-5447. E-mail comments should be sent to recreate@access-board.gov.

2. 36 CFR Part 1191 [Docket No. 98-5] RIN 3014-AA16, 16-21, http://www.access-board.gov/rules/recnprm.htm.

which describes a teeing ground as a rectangular area two club-lengths in depth, with the front and sides defined by the outside limits of two tee-markers.

Accessible Route[3]

This section requires that, where the accessible route is located within the boundary of a golf course, it must be 48 feet wide minimum and connect to the bag drop areas, accessible teeing grounds, and putting greens. Additionally, where handrails are required, the accessible route is required to be 60 feet wide minimum.

The golf subcommittee considered the ADAAG requirements for an accessible route to be impractical on a golf course for several reasons. First, the route of play for a golfer is dependent on where the ball lands and is therefore unpredictable. Secondly, there is an assumption that on most courses, most golfers use a golf car to move throughout the course. Finally, the golf subcommittee raised concerns that requiring an accessible route throughout a course would substantially alter the slopes within a course and eliminate some of the challenge of the game.

As a result, the golf subcommittee recommended that an accessible route only be required to connect course elements from a golf car path or a golf car parking area. This was intended to allow a golfer with a disability to ride in a golf car to reach a point where an accessible route would provide access to various course elements. Public comment received from golf course architects, operators, and the Association of Disabled Golfers generally supported this approach.

The Access Board agrees that making the game of golf accessible to the majority of persons with disabilities can be achieved primarily through the use of golf cars. These proposed guidelines incorporate the concept of providing access through a golf car passage and allow for access to various elements. These proposed guidelines also ensure that all of the amenities (such as snack bars, toilet rooms, and weather shelters) on a course are accessible and are connected by a golf car passage.

Question 1

Should smaller courses (i.e., 3 or 6 holes) have the option of using a golf car passage in lieu of a modified accessible route?

Exception 1

This exception permits the use of a golf car passage in lieu of all or part of an accessible route within the boundary of a golf course. This exception does not apply to practice putting greens and driving ranges since they are not located within a course.

---

3. ADA Accessibility Guidelines for Buildings & Facilities (ADAAG). (2002). http://www.access-board.gov/adaag/html/adaag.htm.

Question 2

The proposed requirements for a golf car passage seek to provide access for players on a golf course. The Board requests comments on how access should be provided for spectators during a golf tournament.

Exception 2

This exception provides that accessible routes within the boundary of a golf course are not required to comply with handrail requirements in ADAAG 4.8.5. It is hazardous for handrails to be located through a green, or on teeing grounds, because of the danger of golf balls ricocheting off rails. Since most elements are required to be accessible from golf car paths, handrails would be of little utility along those routes.

Teeing Grounds[4]

This section requires that where one teeing ground is provided for a hole, it must comply with 15.4.7. If two or more teeing grounds are provided for a hole, at least two teeing grounds must be accessible. The golf subcommittee recommended that as many teeing grounds as possible be made accessible on each hole, but that at least one accessible teeing ground per hole be required. The golf subcommittee based its recommendation on the premise that an accessible route with a running slope not exceeding 1:20 may be required to connect the golf car path and the teeing ground, and that it may not be possible to provide such a route to each teeing ground due to sloped terrain. The exception to 15.4.1, which permits the use of a golf car passage in lieu of an accessible route with the boundary of a golf course, is very flexible and would allow a golfer with a disability to access the teeing ground by using a golf car, instead of providing an accessible route to the area. The Access Board recognizes that some teeing grounds may be located on steep slopes and that it may not be possible to provide a golf car passage to each teeing ground. When golf courses provide several teeing grounds for each hole, the placement of these areas is usually based on skill level (e.g., one set of teeing grounds would be the "pro tee" and the other set would be the "amateur tee"). Golfers with disabilities want the same range of choice to play from different teeing grounds appropriate to their skill levels. The proposed rule would ensure a range of choice for golfers with disabilities.

Driving Ranges and Practice Tees[5]

This section requires that where driving ranges or practice tees are provided, at least five percent, but not less than one, of the practice tees must comply with

4. Id.
5. Id.

15.4.7. This provision applies to practice facilities adjacent to a golf course, in addition to stand-alone facilities.

Weather Shelters[6]

This section requires weather shelters to be designed and constructed to allow a golf car to enter and exit in a forward direction and have a clear floor or ground space 60 feet minimum by 96 feet minimum. This space will allow a golf car to be driven directly into a weather shelter.

Golf Car Passage[7]

This section requires openings at least 60 feet wide at intervals of 75 yards where curbs or other manmade barriers are provided along a golf car passage to prohibit a golf car from entering a fairway. These openings will provide access to fairways at reasonable intervals where golf cars are used to play the game.

15.4.5.1 Width

This section requires a golf car passage to be 48 feet wide minimum. This dimension is based on the standard width of gasoline or electric powered golf cars.

15.4.6 Putting Greens

This section requires putting greens to be designed and constructed to allow a golf car to enter, maneuver within, and exit the putting green. Unlike teeing grounds, each hole of a golf course is provided with only one putting green where the hole is located. This provision supports the use of a golf car on the putting green and requires space to allow a golf car to approach, enter, and exit. This requirement should not impact the design or space required for putting greens.

15.4.7 Teeing Grounds

This section requires teeing grounds to be level with a clear space of 10 feet by 10 feet and be designed and constructed so that a golf car can enter in a forward direction and maneuver. This dimension is wide enough to accommodate a player playing off of the side of a golf car or from a wheelchair. The teeing ground is required to be level since slopes and cross slopes are difficult for wheelchair users to manage even on relatively flat routes of travel.

The technical provisions for teeing grounds require cross slopes no greater than 1:48 in all directions. The Access Board understands that maintaining this slope

6. Id.
7. Id.

may be difficult on turf surfaces due to settling. Drainage problems have also been reported in areas where 1:48 slopes are provided. The rule does not contain any requirements for access to bunkers or other hazards. The golf subcommittee recommended that practice bunkers be made accessible, but not bunkers and hazards on the course.

Miniature Golf Courses[8]

This section requires each hole on a miniature golf course to be accessible. The technical requirements for an accessible hole on a miniature golf course are addressed in 15.5.2 and 15.5.3.

15.5 Exception

This exception permits no more than 50 percent of elevated miniature golf holes to be inaccessible. Since elevated holes are often designed to provide more of a challenge, this provision is proposed to ensure that a person with a disability has adequate opportunities to play some of the more challenging holes. The golf subcommittee recommended that all holes be made accessible. Operators and miniature golf trade groups felt that a requirement for every hole to be accessible would result in flat courses, taking some of the fun and challenge from the game. This proposed exception provides a compromise between the golf subcommittee's recommendation and the concerns of the industry and operators.

15.5.1 Accessible Route

This section requires that at least one accessible route connect start of play areas on each accessible hole. The accessible route connecting each start of play area required to be accessible may be located on the hole or adjacent to the hole. The accessible route must comply with ADAAG 4.3 and 4.8, where the j slope of the route exceeds 1:20.

15.5.1 Exception 1

This exception permits readily removable curbs where the accessible route intersects the playing surface of a hole. The golf subcommittee recommended that the entry and exit points of a miniature golf hole be free of railings, obstacles, and elevation changes. During the comment period for the Advance Notice of Proposed Rulemaking (ANPRM), miniature golf course operators and the industry expressed concerns that this recommendation would significantly alter the play of the game. It was noted that curbs surround the majority of holes on a miniature golf course to prevent a ball from exiting a hole. This proposed exception balances the need for, a person with a disability to access the hole and the concern to keep the ball on the hole.

8. Id.

To maximize the benefit of this feature, it will be important for players using the miniature golf course to know the location of the readily removable curbs. Several options are recommended for operators and designers including signage placed directly on the curb to show that it is removable or including information about the location of these curbs on the scorecard provided for players at the start of the game.

15.5.1 Exception 2

This exception permits a maximum slope of 1:4 for a maximum rise of 4 inches where the accessible route is located on the playing surface of a hole. This exception is only applicable where the accessible route connecting start of play areas is located on the hole. Permitting a greater slope for a limited distance will allow more flexibility in the design of the hole, while still providing access on the hole for the play of the game.

15.5.1 Exception 3

This exception eliminates the requirement for handrails on a ramp located on a miniature golf hole. Handrails are a potential hazard on a hole, because of the danger of golf balls ricocheting off the rails.

15.5.2 Start of Play Areas

This section requires a start of play area to be a 60 feet minimum by 60 feet minimum level area. This level start of play area is necessary so that a person using a wheelchair or other mobility device has sufficient space to maneuver into position to play the game.

15.5.3 Golf Club Reach Range

This section requires that all level areas within an accessible hole be located within 27 feet maximum of an accessible route with a slope not to exceed 1:20. This will allow space for wheelchair users to hit the ball from on the hole or from an accessible route adjacent to the hole. The space requirements incorporate the reach of a golf club. This provision allows persons with disabilities to be within the reach of their ball at all times, while not increasing the size of individual holes.

Other ADA Guidelines for Related Buildings and Facilities on the Golf Course[9]

Once the management of the golf facility has gained adequate information about ADA requirements for the golf course, it needs to gather information about

9. Id.

the buildings and other facilities include in the total golf course facility. After gaining all the pertinent information the next step is to identify how the guidelines apply to the buildings, facilities, and course. For discussion purposes, at least seven facility-related factors are affected by the requirements of the ADA-AGBF: entrances and exterior areas; floor surfaces; stairs, ramps, and elevators; wall fixtures; toilets, lockers, and showers; emergency warning systems; and assistive learning systems. A number of examples of how the ADA-AGBF can apply to each of these factors follows:

Entrances and Exterior Areas

- A facility must provide free and unobstructed access to and egress from a particular area or location for pedestrians and wheelchair users. This requirement refers to all pathways, which may consist of internal walkways and external sidewalks, curb ramps, pedestrian ramps, lobbies, corridors, elevators, activity areas, rest-room facilities, or any combination of these.
- At least one accessible route must be provided within the boundaries of the facility's property that connects parking and public transportation stops with the facility's entrance.
- If the access entrance for individuals with disabilities is located out of the major path of travel, the access door should be automatic. Automatic doors with independent and separate two-level push plates are recommended.
- At least one door at each accessible entrance to the facility must be designed in accordance with the ADA-AGBF In addition, at least one door at each accessible space within the facility must comply with this act.
- All doors must have a minimum width of 32 inches for accessibility.
- Lever hardware must be provided on all accessible doors.
- All hardware on doors must be mounted at 36 inches maximum to the centerline from the floor.
- A wheelchair access symbol must be mounted on all accessible doors.
- Door-mounted door stops or panic bolts must not be installed in the toe-strike zone.
- Doors with closures must be set with 8 1/2 pounds or less of pressure for exterior doors and 5 pounds or less for interior doors.
- Fire doors must not exceed 15 pounds of pressure.
- The appropriate signage denoting accessible parking spaces and building entrances must be provided. This requirement includes signage located at the facility's main entrance that provides directions to all accessible entrances for people with disabilities.
- If passenger loading zones are provided, they must have an access pathway that is 60 inches wide and 20 feet long, adjacent and parallel to the vehicle space.
- All parking spaces for people with disabilities must be located as near as possible to entrances that are accessible to these people.
- A minimum of one parking space per 25 of the total number of spaces available must be for individuals with disabilities. Each parking space

set aside for people with disabilities must be at least 96 inches wide and provide an adjacent 60-inch-wide access pathway.

- The slope of any parking space for people with disabilities must not exceed one quarter inch per foot of parking space in any direction.
- All parking structures must have ceiling clearances of a least eight feet for parking spaces for people with disabilities.
- Signage indicating which parking spaces are for the exclusive use of people with disabilities must be posted.

Floor Surfaces

- Floors within a facility must be at a common level throughout (no more than one quarter inch variance) or must be accessible (connected) by pedestrian ramps, passenger elevators, or special access lifts.
- The maximum height for carpet tile or carpet is one-half inch. In addition, all carpet edges must be fastened to the floor.

Stairs, Ramps, and Elevators

- All activity areas (e.g., weight rooms, exercise classrooms, gymnasiums, courts, and swimming pools) and support areas (e.g., pro shop, food and beverage areas, offices, and sports medicine areas) must be accessible to people with disabilities. An accessible pathway at least 36 inches wide must be provided in all activity areas.
- All steps, stairs, and ramps must be stable, firm, and slip resistant. For interior stairs, the top and bottom stairstep (tread) must be marked by a strip of contrasting color. For exterior steps, every step should be marked with a strip of contrasting color.
- Stairs must have continuous-grasp (1 1/4 to 2 inches in diameter) handrails located on both sides of the stairs. These handrails must be 30 to 34 inches in height. If handrails are not continuous, they must extend 12 inches at the top of the stairs and 12 inches plus a tread width (the width of a stairstep) at the bottom of the stairs.
- Stairs must have uniform riser heights and tread widths.
- Access ramps must be designed to accommodate individuals with disabilities.
- Ramps must be provided on external and internal pathways where there is more than a one-half-inch vertical change in floor elevation.
- Ramps must have slip-resistant surfaces that are stable and firm.
- Ramps must have landing areas of at least 60 inches by 60 inches.
- Ramps must not have slopes greater than 1:12, although a slope of 1:16 may be the most appropriate slope for a club environment.
- Ramp handrails must be continuous grasp, 1 1/4 to 2 inches in diameter, and 30 to 34 inches in height and must be provided wherever the ramp has a rise greater than six inches.
- Whenever possible, ramps should be installed instead of wheelchair lifts. Ramps are usable by everyone, whereas lifts are not. If alternate means

of access are not otherwise available, a wheelchair lift should be put in a facility.

- If installed, a wheelchair lift should be located on major paths of travel.
- If wheelchair lifts are installed, they should have automatic doors and buttons that don't require constant pressure.
- Button heights for any wheelchair lift should be the same as for elevators.
- A wheelchair lift should not go higher than five feet.
- Keys should be required on all unenclosed wheelchair lifts.
- Appropriate signage should be posted for all wheelchair lifts. For example, a sign explaining the location of the key for a lift should be posted in a conspicuous location.
- One passenger elevator must be provided in facilities with more than one floor, and the elevator must serve all floors.
- All elevators in a facility must accommodate wheelchair users.
- Call buttons in the hallway or in elevator lobbies must be mounted at 42 inches above the floor and must be located away from corners.
- All floor buttons inside the elevator must be located away from the corners. These buttons must be mounted horizontally (instead of vertically) on the side panels at the lowest allowable height (35 inches to the lowest button and 48 inches at the highest point is required). All buttons must be raised and at least three-quarters inch in diameter.
- Elevator key locations must be designated by signage.
- The entrance to the elevator must have a minimum width of 36 inches.

Wall Fixtures

- At least 50 percent of all drinking fountains or water coolers provided on each floor of the facility must be in accordance with the ADA-AGBF regarding access for people with disabilities.
- Electrical-cooler water fountains should be installed in the facility as opposed to manual drinking fountains. In the electrical type, a person applies pressure to a button or similar element, whereas in the manual type, a person must turn a handle, which is a more difficult task.
- Telephones must be accessible to people with disabilities. This can be facilitated by mounting the telephones at a height of 48 inches from the center of the coin slot to the finished floor. At least one public phone in the facility must provide a telecommunications device for the deaf (TDD).
- All light and control switches must be located at a maximum height of 36 inches above the finished floor.
- All objects protruding from walls (e.g., cabinets and shelves) must comply with the ADA-AGBF

Toilets, Lockers, and Showers

- Single-accommodation toilet facilities must have sufficient space in the toilet area (room) for a wheelchair (measuring 30 inches wide by 48 inches long) to enter the room and permit the door to close. A minimum turning radius of five feet in the toilet area must be provided for adequate wheelchair maneuverability.

- Designated toilet facilities must be user-friendly for individuals with disabilities.
- At least one water closet must be 60 inches wide for wheelchair access and another must be at least 36 inches wide with grab bars.
- Accessibility signage must be posted on doors.
- Bathroom doors must swing outward to a minimum of 32 inches of clear opening.
- Lever hardware must be placed on both sides of the door.
- Urinals must be 17 inches high.
- Flush valves must be located on the open side of toilet stalls for people with disabilities.
- Lavatories must have space for maneuverability to permit access by people with disabilities.
- Lavatories must be 34 inches maximum in height, 29 inches maximum height to the bottom of the apron from the finished floor.
- All hot water and drain pipes under lavatories must be insulated.
- The faucet-control mixing valve must be operable with one hand. Lever-operated, push-type, and electronically controlled mechanisms are the recommended, acceptable designs for lavatory valves.
- The force to operate the controls of lavatories must require no more than five pounds of pressure.
- The faucet controls and operating mechanisms of lavatories must not require grasping, pinching, or twisting to operate.
- Towel and soap dispensers must be located on a side wall or clear area, not above or between sinks, and should be placed at a height no greater than 36 inches from the floor.
- Lockers must be made accessible to people with disabilities. A path of access not less than 36 inches wide should be provided to these lockers.
- Appropriate signage indicating which lockers are accessible to people with disabilities should be posted in a conspicuous location in the locker room.
- Showers must be made accessible to people with disabilities. Following are design considerations.
- Showers must be at least 36 inches wide and 36 inches deep and must provide an outside clearance of at least 36 by 48 inches.
- Grab bars must be strategically placed adjacent to a reasonable number of showers.
- At least one shower unit must have a handheld apparatus consisting of a hose 60 inches long mounted 48 inches above the floor, or at least one unit must have two shower heads, one 40 inches above the shower floor and the other set at standard height.
- If the unit includes two shower heads, both shower heads must operate independently and have both vertical and horizontal swivel angle adjustments.
- If the unit includes two shower heads, the lower shower head must have a mixing valve operable with one hand.
- Appropriate signage must be posted.

Emergency Warning Systems

- Emergency warning systems, if provided, must include both audible alarms and visual alarms, in accordance with the ADA-AGBF (1991).
- The center of the alarm-initiating device (box) on manual alarm stations must be located at a height not greater than 48 inches above the level of the floor or other surface.

Assistive Listening Systems

- A facility must provide a permanent assistive listening system in any facility area that will be used for meetings or banquets where more than 50 people are present.

A Final Word . . .

In 1991 the federal government published ADA and Accessibility Guidelines for Buildings and Facilities (ADA-AGBF). These guidelines provide for specific information regarding how golf courses facilities must be designed and constructed (and, in some instances, existing buildings modified) so that they are readily accessible to individuals with disabilities.

All golf facilities, by law, must conform to applicable local, state, and federal codes of design and access/admissions regarding access for individuals with disabilities, as specified by the ADA-AGBF, facilities must take every reasonable step to ensure that they are in full compliance with applicable laws. One of the first steps that a facility can undertake to conform to the law is obtain information on the ADA-AGBF. Such information is readily available from both governmental agencies and private concerns. Among the most commonly recommended sources are the following:

Government

Architectural and Transportation Barriers Compliance Board
1111-18th Street N.W., Suite 501
Washington, D.C. 20036-3894
800-USA-ABLE (Voice/TDD)
http://www.atbcb.gov

Publications: ADA Accessibility Guidelines for Building and Facilities; ADA Accessibility Guidelines for Transportation Vehicles; ADA Accessibility Guidelines for Transportation Facilities.

Manuals: ADA accessibility guidelines for transportation vehicles; ADA accessibility guidelines checklist for buildings and facilities; Uniform Federal Accessibility Checklist for Buildings and Facilities.

Private Organizations

Barrier Free Environments, Inc.
P.O. Box 30634
Highway 70 West-Watergarden
Raleigh, NC 27622
919-782-7832 (voice/TDD)

Mainstream, Inc.
3 Bethesda Metro Center, Suite 830
Bethesda, MD 20814
301-654-2400/2401 (voice or TDD)

National Center for Access Unlimited
155 N. Wacker Drive, Suite 315
Chicago, IL 60606
312-368-0380, ext. 49 (voice) or
312-368-0179 (TDD)

Chapter 11

Occupational Safety and Health Act: The Golf Course Worker

Federal laws regulate the safety and health practices of most organizations. The discussion will be limited to laws that affect a majority of organizations, but note that several additional laws exist that cover particular segments of the workforce. For instance, numerous laws pertain to government contractors, to specific states, and to specific industries (e.g., transportation, nuclear power, food, and drug).

The Occupational Safety and Health Act is an example of a federal law regulating the safety and health practices of industry and its workers. The Act outlines duties of employers and employees:

> "(A) Each employer
>
> (1) shall furnish to each of his employees employment and a place of employment which are free from recognized hazards that are causing or are likely to cause death or serious physical harm to his employees;
>
> (2) shall comply with occupational safety and health standards promulgated under this Act.
>
> (B) Each employee shall comply with occupational safety and health standards and all rules, regulations, and orders issued pursuant to this Act which are applicable to his own actions and conduct."[1]

Pursuant to the provisions of this act, the Occupational Health and Safety Administration has enacted rules and regulations for employees in virtually all forms of business. These guidelines include workers involved in all types of golf facility activities. The office of the Secretary of Labor can be contacted for information relative to the particular employment. Section 651 of the Act sets forth purposes and policies:

> "(A) The Congress finds that personal injuries and illnesses arising out of work situations impose a substantial burden upon, and are a hindrance to, interstate commerce in terms of lost production, wage loss, medical expenses, and disability compensation payments.
>
> (B) The Congress declares it to be its purpose and policy, through the exercise of its powers to regulate commerce among the several States and with foreign nations and to provide for the general welfare, to assure so far as

1. OSHA Employee Workplace Rights. (1997). US Department of Labor, Occupational Safety and Health Administration. Http://www.pueblo.gsa.gov/cic_text/employ/osha/osha3021.html.

possible every working man and woman in the Nation safe and healthful working conditions and to preserve our human resources

(1) by encouraging employers and employees in their efforts to reduce the number of occupational safety and health hazards at their places of employment, and to stimulate employers and employees to institute new and to perfect existing programs for providing safe and healthful working conditions;

(2) by providing that employers and employees have separate but dependent responsibilities and rights with respect to achieving safe and healthful working conditions;

(3) by authorizing the Secretary of Labor to set mandatory occupational safety and health standards applicable to businesses affecting interstate commerce, and by creating an Occupational and Health Review Commission for carrying out adjudicatory functions under the Act;

(4) by building upon advances already made through employer and employee initiative for providing safe and healthful working conditions;

(5) by providing for research in the field of occupational safety and health, including the psychological factors involved, and by developing innovative methods, techniques, and approaches for dealing with occupational safety and health problems;

(6) by exploring ways to discover latent diseases, establishing causal connections between diseases and work in environmental conditions, and conducting other research relating to health problems, in recognition of the fact that occupational health standards present problems often different from those involved in occupational safety;

(7) by providing medical criteria which will assure insofar as practicable that no employee will suffer diminished health, functional capacity, or life expectancy as a result of his work experience;

(8) by providing for training programs to increase the number and competence of personnel engaged in the field of occupational safety and health;

(9) by providing for the development and promulgation of occupational safety and health standards;

(10) by providing an effective enforcement program which shall include a prohibition against giving advance notice of any inspection and sanctions for any individual violating this prohibition;

(11) by encouraging the State to assume the fullest responsibility for the administration and enforcement of their occupational safety and health laws by providing grants to the States to assist in identifying their needs and responsibilities in the area of occupational safety and health, to develop plans in accordance with the provisions of this Act, to improve the administration and enforcement of State occupational safety and health laws, and to conduct experimental and demonstrational projects in connection therewith;

(12) by providing for appropriate reporting procedures with respect to occupational safety and health which procedures will help achieve the objectives of this Act and accurately describe the nature of the occupational safety and health problem; and

(13) by encouraging joint labor-management efforts to reduce injuries and disease arising out of employment."[2]

2. Id.

The Occupational Safety and Health Act

The Occupational Safety and Health Act (OSHA) of 1970 is the most comprehensive and wide-ranging legislation in this area applying to nearly all U.S. workplaces. The act aims to ensure safe working conditions for every American worker by:

- Setting and enforcing workplace safety standards,
- Promoting employer-sponsored educational programs that foster safety health, and
- Requiring employers to keep records regarding job-related safety and he matters.

Three separate agencies were created by the act:

- The Occupational Safety and Health Administration (OSHA) develops enforces health and safety standards.
- The Occupational Safety and Health Review Commission hears appeals from employers who wish to contest OSHA rulings.
- The National Institute for Occupational Safety and Health conducts health and safety research to suggest new standards and update previous ones.[3]

OSHA Standards

The following discussion focuses on the safety standards imposed by OSHA and how they are enforced. OSHA has issued literally thousands of safety and health standards. Areas of basic concern include fire safety, personal protection equipment, electrical safety, basic housekeeping, and machine guards. Each standard specifies such things as permissible exposure limit, monitoring requirements, methods of compliance, personal protective equipment, hygiene facilities, training, and record keeping. To comply with these standards, most mid- to large-sized organizations employ safety professionals to keep up with them and ensure that each is being met.

Enforcement of OSHA Standards

Companies with more than 10 employees are subject to routine OSHA inspections. Companies with fewer than 10 employees are exempt from such inspections, but can be investigated if a safety-related problem is brought to the attention of OSHA.

OSHA conducts inspections based on the following priority classifications, which are listed in order of importance:

"– *Imminent danger*: OSHA gives top priority to workplace situations that present an "imminent danger" of death or serious injury to employees. The company must take immediate corrective action.

3. Id.

- *Fatality or catastrophe investigations*: The second highest priority is - given to sites that have experienced an accident that has caused at least one employee to die or five or more to be hospitalized. The inspection aims to determine the cause of the accident and whether any violation of OSHA standards contributed to it.
- *Employee complaint investigations*: OSHA responds third to employee complaints about unsafe working conditions. The speed with which OSHA responds depends on the seriousness of the complaint.
- *General programmed inspections*: OSHA will also inspect an organization if its lost workday injury rate is above the national norm for that industry."[4]

When an OSHA inspection reveals that an employer has violated one of its standards, it issues a citation. The citation, posted near the cite of the violation, lists the nature of the violation, the abatement period (i.e., the time frame within which company must rectify the problem), and any penalty levied against the employer. Willful violations (i.e., those that an employer intentionally and knowingly commits) carry a penalty of up to $70,000 for each offense. If a death occurs because of a willful violation, the employer may be both fined and imprisoned.[5]

Major OSHA Provisions Affecting Employers

The Occupational Health and Safety Act requires that in areas in which no standards have been adopted, the employer has a general duly to provide safe and healthy working conditions. Employers who know of, or who should reasonably know of, unsafe or unhealthy conditions can be cited for violating the general duty clause. Also, employers are responsible for knowing about and informing their employees of safety and health standards established by OSHA, and for displaying OSHA posters in prominent places. In addition, employers are required to enforce the use of personal protective equipment and to provide communications to make employees aware of safety considerations. The act also states that employees who report safety violations to OSHA cannot be punished or discharged by their employers.

Refusing Unsafe Work

Union as well as nonunion workers have, at times, refused to work when they considered the work unsafe. Although such actions may appear to be insubordination, in many cases they are not. The following are current legal conditions for refusing work because of safety concerns:

- The employee's fear is objectively reasonable.
- The employee has tried to have the dangerous condition corrected.
- Using normal procedures to solve the problem has not worked.

4. Id.
5. Id.

Enforcement of Standards

To implement OSHA, specific standards were established regulating equipment and working environments. National standards developed by engineering and quality control groups are often used. Exhibit 11.1 shows the OSHA standard for personal protective equipment (PPE) as an illustration. OSHA rules and standards often are very complicated and technical. Small-business owners and managers who do not have specialists on their staffs may find the standards difficult to read and understand. In addition, the presence of many minor standards has hurt OSHA's credibility.

Exhibit 11.1

OSHA Standard 1910.132

General Requirements for Personal Protective
Equipment for General Industry

OSHA requires employers to:

- Perform a hazard assessment and equipment selection.
- Inform all affected employees of the hazards and the type of equipment that will be used to protect them.
- Ensure that each employee is properly fitted.
- Verify that the required workplace hazard assessment has been performed through a written certification that identifies the workplace and the person certifying that the evaluation has been approved.
- Mandate that defective or damaged PPE shall not be used and determine the extent of applicable "defect or damage."
- Train each employee to know, at a minimum, the following—when PPE is necessary—what PPE is necessary; how to properly don, doff, adjust, and wear PPE; PPE's limitations; and proper care, maintenance, life, and disposal of PPE.
- Test employees or otherwise ensure that employees can demonstrate understanding of the training covered and the ability to use the PPE properly before being allowed to perform work requiring the use of PPE. The employer must first define the learning objectives of the training required.
- Retrain an employee when there is reason to believe that an affected employee who has undergone training does not have the understanding and skill required.

Verify that each affected employee has received and understands the required training thorough a written certification bearing the name of each employee trained and the subjects of certification.

Source: 29 CFR 1910.

Personal Protective Equipment (PPE)

One goal of OSHA has been to develop standards for personal protective equipment (refer again to Exhibit 11.1). These standards require that employers conduct analyses of job hazards, provide adequate PPE to employees in those jobs, and train employees in the use of PPE.

Bloodbourne Pathogens

OSHA issued a standard "to eliminate or minimize occupational exposure to hepatitis B virus (HBV), human immunodeficiency virus (HIV), and other bloodborne pathogens." This regulation was developed to protect employees from AIDS who regularly are exposed to blood and other such substances. Obviously, health-care laboratory workers, nurses, and medical technicians are at greatest risk. However, all employers covered by OSHA regulations must be prepared in workplaces where cuts and abrasions are common. Employers with the most pronounced risks are required to have written control and response plans to train workers in following the proper procedures.[6]

Hazard Communication Standard (Employee Right-to-Know Law)

Congress enacted the Hazard Communication Standard (more commonly referred to as the Employee Right-to-Know Law) in 1984. This law gives workers the right to know what hazardous substances they are dealing with on the job. A substance is considered hazardous if exposure to it can lead to acute or chronic health problems.

Exhibit 11.2

Provisions of the Employee Right-To-Know Law

1. Develop a written hazard communication policy describing how the organization is complying with the law. The policy should indicate:
   - What constitutes a hazardous substance
   - What hazardous materials are used by the organization
   - How information concerning hazardous materials is transmitted to employees
   - How, when, and by whom employees are to be trained in the right-to-know program
2. Provide Material Safety Data Sheets (MSDS) for each substance in use at the workplace. The MSDS should specify:
   - The substance's hazardous components, chemical ID, common names, and worker exposure limits
   - The substance's physical and chemical characteristics, such as boiling point, melting point, and water solubility
   - The physical hazards stemming from the use of this substance, such as fire or explosion, and ways to handle these hazards
   - The substance's reactivity (i.e., whether the substance is stable) and situations to avoid so it will not react

---

6. Bloodborne Pathogens. (1999). Http://victusinc.com/English/icu/OSHAeng.htm.

- The health hazards posed by the substance; the MSDS should specify how the chemical could enter the body and the possible health hazards upon exposure
- Precautions for safety handling and use (i.e., what to do if it spills or leaks; how to dispose of the substance; how to handle the substance properly; how to store it).

3. Clearly label each container housing a chemical. The container label should:
   - The name of the chemical
   - The name of the manufacturer of the chemical
   - The physical hazards associated with the chemical (e.g., Will it explode? Will it catch fire? Is it radioactive?)
   - The health hazards associated with the chemical (e.g., Is it toxic? Could it cause cancer? Is it an irritant?)
   - The protective clothing, equipment, and procedures that are recommended when working with this chemical.
4. Train all employees on how to deal safely with the chemical substance. The training should cover:
   - How to properly handle and store the chemical
   - The appropriate action to take when coming into contact with the substance
   - Safety precautions, protective equipment, and first aid
   - How to detect hazardous substance exposure (e.g., distinct odors) and how to read monitoring devices.[7]

Specific provisions of the Employee Right-to-Know Law are spelled out in Exhibit 11.2. In brief, the law requires all organizations to (1) develop a system for inventorying hazardous substances, (2) label the containers of these substances, and (3) provide employees with needed information and training to handle and store these substances safely.

OSHA Inspections

The Occupational Safety and Health Act provides for on-the-spot inspections by OSHA representatives, called compliance officers or inspectors. Under the original act, an employer could not refuse entry to an OSHA inspector. Further, the original act prohibited a compliance officer from notifying an organization before an inspection. Instead of allowing an employer to "tidy up." This no-knock provision permits inspection of normal operations. The provision was challenged in numerous court suits.

Dealing with an Inspection

When an OSHA compliance officer arrives, managers should ask to see the inspector's credentials. Next, the human resource representative for the employer should insist on an opening conference with the compliance officer. The compliance officer may request that a union representative, an employee, and a company representative be present while the inspection is conducted. In the inspection, the officer checks organizational records to see if they are being maintained and to determine the number of accidents that have occurred. Following this re-

7. See OSHA at 3.

view of the safety records, the officer conducts an on-the-spot inspection and may use a wide variety of equipment to test compliance with standards. After the inspection, the compliance officer can issue citations for any standards and provisions of the act.

Citations and Violations

While OSHA inspectors can issue citations for violations of the provisions of the act, whether a citation is issued depends on the severity and extent of the problems, and on the employer's knowledge of violations. In addition, depending on the nature and number of violations, penalties can be assessed against employers. The nature and extent of the penalties depend on the type and severity of the violations as determined by OSHA officials.

There are five types of violations, ranging from severe to minimal, including a special category for repeated violations:

"– *Imminent danger*: When there is reasonable certainty that the condition will cause death or serious physical harm if it is not corrected immediately. An imminent-danger citation is issued and a notice posted by an inspector. Imminent-danger situations are handled on the highest-priority basis. They are reviewed by a regional OSHA director and must be corrected immediately. If the condition is serious enough and the employer does not cooperate, a representative of OSHA may go to a federal judge and obtain an injunction to close the company until the condition is corrected. The absence of guard railings to prevent employees from falling into heavy machinery is one example.

– *Serious*: When a condition could probably cause death or serious physical harm, and the employer should know of the condition, a serious-violation citation is issued. Examples are the absence of a protective screen on a lathe or the lack of a blade guard on an electric saw.

– *Other than serious*: Other-than-serious violations could have an impact on employees' health or safety but probably would not cause death or serious harm. Having loose ropes in a work area might be classified as an other-than serious violation.

– *De minimis*: A *de minimis* condition is one that is not directly and immediately related to employees' safety or health. No citation is issued, but the condition is mentioned to the employer. Lack of doors on toilet stalls is a common example of a *de minimis* violation.

– *Willful and repeated*: Citations for willful and repeated violations are issued to employers who have been previously cited for violations. If an employer knows about a safety violation or has been warned of a violation and does not correct the problem, a second citation is issued. The penalty for a willful and repeated violation can be very high. If death results from an accident that involves such a safety violation, a jail term of six months can be imposed on responsible executives or managers."[8]

---

8. Id.

Record-Keeping Requirements

OSHA has established a standard national system for recording occupational injuries, accidents, and fatalities. Employers are generally required to maintain a detailed annual record of the various types of accidents for inspection by OSHA representatives and for submission to the agency. Employers that had good safety records in previous years and have fewer than 10 employees are not required to keep detailed records. Those organizations required to complete OSHA 200 reports are:

- Firms having frequent hospitalizations, injuries, or illnesses,
- Firms having work-related deaths, and
- Firms included in OSHA's annual labor statistics survey.

No one knows how many industrial accidents go unreported. It may be many more than anyone suspects, despite the fact that OSHA has increased its surveillance of accident-reporting records. OSHA guidelines state that facilities whose accident record is below the national average rarely need inspecting.

Accident Frequency Rate

Accident frequency and severity rates must be calculated. Regulations from OSHA require organizations to calculate injury frequency rates per 100 full-time employees on an annual basis. Employers compute accident severity rates by figuring the number of lost-time cases, the number of lost workdays, and the number of deaths. These figures are then related to total work hours per 100 full-time employees and compared with industry-wide rates and other employers' rates.

Reporting Injuries and Illnesses

Four types of injuries or illnesses have been defined by the Occupational Safety and Health Act of 1970:

"– *Injury- or illness-related deaths*;
- *Lost-time or disability injuries*: These include job-related injuries or disabling occurrences that cause an employee to miss his or her regularly scheduled work on the day following the accident.
- *Medical care injuries*: These injuries require treatment by a physician but do not cause an employee to miss a regularly scheduled work turn; and
- *Minor injuries*: These injuries require first-aid treatment and do not cause an employee to miss the next regularly scheduled work turn."[9]

The record-keeping requirements for these injuries and illnesses are summarized in Figure 11.1. Notice that only minor injuries do not have to be recorded for OSHA. Managers may attempt to avoid reporting lost time or medical care injuries. For example, if several managers are trained in first aid, some minor injuries can be treated at the worksite.

9. Id.

Figure 11.1

Guide to Recordability of Cases under OSHA[10]

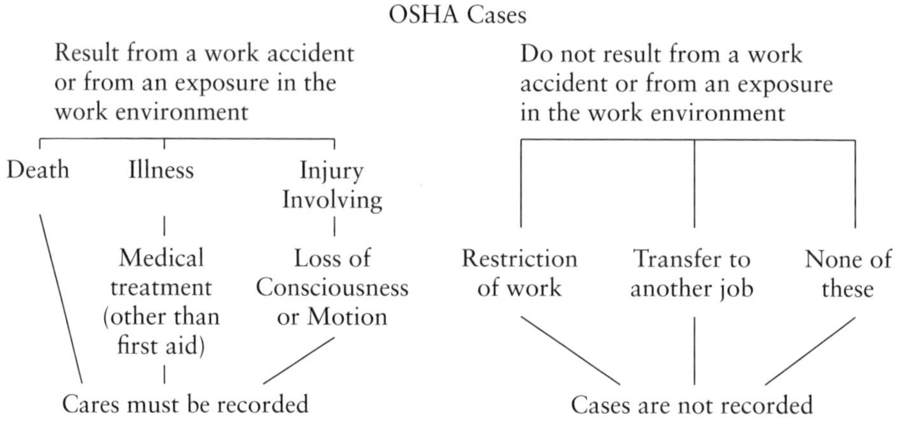

Safety Management

Effective safety management requires an organizational commitment to safe working conditions. But more importantly, well designed and managed safety programs can pay dividends in reduced accidents and the associated costs, such as workers' compensation and possible fines. Further, accidents and other safety concerns do respond to management efforts emphasizing safety. The difference between firms with good safety performance and those OSHA has targeted as being well below the industry average often is an effective safety management program.

An Effective Safety Management Program

An effective safety management program usually entails the following:

- Organizational commitment and responsibility,
- Safety policies and discipline,
- Safety training and communications,
- Safety committees,
- Inspection, accident investigation, and research, and
- Evaluation of safety efforts.

Organizational Commitment and Responsibility

At the heart of safety management is an organizational commitment to a comprehensive safety effort. This effort should be coordinated from the top level of management to include all members of the organization. It also should be reflected in man-

10. Id.

agerial actions. If the president of a small electrical manufacturing firm does not wear a hard hat in the manufacturing shop, he can hardly expect to enforce a requirement that all employees wear hard hats in the shop. Unfortunately, sincere support by top management often is missing from safety programs. However, the importance of a real commitment to safety is strongly demonstrated by some public and private organizations, which choose to reject contract bids from firms with poor safety records.

There are three different approaches that an employer might choose in managing safety. Successful programs may use all three in dealing with safety issues. Figure 11.2 shows the organizational, engineering, and individual approaches and their components.

The focus of any systematic approach to safety is the continued diligence of workers, managers, and others. Employees who are not reminded of safety violations, who are not encouraged to be safety conscious, or who violate company safety rules and policies are not likely to be safe.

Figure 11.2

Approaches to Effective Safety Management

Organization Approach

- Designing jobs
- Developing and Implementing Safety Policies
- Using Safety Committee
- Coordinating Accident investigations

Engineering Approach

- Designing work environment
- Reviewing equipment
- Applying ergonomic principles

Individual Approach

- Reinforcing safety motivation and attitudes
- Providing employee safety training
- Rewarding safety through incentive programs

Safety Policies and Discipline

Designing safety policies and rules and disciplining violators, are important components of safety efforts. Frequently reinforcing the need for safe behavior and supplying feedback on positive safety practices also are extremely effective in improving worker safety.

Consistent enforcement has been used by employers as a defense against OSHA citations. In one situation, a utility foreman was electrocuted while operating an overhead crane. However, the company was exonerated because it had consistently enforced safety rules and penalized violators. The employee who was killed had violated a safety rule for grounding equipment even though the company had given him regular safety training, had posted signs prominently, and had warned all employees about grounding equipment. The OSHA district director ruled that the employee's action was an isolated incident and management was not to blame.

Safety Training and Communications

One way to encourage employee safety is to involve all employees at various times in safety training sessions and committee meetings and to have these meetings frequently. In addition to safety training, continuous communication to develop safety consciousness is necessary. Merely sending safety memos is not enough. Posting safety policies and rules is part of this effort. Contests, incentives, and posters are all ways to heighten safety awareness. Changing safety posters, continually updating bulletin boards, and posting safety information in visible areas also are recommended. Safety films and videotapes are additional ways to communicate safety ideas.

Safety Committees

Workers frequently are involved in safety planning through safety committees, composed of workers from a variety of levels and departments. A safety committee generally has regularly scheduled meetings, specific responsibilities for conducting safety reviews, and makes recommendations for changes necessary to avoid future accidents. Usually, at least one member of the committee is from the human resources unit.

Care must be taken that managers do not compose a majority on a safety committee. Otherwise, the employer may be in violation of some provisions of the National Labor Relations Act. The act prohibits employers from dominating a labor organization. Some safety committees have been ruled to be labor organizations because they deal with working conditions.

In approximately 32 states, all but the smallest employers may be required to establish safety committees. From time to time, legislation has been introduced at the federal level to require joint management/employee safety committees. But as yet, no federal provisions have been enacted. Figure 11.3 shows a job description for a safety committee.

Figure 11.3

Responsibilities of a Safety Committee

Huckleberry Finn Country Club
Safety Committee

Function: To eliminate workplace hazards that are capable of causing significant injury or illness.

Mission: To foster a spirit of open communication and cooperation in resolving all issues that pertain to employee safety and health.

Responsibilities:

- Review the results of workplace safety inspections to identify and analyze hazards.
- Review accident and injury reports (including close calls) to identify and analyze hazards.
- Review and act upon safety and health concerns, suggestions, and needs communicated by employees and supervisors.
- Review workplace hazard assessments.
- Conduct semiannual walk-through safety inspections.
- Identify and communicate specific safety and health related needs and improvements to the employer, supervisors, and employees.
- Perform an annual audit of the safety and health program.

Source: Adapted from Dennis Zimet, "A Comprehensive Safety and Health Program for the Small Employer," *Occupational Health & Safety*, October 1997, 129.

Inspection, Accident Investigation, and Research[11]

It is not necessary to wait for an OSHA inspector to inspect the work area for safety hazards. Inspections may be done by a safety committee or by a safety coordinator. They should be done on a regular basis, because OSHA may inspect organizations with above average lost workday rates more frequently.

When accidents occur, they should be investigated by the employer's safety committee or safety coordinator. In investigating the scene of an accident, it is important to determine the physical and environmental conditions that contributed to the accident. Poor lighting, poor ventilation, and wet floors are some possible contributors. Investigation at the scene should be done as soon as possible after an accident to ensure that the conditions under which the accident occurred have not changed significantly. One way to obtain an accurate view of the accident scene is with photographs or videotapes.

The second phase of the investigation is the interview of the injured employee, his or her supervisor, and witnesses to the accident. The interviewer attempts to determine what happened and how the accident was caused. These interviews may also generate some suggestions on how to prevent similar accidents in the future. In the third phase, based on observations of the scene and interviews, investigators complete an accident investigation report. This report form provides the data required by OSHA.

Finally, recommendations should be made on how the accident could have been prevented, and on what changes are needed to avoid similar accidents. Identifying why an accident occurred is useful, but taking steps to prevent similar accidents from occurring also is important.

Closely related to accident investigation is research to determine ways of preventing accidents. Employing safety engineers or having outside experts evaluate the safety of working conditions is useful. If many similar accidents seem to occur in an organizational unit, a safety education training program may be necessary to emphasize safe working practices. As an example, a publishing company reported a greater-than-average number of back injuries among employees who

11. Id.

lifted heavy boxes. Safety training on the proper way to lift heavy objects was initiated to reduce the number of back injuries.

A Final Word . . .

Organizations should monitor and evaluate their safety efforts. Just as organizational accounting records are audited, a firm's safety efforts should be audited periodically as well. Accident and injury statistics should be compared with previous accident patterns to identify any significant changes. This analysis should be designed to measure progress in safety management. A manager at a hospital might measure its safety efforts by comparing the hospital's accident rate with hospital industry figures and with rates at other hospitals of the same size in the area.

Epilogue

Risk Management

It has been observed by many in the golf world that the golf-related litigation has been so numerous that one might think golf is the most hazardous sport played in the nation. Further, it has become an almost universally accepted fact that any injury that occurs on a golf course is automatically covered under the doctrine of assumption of risk. While this doctrine in many states is a reliable defense, it is not a panacea for guaranteed protection in golf-related injury cases. However, the courts have made several points over the years regarding the doctrine of assumption of risk that apply to all golfers:

- It must be proven that the injured employee, golfer, and/or spectator had general knowledge about the specific danger or risk involved in the activity.
- The golfer must have not only understood the danger or risk but also appreciated the particular danger or risk and the magnitude of the danger or risk involved in the activity.
- The golfer must have volunteered to participate in the activity freely.

Risk Management: A Golf Course Manager's Duty

It is the primary duty of a golf course manager to manage the risks of a golf facility. The manager must have a sound risk management plan design to make the golf facility safe for employees, golfers, and/or spectators. Once a risk management plan is in place it will hopefully prevent most accidents. However, if an accident should occur and a lawsuit is initiated, the risk management plan is evidence of having acted as a reasonable person and responsibly.

Risk Management Plan

A risk management is a total plan that analyzes where and why accidents may occur and how the hazards might be controlled. The risk management plan, if designed properly, will be able to accurately determine which calculated risks are acceptable. The plan will effectively integrate safety with accident prevention and sound insurance policies which includes regularly inspecting facilities and equipment and training personnel in accident prevention. A risk management plan has been recognized by the courts and insurance providers as a pro-active approach to managing risk and ensuring safety.

Components of a Risk Management Plan

Before a risk management plan can be developed, the golf course manager must establish a risk management committee. The golf course manager becomes the risk management coordinator who should be advised by a legal and insurance consultant. These consultants would become advisors for the committee. The committee should have representation from all areas of the golf course including, but not limited to, grounds maintenance, clubhouse, kitchen, and proshop. The committee needs to work closely with the governing body to develop a philosophy and policy statement. Once the philosophy and policy statements have been established, a needs assessment should be completed followed by the establishment of goals and objectives for the plan.

Risk Identification

Once the Risk Management Committee has been established, philosophy and policy statements put in place, a needs assessment completed, and goals and objectives drafted, it is time for the committee to identify the dangers and risks to be dealt with to make the facility safe for employees, golfers, and/or spectators. When identifying dangers and risks, the committee must consider three issues—probability of loss, severity of loss, and site and facility development. The committee should review the following common causes of accidents and injuries for employees, golfers, and/or spectators to determine if any apply to the golf facility in question:

"– design and construction of the golf facility and equipment including clubhouse, course, driving range, shelters, chemical storage, cart storage, carts, fences, maintenance buildings, etc.
- protection of private property either nearby housing or passing vehicles
- course maintenance in general
- cart path design and maintenance
- bridge design and maintenance
- weather monitoring system and weather alert system
- application and storage of chemicals
- maintenance of all equipment in safe operating condition
- compliance with OSHA rules and regulations
- training of personnel."[1]

The following are common sources of potential risk on a golf course that should be carefully considered during a risk identification inspection of the facility:

"– poorly maintained cart paths with pot holes and drop-offs
- bridges without handrails (42") or safety barrier
- lack of guard rails on cart paths with steep drop-offs
- lack of ground fault interrupters
- lack of proper markings in areas where both vehicle and cart traffic are present

1. Unpublished research. Appalachian State University, 2002, Bouldin.

- lack of tee box protection from errantly hit balls
- lack of protection for passing vehicles on main highway
- lack of signage near large water hazards
- lack of proper drainage/standing water on cart paths
- dangerous cart path locations
- lack of directional signage for cart paths
- lack of speed limit or other control (i.e., slow, stop, yield, etc) signage on cart paths
- lack of handicapped accessibility on the course and in the clubhouse
- improperly stored maintenance equipment
- improperly stored chemicals
- improper application of chemicals
- lack of tree grooming near cart paths
- lack of emergency action plan
- no extreme weather warning system
- lack of lightning safe shelters
- lack of a weather warning system
- lack of cart paths
- improperly designed course restroom facilities
- lack of accessible drinking water throughout the course
- poorly designed locker rooms and shower areas
- unsafe bleachers (i.e., loose seats or foot stands, protruding bolts or nails, loose/uncapped bolts, no handrails, no top back rails, no side rails, lack of proper stairways)
- bleachers that do not meet current safety standards to protect children
- lack of clearly marked pedestrian crosswalks in parking areas as well as across roadways
- water valves and hoses not properly covered
- unmarked open drains
- lack of signage describing any dangerous animals, snakes, or reptiles
- steep banks not roped off
- holes not properly marked for number, yardage, or layout
- exposed irrigation heads"[2]

As the dangers and risks are being identified it is important to determine the frequency and magnitude of the risk in order to eventually establish a danger priority for the risk. Using the sample risk identification and prioritization form outlined in Figure E.1, the danger or risk would be identified and assessed. The reviewer would assign a score of 1 to 5 for frequency of exposure to an employee, golfer, and/or spectator. A score of one equals very little exposure whereas a score of five equals very frequent exposure. When determining magnitude (seriousness of danger or damage), the reviewer, using the same scale, would score a one for very little danger or damage and a five for great danger or damage.

2. Id.

Figure E.1

Mark Twain Championship Golf Course

Risk Identification and Prioritization Tool

Dangers/Risks	Frequency	Magnitude	Priority Score	Priority
Lightning	3	5	8	1
Hitting passing vehicle	1	2	3	3
Pot Holes in cart path	1	2	3	3
Poisonous snakes on course	1	5	6	2
Alligators on course	2	5	7	2

For example, lightning is a common problem for the Mark Twain Championship Golf Course. The reviewer might score this risk under frequency as a four and a five for magnitude. The total priority score for lightning would be nine. The same reviewer, however might score a problem with a golfer hitting a passing vehicle a one for frequency and a two for magnitude. The total priority score for hitting a passing vehicle would be three. The priority rating of danger for lightning would be one and hitting a passing vehicle a four based on the priority table below (see E.2). The risk management coordinator would be more concerned about providing solutions to a priority one then s/he would for priority four. The risk manager would not ignore either, only respond quicker to the priority ones then fours.

Figure E.2

Priority Score Conversion Table to Priority Rating

Priority scores	Priority
9-10	1
7-8	2
5-6	3
3-4	4
1-2	5

The next step in the risk management process would be to determine the most appropriate solution or treatment for the problem.

Risk Treatment

Once the dangers and risks have been identified, analyzed, and classified, the next task is to decide on how to treat the risk. There are four options that exist to treat a risk including avoid, reduce, retain, and transfer. Avoidance (avoid) is making conscious decisions not to accept the specific danger or risk. Reduction (reduce) is using additional safety equipment or structures (i.e., fences, lightning protected shelters, protected containers for chemicals, gasoline, and diesel fuel) and/or procedures (i.e., regular inspections, maintenance schedules, and staff training) that are designed to reduce potential accidents. Retention (retain) is an intentional decision to continue using the area and equipment with planned consideration of the risks (i.e., warnings and waivers). At last, transferring (transfer) the responsibility to the employees, players, and/or participants by informing them of high risk activity situations and to an insurance carrier. The risk management coordinator may decide to employ more than one treatment to the situation to make the area safer. For example, a tee box is located too close to another tee box and golfers have been hit by errant balls while teeing off or waiting to tee off. The risk management coordinator decides that s/he cannot move the tee box and recognizes that there is a safety problem. S/he decides to erect a fence on heavy gage metal poles and small mesh fencing material to stop the errant balls. S/he also erects signage on both tees to make the golfers aware of the problem. This solution used three forms of treatment—reduce (fence), retain (did not eliminate tee box), and transfer (transferred the risk to the golfers).

Risk Management Plan Implementation

The risk management coordinator should oversee and monitor the implementation of the risk management plan. The risk management plan should provide for the following types of forms (see appendices for sample copies): waiver and release form, release form, agreement to participate, golf risk assessment tool, golf cart inspection form, warning, injury report, tournament checklist, maintenance report, inspection monitoring report, and ADA checklist.

Further, the plan should describe how to activate emergency procedures for injuries and bad weather. It should have an established training program for all personnel to include first aid and CPR. Finally, an accurate record of all accidents and injuries should be maintained and reviewed regularly.

Risk Management Plan Evaluation

The risk management plan should be implemented as soon as possible and evaluated annually by the risk management committee and its advisors. The annual evaluation would be completed by the risk management coordinator and a report submitted to the risk management committee for its review. The annual report would include, but not be limited to, a review of current dangers and risks (i.e., a new review of facilities and equipment should be done annually), an update on progress being made to reduce risks and improve facility safety (i.e., a chart outlining progress on the prioritized list of previous dangers and risks), a review of facility maintenance (i.e., a review of all policies and procedures related to facility and equipment maintenance), a review of staff training that has taken place (i.e., a chart outlining training provided and those who attended), a review of all accidents and injuries (i.e., a chart outlining accidents and injuries and what was done for the victims initially as well as follow-up), a review of current and pending litigation (i.e., a chart outlining cases and current status), and recommendations for changes in polices and procedures (i.e., modify maintenance procedures for new golf carts to coincide with manufacturer's suggested maintenance schedule), maintenance needs (i.e., adding lightning protection to shelters and maintenance facilities), and additional facilities needed to improve safety (i.e., lightning protected shelters).

Golf Course Safety Procedures

Every golf course should have established safety procedures for employees, players, and/or spectators to observe while working, playing, and watching. These procedures are based on the established policies and protocols of the specific golf course. Most insurance consultants would expect to see these procedures developed and in place. The following is a sample of golf course safety procedures commonly found throughout the United States:

"Push Mowers

1. Never operate a mower until proper instruction has been provided.
2. Check mower to ensure it is mechanically sound and ready to operate.
3. Service before starting: check oil level, air filter, and fuel level.
4. Gasoline is highly flammable. Handle it carefully.
   - Use an approved gasoline container.
   - Do not fill the gasoline tank indoors while the engine is running, or while the engine is still hot.
   - Do not overfill. Wipe off any spilled gasoline before starting.
   - Do not smoke while handling gasoline.
   - Always use a funnel or gasoline container with a spout.
   - Do not mix fuel unless you have been cleared to do so.
5. Wear long pants and substantial shoes. Never operate a mower while wearing sandals, tennis shoes, sneakers, or shorts.
6. Do not store mower near any open flame or where gasoline fumes may be ignited by a spark.
7. Do not mow in areas where there are people, especially children.
8. Do not blow grass toward windows or onto sidewalks and streets.
9. Do not mow in the same direction every time; change mowing patterns.
10. Do not mow over litter or paper. Remove sticks, stones, wire, or any other debris that might be picked up and thrown by a blade.
11. Do not bump trees with mower.
12. Do not lift mowers by yourself. Find someone to help you.
13. Never attempt to make a wheel height adjustment while the engine (motor) is running.
14. Plan the cutting operation so it is not necessary to pull the mower rearward towards you, particularly on a downgrade.
15. When you mow on rough terrain or in high grass or weeds, the blade should be set at the highest cutting point to minimize debris being ejected from the mower.
16. Do not put hands or feet under rotating parts. Keep clear of the discharge opening at all times.
17. Stop the blades when crossing gravel drives, walks, or roads.

18. After striking a foreign object, stop the engine (motor), remove the wire from the spark plug, thoroughly inspect the mower for any damage, and repair it before restarting and operating the mower.
19. If the equipment should start to vibrate abnormally, stop the engine (motor) and check immediately for the cause. Vibration is generally a warning for trouble.
20. Stop the engine (motor) whenever you leave the equipment, before cleaning the mower housing, and when making any repairs or inspections. Employees should wear gloves when changing the blades on a mower.
21. When cleaning, repairing, or inspecting mowers, make certain the blade and all moving parts have stopped. Disconnect the spark plug wire and keep it away from the plug to prevent accidental starting.
22. Mow across the face of slopes, never up and down. Exercise extreme caution when changing direction on slopes. Do not mow excessively steep slopes.
23. Never operate the mower without proper guards, plates, or other protective devices in place.
24. Give complete and undivided attention to the job at hand.
25. Keep in step with the mower. Do not lag behind or let it pull so you will not be in full command of the machine. Do not run.
26. When operating the mower, use the handle to push or pull the mower. Do not push or pull on the deck with hands or feet.
27. Wash off the deck and the engine at the end of every day.
28. Wear protective head gear at all times when working on or transporting across a golf course. Use eye and ear protection whenever conditions indicate such precautions are advisable.

Riding Equipment

1. Never operate equipment until proper instruction has been provided.
2. Check equipment to be sure it is in good mechanical condition.
3. Service before starting: check all fluid levels, air filter, fuel filter, and lubricate grease fittings.
4. Use appropriate fuel: diesel or gasoline.
5. Gasoline is highly flammable. Handle it carefully.
   - Use an approved gasoline container.
   - Do not fill the gasoline tank indoors while the engine is running or while the engine is still hot.
   - Do not overfill. Wipe off any spilled gasoline before starting.
   - Do not smoke while handling gasoline.
   - Always use a funnel or gasoline container with a spout.
   - Do not mix fuel unless you have been cleared to do so.
6. After starting engine, if there is any indication that the unit is not working properly, shut it down and seek a mechanic's help. Abnormal noises, difficult steering, or slow hydraulic response all indicate that there is a problem.
7. Do not park equipment near any open flame or where sparks might ignite gasoline or diesel fuel.
8. Be extremely careful when operating equipment near people, especially children.
9. Do not blow grass toward windows or onto sidewalks and streets.

10. Do not mow in the same direction every time; change mowing patterns.
11. Do not mow over litter or paper. Remove sticks, stones, wire, or any other debris that might be picked up and thrown by a blade.
12. Do not bump trees with mower.
13. Do not risk a back injury by trying to lift or push stuck equipment back. Get help.
14. Never attempt to make a wheel height adjustment while the engine (motor) is running.
15. Do not put hands or feet under rotating parts. Keep clear of the discharge opening at all times.
16. Stop the blades when crossing gravel drives, walks, or roads.
17. After striking a foreign object, stop the engine (motor), remove the wire from the spark plug, thoroughly inspect the mower for any damage, and repair it before restarting and operating the mower.
18. If the equipment should start to vibrate abnormally, stop the engine. Vibration is generally a warning for trouble.
19. Stop the engine (motor) whenever you leave the equipment, before cleaning the mower housing, and when making any repairs or inspections. Employees should wear gloves when changing the blades on a mower.
20. When cleaning, repairing, or inspecting mowers, make certain the blade and all moving parts have stopped.
21. Mow across the face of slopes, never up and down. Exercise extreme caution when changing direction on slopes. Do not mow excessively steep slopes.
22. Never operate the mower without proper guards, plates, or other protective devices in place.
23. Give complete and undivided attention to the job at hand.
24. Wash equipment at the end of each day.
25. Always wear protective head gear when working on a golf course. Do not wear loose fitting clothing which might become caught in rotating parts.
26. Use extreme care when operating turf equipment on slopes. Turf tires have little traction on wet turf and may not stop even when brakes are applied.
27. Use extreme caution when operating equipment with a high center of gravity. Buckets of backhoes and loaders should be carried as low as possible to lower center of gravity and reduce tipping.
28. Operating speed should be gauged by the type of terrain being crossed. Reduce speed as terrain becomes more sloping or rougher.
29. Be careful when operating equipment near lake edges or sand bunker edges. Equipment weight can often cause the edges to cave in.
30. When using excavating equipment, be certain the area is free of underground utilities such as electric, irrigation, water, or drain lines.
31. Always wear eye and ear protection when conditions indicate such use is needed.
32. Never allow anyone to ride on a piece of equipment unless it is designed to carry more than one person.
33. Always allow the engine to settle into ideal speed before turning off. Never kill an engine when it is at operating speed unless it is an emergency.
34. Report any needed service or repair to the mechanic so the equipment can be ready for the next shift.

Edgers, Weedeaters, and Blowers

1. Check and service equipment before starting
2. Gasoline is highly flammable. Handle it carefully.
   - Use an approved gasoline container.
   - Do not fill the gasoline tank indoors while the engine is running or while the engine is still hot.
   - Do not overfill. Wipe off any spilled gasoline before starting.
   - Do not smoke while handling gasoline.
   - Always use a funnel or gasoline container with a spout.
   - Do not mix fuel unless you have been cleared to do so.
3. Wear appropriate safety goggles, face shields, and hearing protection.
4. Use extreme caution when operating equipment around people.
5. Take appropriate tools and supplies with you.
6. Do not hit landscape plants with weedeater line.
7. Always set weedeaters on a solid surface when starting.
8. Allow engine time to cool before refueling.
9. Wash equipment and store properly when finished.
10. Never leave small equipment unattended. (It could easily be stolen.)

Spraying Pesticides

1. Apply pesticides only under the direction of a licensed pesticide applicator.
2. The pesticide label contains all information on safety, handling, and use of pesticides. Read and follow the label instructions.
3. Check equipment to make sure it is in proper working condition and correctly calibrated.
4. Know the target pest and chemical being used.
5. Wear proper clothing, rubber gloves, and eye and breathing protection.
6. Never come in direct contact with the chemical being used. Should that happen, wash immediately.
7. Wash spray equipment and clean filters thoroughly before and after each spray application to reduce chances of contamination.
8. Take every possible precaution to prevent the accidental use of the wrong chemical. Store herbicides separately from insecticides and fungicides.
9. Store chemicals only in original containers.
10. Maintain proper spray records according to the Department of Agriculture requirements.
11. Dispose of empty containers properly.
12. Mix only the quantity of materials needed. The best way to dispose of excess tank mix is to spray it out.
13. Store all pesticides and fertilizers in appropriate storage containers in safe areas.
14. Construct a wash area for equipment washing and pesticide mixing that has proper drainage to protect the environment."[3]

3. Unpublished research. Appalachian State University, 2001, Andrea Pellicco.

A Final Word . . .

Beware has become the byword when it comes to accidents and injuries that lead to liabilities at a golf course. In this litigious society, settlements and verdicts from lawsuits are increasing at a very rapid rate. These suits are not just from players and spectators but employees as the number of workers' compensation claims sky rockets and insurance premiums increase proportionately. The cost to defend a suit, pay a claim, contest a citation, or pay a fine can be devastating. The most effective way to minimize liability exposure is to develop a sound risk management plan.

Risk management is the process of identifying, evaluating, and managing existing and/or potential hazards or conditions that may lead to accidents and injuries and/or damages to property. The accidents and injuries and damage to property always lead to litigation. A sound risk management plan will result in a reduction in injury rates and reduce costs.

Appendices

Performance Review

Source: Indiana State University, Human Resources

Employee Name:
Job Title:
Department:
Review Period Start:
Review Period End:
Last Review Date:
Reviewer Name:
Reviewer Title:

PERFORMANCE ELEMENTS

		RATINGS
Low	=	Unsatisfactory
		Needs improvement
		Meets job requirements
		Exceeds job requirements
High	=	Outstanding

Job Knowledge

	NIA	Low	<—	—	—>	High
Competent in required job skills and knowledge	❑	❑	❑	❑	❑	❑
Exhibits ability to learn and apply new skills	❑	❑	❑	❑	❑	❑
Keeps abreast of current developments	❑	❑	❑	❑	❑	❑
Requires minimal supervision	❑	❑	❑	❑	❑	❑
Displays understanding of how job relates to others	❑	❑	❑	❑	❑	❑
Uses resources effectively	❑	❑	❑	❑	❑	❑
Overall	❑	❑	❑	❑	❑	❑

Quality

	NIA	Low	<—	—	—>	High
Demonstrates accuracy and thoroughness	❑	❑	❑	❑	❑	❑
Displays commitment to excellence	❑	❑	❑	❑	❑	❑
Looks for ways to improve and promote quality	❑	❑	❑	❑	❑	❑
Applies feedback to improve performance	❑	❑	❑	❑	❑	❑
Monitors own work to ensure quality	❑	❑	❑	❑	❑	❑
Overall	❑	❑	❑	❑	❑	❑

Quantity

	NIA	Low	<—	—	—>	High
Meets productivity standards	❑	❑	❑	❑	❑	❑
Completes work in timely manner	❑	❑	❑	❑	❑	❑
Strives to increase productivity	❑	❑	❑	❑	❑	❑
Works quickly	❑	❑	❑	❑	❑	❑
Achieves established goals	❑	❑	❑	❑	❑	❑
Overall	❑	❑	❑	❑	❑	❑

Cooperation

	NIA	Low	<——	——	——>	High
Establishes and maintains effective relations	❑	❑	❑	❑	❑	❑
Exhibits tact and consideration	❑	❑	❑	❑	❑	❑
Displays positive outlook and pleasant manner	❑	❑	❑	❑	❑	❑
Offers assistance and support to co-workers	❑	❑	❑	❑	❑	❑
Works cooperatively in group situations	❑	❑	❑	❑	❑	❑
Works actively to resolve conflicts	❑	❑	❑	❑	❑	❑
Overall	❑	❑	❑	❑	❑	❑

Problem Solving

	NIA	Low	<——	——	——>	High
Identifies problems in a timely manner	❑	❑	❑	❑	❑	❑
Gathers and analyzes information skillfully	❑	❑	❑	❑	❑	❑
Develops alternative solutions	❑	❑	❑	❑	❑	❑
Resolves problems in early stages	❑	❑	❑	❑	❑	❑
Works well in group problem solving situations	❑	❑	❑	❑	❑	❑
Overall	❑	❑	❑	❑	❑	❑

Dependability

	NIA	Low	<——	——	——>	High
Responds to requests for service and assistance	❑	❑	❑	❑	❑	❑
Follows instructions, responds to management direction	❑	❑	❑	❑	❑	❑
Takes responsibility for own actions	❑	❑	❑	❑	❑	❑
Commits to doing the best job possible	❑	❑	❑	❑	❑	❑
Keeps commitments	❑	❑	❑	❑	❑	❑
Meets attendance and punctuality guidelines	❑	❑	❑	❑	❑	❑
Overall	❑	❑	❑	❑	❑	❑

Initiative

	NIA	Low	<——	——	——>	High
Volunteers readily	❑	❑	❑	❑	❑	❑
Undertakes self-development activities	❑	❑	❑	❑	❑	❑
Seeks increased responsibilities	❑	❑	❑	❑	❑	❑
Takes independent actions and calculated risks	❑	❑	❑	❑	❑	❑
Looks for and takes advantage of opportunities	❑	❑	❑	❑	❑	❑
Asks for help when needed	❑	❑	❑	❑	❑	❑
Overall	❑	❑	❑	❑	❑	❑

Planning & Organization

	NIA	Low	<——	——	——>	High
Prioritizes and plans work activities	❑	❑	❑	❑	❑	❑
Uses time efficiently	❑	❑	❑	❑	❑	❑
Plans for additional resources	❑	❑	❑	❑	❑	❑
Integrates changes smoothly	❑	❑	❑	❑	❑	❑
Sets goals and objectives	❑	❑	❑	❑	❑	❑
Works in an organized manner	❑	❑	❑	❑	❑	❑
Overall	❑	❑	❑	❑	❑	❑

Judgment

	NIA	Low <——			——>	High
Displays willingness to make decisions	❑	❑	❑	❑	❑	❑
Exhibits sound and accurate judgment	❑	❑	❑	❑	❑	❑
Supports and explains reasoning for decisions	❑	❑	❑	❑	❑	❑
Includes appropriate people in decision-making process	❑	❑	❑	❑	❑	❑
Makes timely decisions	❑	❑	❑	❑	❑	❑
Overall	❑	❑	❑	❑	❑	❑

Oral Communications

	NIA	Low <——			——>	High
Speaks clearly and persuasively	❑	❑	❑	❑	❑	❑
Listens and gets clarification	❑	❑	❑	❑	❑	❑
Responds well to questions	❑	❑	❑	❑	❑	❑
Demonstrates group presentation skills	❑	❑	❑	❑	❑	❑
Participates in meetings	❑	❑	❑	❑	❑	❑
Overall	❑	❑	❑	❑	❑	❑

Written Communications

	NIA	Low <——			——>	High
Writes clearly and informatively	❑	❑	❑	❑	❑	❑
Edits work for spelling and grammar	❑	❑	❑	❑	❑	❑
Varies writing style to meet needs	❑	❑	❑	❑	❑	❑
Presents numerical data effectively	❑	❑	❑	❑	❑	❑
Overall	❑	❑	❑	❑	❑	❑

SUMMARY

PLANS FOR IMPROVEMENT

EMPLOYEE COMMENTS

Employee Acknowledgment

I have reviewed this document and discussed the contents with my manager. My signature Means that I have been advised of my performance status and does not necessarily imply that I agree with the evaluation.

____

Employee Signature/Date

REVIEWER COMMENTS

____

Reviewer Signature/Date

Job Description

Source: Indiana State University, Human Resources

Job Title: Golf Course Laborer
Department:
Reports To:
FLSA Status:
Prepared By:
Prepared Date:
Approved By:
Approved Date:

SUMMARY

Maintains grounds and turf of golf course in playing condition as directed by Head Greenskeeper by performing the following duties.

ESSENTIAL DUTIES AND RESPONSIBILITIES include the following. Other duties may be assigned.

Operates tractor to till, cultivate, and grade new turf areas, to apply prescribed amounts of lime, fertilizer, insecticide, and fungicide, and to mow rough and fairway areas at designated cut, exercising care not to injure turf or shrubs.

Operates hand or power mower to cut turf on green and tee areas.

Connects hose and sprinkler systems at designated points on course to irrigate turf.

Digs and rakes ground to prepare new greens, grades and cleans traps, and repairs roadbeds.

Plants, trims, and sprays trees and shrubs.

SUPERVISORY RESPONSIBILITIES

QUALIFICATIONS To perform this job successfully, an individual must be able to perform each essential duty satisfactorily. The requirements listed below are representative of the knowledge, skill, and/or ability required. Reasonable accommodations may be made to enable individuals with disabilities to perform the essential functions.

EDUCATION and/or EXPERIENCE

LANGUAGE SKILLS

MATHEMATICAL SKILLS

REASONING ABILITY

CERTIFICATES, LICENSES, REGISTRATIONS

PHYSICAL DEMANDS The physical demands described here are representative of those that must be met by an employee to successfully perform the essential functions of this job. Reasonable accommodations may be made to enable individuals with disabilities to.perform the essential functions.

WORK ENVIRONMENT The work environment characteristics described here are representative of those an employee encounters while performing the essential functions of this job. Reasonable accommodations may be made to enable individuals with disabilities to perform the essential functions.

Job Description

Source: Indiana State University, Human Resources

Job Title: Accounting Clerk
Department:
Reports To:
FLSA Status:
Prepared By:
Prepared Date:
Approved By:
Approved Date:

SUMMARY

Computes, classifies, records, and verifies numerical data for use in maintaining accounting records by performing the following duties.

ESSENTIAL DUTIES AND RESPONSIBILITIES include the following. Other duties may be assigned.

Compiles and sorts documents, such as invoices and checks, substantiating business transactions.

Verifies and posts details of business transactions, such as funds received and disbursed, and totals accounts to ledgers or computer spreadsheets and databases.

Computes and records charges, refunds, cost of lost or damaged goods, freight charges, rentals, and similar items.

Prepares vouchers, invoices, checks, account statements, reports, and other records and reviews for accuracy.

Reconciles bank statements.

Monitors loans and accounts payable and receivable to ensure that payments are up to date.

Reconciles report discrepancies and problems.

Codes data for input to financial data processing system according to company procedures.

Reviews computer printouts against manually kept ledgers and makes corrections.

SUPERVISORY RESPONSIBILITIES

QUALIFICATIONS To perform this job successfully, an individual must be able to perform each essential duty satisfactorily. The requirements listed below are representative of the knowledge, skill, and/or ability required. Reasonable accommodations may be made to enable individuals with disabilities to perform the essential functions.

EDUCATION and/or EXPERIENCE

LANGUAGE SKILLS

MATHEMATICAL SKILLS

REASONING ABILITY

CERTIFICATES, LICENSES, REGISTRATIONS

PHYSICAL DEMANDS The physical demands described here are representative of those that must be met by an employee to successfully perform the essential functions of this job. Reasonable accommodations may be made to enable individuals with disabilities to perform the essential functions.

WORK ENVIRONMENT The work environment characteristics described here are representative of those an employee encounters while performing the essential functions of this job. Reasonable accommodations may be made to enable individuals with disabilities to perform the essential functions.

Huckleberry Finn Championship Golf Club
Waiver and Release Form

Disclaimer: Huckleberry Finn Championship Golf Club (HFCGC) is not responsible for any injury (or loss of property) suffered while participating in club activities, using equipment, or on club premises, for any reason whatsoever, inducting ordinary negligence on the part of HFCGC, its agents, or employees.

In consideration of my membership and being able to use Huckleberry Finn Championship Golf Club facilities and equipment, I hereby release and covenant not to sue HFCGC, its owners, its employees, instructors, or agents, from any and all present and future claims resulting from ordinary negligence on the part of HFCGC or others listed for loss, damage, or theft of personal property, personal injury, or death, arising as a result of using the facilities and equipment of HFCGC and engaging in any HFCGC activities or any activities incidental thereto, wherever, whenever, or however the same may occur. I hereby voluntarily waive any and all claims resulting from ordinary negligence, both present and future, that may be made by me, my family, estate, heirs, or assigns.

Further, I am aware that golf club activities may include vigorous cardiovascular activity beyond playing golf (i.e., aerobics, bicycles, steppers, swimming, or tennis). I understand that these and other physical activities at HFCGC involve certain risks, including but not limited to, death, serious neck and spinal injuries resulting in complete or partial paralysis, heart attacks, and injury to bones, joints, or muscles. I am voluntarily participating in club activities with knowledge of dangers involved and hereby agree to accept any and all inherent risks of property damage, personal injury, or death.

I further agree to indemnify and hold harmless HFCGC and others listed for any and all claims arising as a result of my engaging in club activities or any activities incidental thereto, wherever, whenever, or however the same occur.

I understand that this waiver is intended to be as broad and inclusive as permitted by the laws of this state (specify) and agree that if any portion is held invalid, the remainder of the waiver will continue in full legal force and effect. I further affirm that the venue for any legal proceedings shall be in this state (specify).

I affirm that I am of legal age and am freely signing this agreement. I have read this form and fully understand that by signing this form, I am giving up legal rights and/or remedies which may be available to me for the ordinary negligence of HFCGC or any of the parties listed above.

Date: ____

Signature of Participant: ______________________________

Signature of Parent of Minor: __________________________

Huckleberry Finn Championship
Eighteen Hole Golf Course, Hannibal, MO
Release Form

I, (name) hereby authorize ORGANIZATION XYZ to obtain any and all pertinent information pertaining to any charges, allegations, and/or convictions of any kind I may have had or are currently pending relating to any state, federal or international criminal law violations. Such information can include, but is not limited to, any allegations charges or convictions for crimes committed against children, people, and crimes involving moral turpitude. Such information can be obtained from such sources as any and all law enforcement agencies of this state, other states, federal agencies, and international law enforcement agencies to full extent permitted by law.

Social Security Number: ______________________________

LIST All states and counties which you have lived in over the past ten years:

____

____

Have you ever been convicted of any felony? Yes No

If yes, please describe the conviction and when you were convicted.

____

____

I affirm, under the penalty of perjury, that the following is true and correct information and I would testify accordingly if called to testify in any court of law.

Signature: ______________________________

Date: ______________________________

Huckleberry Finn Championship Eighteen Hole Golf Course, Hannibal, MO

Agreement to Participate (Acknowledgement of Risks)

I am aware that the activities I am participating in, under the arrangements of Huckleberry Finn Championship Golf Course [HFCGC]; its agents, employees, and associates, involves certain inherent risks. I recognize that white water rafting ... and other activities, scheduled or unscheduled have an element of risk which combined with the forces of nature, acts of commission, or omission, by participants or others, can lead to injury or death.

I also state and acknowledge that the hazards include, but are not limited to the loss of control, collisions with rocks, trees and other man made or natural objects, whether they are obvious or not obvious, flips, immersions in water, hypothermia, and falls from vessels, vehicles, animals, or on land.

I understand that any route or activity, chosen as a part of our outdoor adventure may not be the safest, but has been chosen for its interest and challenge... (... understand and agree that any bodily injury, death or loss of personal property, and expenses thereof, as a result of my... participation in any scheduled or unscheduled activities, are my responsibility. I hereby acknowledge that I and my family... have voluntarily applied to participate in these activities. I do hereby agree that I and my family... are in good health with no physical defects that might be injurious to me and that I and my family are able to handle the hazards of traffic, weather conditions, exposure to animals, walking, riding, and all and any similar conditions associated with the activities we have contracted for...

I and my family... agree to follow the instructions and commands of the guides, wranglers, and others in charge at HFCGC with conducting activities in which I and my family are engaged.

Further, and in consideration of, and as part payment for the right to participate in such trips or other activities... I have and do hereby assume all the above risks and will hold Brown's Fort... its agents, employees, and associates harmless from any and all liability, action, causes of action, debts, claims, and demands of any kind or nature whatsoever which I now have or which may arise out of, or in connection with, my trip or participation in any other activities. The terms of this contract shall serve as a release and assumption of risk for my heirs, executors and administers and for all members of my family, including any minors accompanying me... I have carefully read this contract and fully understand its contents. I am aware that I am releasing certain legal rights that I otherwise may have and I enter into this contract in behalf of myself and my family of my own free will.

Huckleberry Finn Championship Eighteen Hole Golf Course, Hannibal, MO

Illustrative Agreement to Participate (for Use with Adults)

Agreement to Participate in Golf

(Substitute Information Appropriate to other Activities for Italicized Sections)

Participation in all sports and physical activities involves certain inherent risks and, regardless of the care taken, it is impossible to ensure the safety of the participant. golf is an activity requiring considerable coordination, and agility. It can involve physical activity for as long as three hours or more, and being alert to fast moving objects. While it is a reasonably safe sport as long as safety guidelines are followed, some elements of risk cannot be eliminated from the activity.

A variety of injuries may occur to a golf participant. Some examples of those injuries are:

1. *Minor injuries such as scrapes, bruises, strains, and sprains;*
2. *More serious injuries such as broken bones, cuts, concussions, and loss of vision;*
3. *Catastrophic injuries such as heart attacks, stroke, heat exhaustion, heat stroke, and death.*

These, and other injuries, sometime occur in golf as a result of hazards or accidents such as slips, being struck by a golf ball, being struck by a golf club, colliding with a golf cart, falling out of a golf cart, stress placed on the cardiovascular system due to heat and humidity, and being struck by lightning.

To help reduce the likelihood of injury to yourself and to other participants, participants are expected to follow the following rules:

1. *All participants are expected to wear proper footwear;*
2. *All participants should stay out of golf cart paths;*
3. *All participants are expected to stay away from players swinging clubs;*
4. *All participants are expected to warn others of balls coming to close to another participant; and*
5. *All participants are expected to follow all posted safety rules.*

I agree to follow the preceding safety rules, all posted safety rules, and all rules common to the sport of golf. Further, I agree to report any unsafe practices, conditions, or equipment to the management.

I certify that (1) I possess a sufficient degree of physical fitness to safely participate in golf, (2) I understand that I am to discontinue activity at any time I feel undue discomfort or stress, and (3) I will indicate below any health-related conditions that might affect my ability to play racquetball and I will verbally inform activity management immediately.

Circle: Diabetes Heart Problems Seizures Asthma Other: __________

I have read the preceding information and it has been explained to me. I know, understand, and appreciate the risks associated with participation in racquetball and I am voluntarily participating in the activity. In doing so, I am assuming all of the inherent risks of the sport. I further understand that in the event of a medical emergency, management will call EMS to render assistance and that I will be financially responsible for any expenses involved.

Signature of Participant Date

WAIVER OF LIABILITY: In consideration of being permitted to play racquetball, on behalf of myself, my family, my heirs, my assigns, my executors, and administrators, I hereby release the service provider from liability for injury, loss, or death to myself, while using the facility, equipment, or in any way associated with participating in the activity of racquetball now or in the future, resulting from the ordinary negligence of the service provider, its agents, or employees.

Signature of Participant Date

Huckleberry Finn Championship Eighteen Hole Golf Course, Hannibal, MO

Illustrative Agreement to Participate (for Use with Minors)

Agreement to Participate in Golf

(Substitute Information Appropriate to other Activities for Italicized Sections)

Participation in all sports and physical activities involves certain inherent risks and, regardless of the care taken, it is impossible to ensure the safety of the participant. golf is an activity requiring considerable coordination, and agility. It can involve physical activity for as long as three hours or more, and being alert to fast moving objects. While it is a reasonably safe sport as long as safety guidelines are followed, some elements of risk cannot be eliminated from the activity.

A variety of injuries may occur to a golf participant. Some examples of those injuries are:

1. *Minor injuries such as scrapes, bruises, strains, and sprains;*
2. *More serious injuries such as broken bones, cuts, concussions, and loss of vision;*
3. *Catastrophic injuries such as heart attacks, stroke, heat exhaustion, heat stroke, and death.*

These, and other injuries, sometime occur in golf as a result of hazards or accidents such as slips, being struck by a golf ball, being struck by a golf club, colliding with a golf cart, falling out of a golf cart, stress placed on the cardiovascular system due to heat and humidity, and being struck by lightning.

To help reduce the likelihood of injury to yourself and to other participants, participants are expected to follow the following rules:

1. *All participants are expected to wear proper footwear;*
2. *All participants should stay out of golf cart paths;*
3. *All participants are expected to stay away from players swinging clubs;*
4. *All participants are expected to warn others of balls coming to close to another participant; and*
5. *All participants are expected to follow all posted safety rules.*

I agree to follow the preceding safety rules, all posted safety rules, and all rules common to the sport of golf. Further, I agree to report any unsafe practices, conditions, or equipment to the management.

I certify that (1) I possess a sufficient degree of physical fitness to safely participate in golf, (2) I understand that I am to discontinue activity at any time I feel undue discomfort or stress, and (3) I will indicate below any health-related conditions that might affect my ability to play racquetball and I will verbally inform activity management immediately.

Circle: Diabetes Heart Problems Seizures Asthma Other: __________

I have read the preceding information and it has been explained to me. I know, understand, and appreciate the risks associated with participation in racquetball and I am voluntarily participating in the activity. In doing so, I am assuming all of the inherent risks of the sport. I further understand that in the event of a medical emergency, management will cal! EMS to render assistance and that 1 will be financially responsible for any expenses involved.

Signature of Participant Date

Signature of Parent Date

Possible Consequences of Injury. Two areas should be covered in this section. First, the participant should be made aware of the types of accidents that may occur in the specific physical activities involved. Insignificant accidents that are common to the activity (slips while performing aerobics), as well as some serious accidents that occur occasionally (losing control of weights so that they fall on the lifter) should be delineated.

Second, a list of some of the injuries that can occur in the particular physical activity should be included. Minor injuries that are common (e.g., bruises, strains, pulled muscles, sprains), some more serious injuries (e.g., ruptured disks, broken bones, concussions), as well as catastrophic injuries (e.g., paralysis and death) should be specified. Phrases such as "some of the..." "injuries such as..." and "including, but not limited to..." in listing both accidents and injuries should be utilized. It is critical that the accidents and injuries be specific to the activity for which the agreement applies. A generic agreement to participate would not be effective because one of the purposes of such documents is to show that the participant was aware of the risks of the particular activity.

Huck Finn Links
Golf Risk Assessment Tool

Date:
Person Making Review:
Course Name:

Hole No.:	Par:		
Yardage:	Front Tee:	Middle Tee:	Back Tee:

Average Width of Fairway:
Injuries on Hole in Last 5 Years: Include a diagram of each hole (Set out distances from nearest fairways, tees, greens, etc.)

Hole	Yes	No
1		
2		
3		
4		
5		
6		
7		
8		
9		
10		
11		
12		
13		
14		
15		
16		
17		
18		

Risk of Balls Landing on Tee From Adjacent Holes:

1	10
2	11
3	12
4	13
5	14
6	15
7	16
8	17
9	18

Existing Protection:

Hole	Screens	Trees	Shrubs
1			
2			
3			
4			
5			
6			
7			
8			
9			
10			
11			
12			
13			
14			
15			
16			
17			
18			

Other Protection Needed:

Hole	Screen(s)	Trees	Shrubs	None
1				
2				
3				
4				
5				
6				
7				
8				
9				
10				
11				
12				
13				
14				
15				
16				
17				
18				

TEE SHOT:

Hole	Open	Trees	Other obstacles near tee	Blind/Partially Blind
1				
2				
3				
4				
5				
6				
7				
8				
9				
10				
11				
12				
13				
14				
15				
16				
17				
18				

Probability of hitting tee shot onto adjacent: After each of the following areas indicate for each hole whether or not there is a high (H), medium (M), or low (L) probability.

Fairways:

Tees:

Greens:

Property or Roadway:

Existing Protection:

Trees

Rough

Other Barriers

Suggested Changes:

MIDDLE SHOT: Using the following adjectives or phrases how would you best describe each hole relative to a middle shot—open, trees, other obstacles near shot area, blind, partially blind, and what is the probability of hitting tee shot onto adjacent (high [H], medium [M], low [L]).

Fairways:

Tees:

Greens:

Property or Roadway:

Existing Protection:

Trees

Rough

Other Barriers

Suggested Changes:

APPROACH SHOT: Using the following adjectives or phrases how would you best describe each hole relative to a middle shot—open, trees, other obstacles near shot area, blind, partially blind, and what is the probability of hitting tee shot onto adjacent (high [H], medium [M], low [L]).

Fairways:

Tees:

Greens:

Property or Roadway:

Existing Protection:

Trees

Rough

Other Barriers

Suggested Changes:

CART PATH:

Construction: ❑ Concrete ❑ Asphalt ❑ Other:

Location: ❑ Left Side of Fairway ❑ Right Side of Fairway ❑ Both

Terrain: ❑ Level ❑ Moderate Incline ❑ Steep

Nature of Path: ❑ Straight ❑ Curves ❑ Sharp Curves

Safety features: ❑ Existing Warning Signs ❑ Rails

Prior Cart Accidents in Past 5 Years: ❑ Yes ❑ No Number:

Suggested Changes:

Other Features of Hole Which Pose Risks:

Most Dangerous Feature of Hole:

Most Needed Safety Feature:

How is gasoline or diesel fuel stored: ❑ Underground ❑ Above ground

How are chemicals stored:

Is the person(s) who apply chemicals licensed: ❑ Yes ❑ No

List and describe the insurances held by the organization:

Does the organization have a risk management plan: ❑ Yes ❑ No

Does the organization have a risk management committee: ❑ Yes ❑ No

Who is in charge of risk management for the organization:

Final Suggested Changes in Order of Priority:

Mark Twain Links
Golf Cart Inspection Form

Date: ____________ Time: ____________ Inspected by: ____________

	Brakes				Steering	Tires			Safety Features		
	Daily Pedal Test			Weekly	Check	Visual		Weekly	Reverse	Safety Sticker	Bumpers &
Cart #	Forward	Reverse	Park	Inspection	Daily	Damage	Air P.	Air Guage	Warning Signal	in Place	Seat Rails

Huckleberry Finn Championship
Eighteen Hole Golf Course, Hannibal, MO
Golf Cart Rental Contract

Golf car is hereby leased for not more than number of holes stated below and/or time stated below, and if LESSEE retains said golf car after expiration, such retention shall be construed as a continuance of this lease at the same rental, and under same terms, until said golf car is so returned to LESSOR.

The intent of this agreement is that LESSOR is hereby renting said golf car only.

Lessee agrees to keep said golf car in the same condition as when received. It is expressly understood and agreed that LESSOR shall not be liable for negligence or damages of any kind whatsoever, whether to person and/or property, and/or for loss of time, and/or any other loss, arising from the use of, operation of, or in any way connected with, the said golf car or to any part thereof, from whatever cause arising. LESSEE agrees to hold LESSOR free from all such damages. LESSEE SHALL BE LIABLE AND RESPONSIBLE TO LESSOR FOR ANY AND ALL DAMAGES TO THE GOLF CAR OCCURRING DURING THE RENTAL PERIOD AND ANY EXTENSIONS THEREOF, EXCLUDING ORDINARY WEAR, AND LESSEE SHALL PROMPTLY PAY ALL REPAIR/ REPLACEMENT CHARGES INCURRED BY LESSOR IN REPAIRING REPLACING OR OTHERWISE SERVICING THE GOLF CAR AS A RESULT OF SUCH DAMAGES, AS WELL AS ALL OTHER INCIDENTAL AND CONSEQUENTIAL DAMAGES INCURRED BY LESSOR.. Lessee agrees to keep said golf car in LESSEE's custody and not to sublease or re-rent same. LESSEE HEREBY CERTIFIES THAT HE HAS FULL KNOWLEDGE OF THE OPERATION OF THE GOLF CAR.

The full agreement between the LESSOR and LESSEE is contained herein, and time is made of the essence of this agreement. The receipt of above golf car, in good order and repair is hereby acknowledged by LESSEE.

NO MORE THAN 2 PERSONS OR 2 SETS OF CLUBS LESSEE IS RESPONSIBLE FOR GOLF CAR DAMAGE

Lessee Name (Please Print): ______________________________

Address: ______________________________

____

____

Driver's License No.: ______________________________

State: ______________________________

Phone: ______________________________

Signature: ______________________________

❑ 18 Holes: 6 Hour Maximum

❑ 9 Holes: 2 1/2 Hour Maximum

CART NO.: ______________________________

TIME: ________ DATE: _________ AMOUNT:

Huckleberry Finn Championship Eighteen Hole Golf Course, Hannibal, MO

Warnings

Things to avoid when playing to increase player safety.

These general warnings should be posted around the golf course and printed on the backside of the score card.

1. No more than two per cart golf with only two sets of clubs.
2. The consumption of alcoholic beverages can be dangerous to the consumer as well as other participants on the course.
3. Abide by the speed limits (5 MPH or as posted) when operating golf carts.
4. Do not drink and drive.
5. Make sure the brake is on before leaving golf carts.
6. Give your partner adequate room the swing the club.
7. Do not throw your clubs.
8. Do not tee off until the party in front has reach a distance beyond your ability to reach.
9. Leave the course immediately at the first sight of lightning.
10. Do not enter water hazards sharp drop offs.
11. Give the universal golf warning "fore" when your ball is heading directly toward another person.

Huckleberry Finn Championship
Eighteen Hole Golf Course, Hannibal, MO
Injury Report

Name of Injured: ______________________________

Address: ______________________________

Phone: ______________________________

Responder Name: ______________________________

Date: __________ Weather Condition: ❑ Clear/Sunny ❑ Cloudy/Wet ❑ Hot/Humid ❑ Cold/Windy

Type of Injury: ❑ abrasion ❑ laceration ❑ incision ❑ tear ❑ puncture ❑ sprain ❑ strain ❑ simple fracture ❑ compound fracture ❑ broken tooth ❑ eye injury ❑ snake bite ❑ other: ______________________________

Location on body:

❑ right lower arm	❑ left lower arm	❑ right upper arm
❑ left upper arm	❑ right hand	❑ left hand
❑ right lower leg	❑ left lower leg	❑ right upper leg
❑ left upper leg	❑ right foot	❑ left foot
❑ head	❑ neck	❑ stomach
❑ lower back	❑ upper back	❑ genital area

❑ Other: ______________________________

Drugs being used: ______________________________

____

Drug Allergies: ______________________________

Known Medical Conditions: ______________________________

____

Treatment provided: ______________________________

____

____

____

Transported where: ______________________________

How Transported: ______________________________

Follow-up: ______________________________

Witnesses: ______________________________

____

____

____

Additional Comments: ______________________________

____

____

____

Nike Tour Pre-Tournament Safety Checklist

(This has been reproduced with permission of the PGA Tour and Nike Tour.)

PGA TOUR

112 TPC Boulevard
Pointe Vedra Beach, FL 32082
(204) 285-3700

Name of event: Date of Event:

Location: Date of Inspection:

Tournament Coordinator: ______________________________

(Name) (Phone #)

Designated SAFETY COORDINATOR: ______________________________

(Name) (Phone #)

INSTRUCTIONS: Please complete this form entirely, and respond to all items. Any "NO" responses will indicate that a deficiency exists and therefore should be corrected before the tournament begins. This survey should be completed prior to the tournament with items periodically inspected throughout the event. After your tournament, please send the completed form to: PGA TOUR, 112 TPC Boulevard, Ponte Vedra Beach, FL 32082.

A. PATRON PARKING	Yes	No	N/A
1. Vehicle and pedestrian traffic flow patterns have been reviewed and clearly laid out.	❑	❑	❑
2. Entrance, exits, and parking areas clearly marked.	❑	❑	❑
3. Traffic control provided by local law enforcement personnel, parking controlled by same or security.	❑	❑	❑
4. Pedestrian crosswalks clearly marked, signs, etc.	❑	❑	❑
5. Crosswalks controlled by crossing guards and/or other control devices. Shuttle bus pick-up/drop-off areas marked.	❑	❑	❑
6. Walking surfaces checked for and cleared of tripping hazards, holes, posts, stumps, etc.	❑	❑	❑
7. Parking areas receive regular security patrols.	❑	❑	❑

Explain Deficiencies/Method to Correct:

B. COURTESY CARS/VALET PARKING	Yes	No	N/A
1. Courtesy cars stored/parked in well lighted area	❑	❑	❑
2. Parking area secured and regularly patrolled by security.	❑	❑	❑
3. Vehicle doors locked, parking brakes set.	❑	❑	❑
4. Parking area is on "high ground" not subject to flooding.	❑	❑	❑
5. Golf carts prohibited from entering valet parking drop-off/pick-up area.	❑	❑	❑
6. Valet parking areas free from tripping hazards-curbs clearly marked.	❑	❑	❑

Explain Deficiencies/Method to Correct:

C. CLUBHOUSE/TEMPORARY STRUCTURES

(Concession stands, restrooms, tents, etc.)	Yes	No	N/A
1. Steps, uneven surfaces marked and free of tripping hazards.	❑	❑	❑
2. Stairs, ramps, etc. provided with handrails	❑	❑	❑
3. Balconies, porches, mezzanines provided with guard rails (42"h).	❑	❑	❑
4. Adequate exits provided and clearly marked for all assembly areas.	❑	❑	❑
5. Room, tent capacities posted and enforced.	❑	❑	❑
6. Emergency lighting units provided and inspected (assembly, dining, banquet areas, etc).	❑	❑	❑
7. Clubhouse equipped with operating smoke/fire alarm systems.	❑	❑	❑
8. Fire extinguishers available for all structures charged and accessible.	❑	❑	❑
9. Counters, tables, chairs, etc. have been inspected, secured, and free from defects.	❑	❑	❑
10. "Wet Floor"signs available and used as required.	❑	❑	❑
11. Doors in assembly area open outward.	❑	❑	❑
12. Compressed gas/fuel cylinders properly marked and secured in upright position.	❑	❑	❑

Explain Deficiencies/Method to Correct:

D. BLEACHERS, GRANDSTANDS, SCOREBOARDS	Yes	No	N/A
1. Portable units are aluminum ( ), wood ( ), combination ( ), rigidly constructed with cross ( ) stringers and erected by qualified personnel.	❑	❑	❑
2. Benches seating free of splinters, pinchpoints, defects, etc.	❑	❑	❑
3. Bleachers provided with footboards at all tiers.	❑	❑	❑
4. Safety guard rails (42"h) with midrails provided along top and sides of bleachers, grandstands, etc.	❑	❑	❑
5. Handrails provided for all stairs, ramps, etc.	❑	❑	❑
6. Bleachers supported by flat metal baseplates, located on stable ground, adequately secured.	❑	❑	❑
7. Scoreboards and platforms secured and free of tripping hazards.	❑	❑	❑
8. Safety guard rails (42"h) provided for all scoreboard platforms located more than 30" above the ground. Stairs, ramps equipped with hand rails.	❑	❑	❑

Explain Deficiencies/Method to Correct:

E. ELECTRICAL/TV/RADIO	Yes	No	N/A
1. Power supply sources, remote units, antennas are segregated and posted.	❑	❑	❑
2. All wiring and power cables elevated (101h) where possible, bundled and wrapped with contrast markings, protected from damage by vehicles.	❑	❑	❑

		Yes	No	N/A
3.	Exterior wiring (permanent or temporary) should be installed in accordance to the National Electric Code, properly grounded and inspected.	❑	❑	❑
4.	TV/Radio platforms—scaffolding is stable, on flat surfaces, baseplates used, guyed on 4 sides and secured. (Bases and guy wire anchors have been roped off from spectator area).	❑	❑	❑
5.	Ground cables laid to minimize tripping hazards cable covers used at walkways and other high traffic areas.	❑	❑	❑

Explain Deficiencies/Method of Correct:

F. PLAYING COURSE		Yes	No	N/A
1.	All bridges, elevated walkways equipped with guard rails (42"h)	❑	❑	❑
2.	Foliage/branch cut to 81 height clearance.	❑	❑	❑
3.	Dangerous foliage, sprinkler heads, control valves, equipment, electrical apparatus, holes, steep banks, water hazards, etc. roped off/posted or access restricted.	❑	❑	❑
4.	Rest areas, benches, water fountains, etc. inspected for defects.	❑	❑	❑
5.	Golf cart paths are free from obstructions, uneven surfaces, over-hanging foliage (below 8'h)	❑	❑	❑
6.	Tee boxes, fairways, greens are adequately roped off per PGA specifications as minimum requirements. Distances should be increased/ adjusted for high hazard areas to prevent golf shot/ spectator contact (Marshals should provide daily feedback)	❑	❑	❑
7.	Marshals should be stationed at all crosswalk areas, tee boxes, greens, etc.	❑	❑	❑
8.	Spectator traffic areas are free of tripping hazards, wet walking surfaces, insect-ant hills, etc.	❑	❑	❑
9.	Practice driving range has been properly segregated/fenced off	❑	❑	❑

Explain Deficiencies/Method to Correct:

G. EMERGENCY PROVISIONS		Yes	No	N/A
1.	Emergency action plans have been developed, written, and are operational.	❑	❑	❑
2.	Independent licensed/certified emergency services secured.	❑	❑	❑
3.	Tournament emergency stations both primary and remote have been clearly designated with directions posted throughout the course (first aid, security, etc.)	❑	❑	❑
4.	Public emergency services have been notified with emergency phone numbers posted.	❑	❑	❑
5.	Emergency vehicles have unrestricted access to any point or location on the course. Possible problem areas have been identified and considered in the written emergency plan	❑	❑	❑
6.	Two-way communication devices/system will be utilized including use of a designated exclusive emergency channel	❑	❑	❑

	Yes	No	N/A
7. Inclement weather plan has been developed, warning signal system operational.	❑	❑	❑

Explain Deficiencies/Method to Correct:

H. GENERAL	Yes	No	N/A
1. Certificates of Insurance are on file for all sub-contractors, suppliers, vendors, TV/Radio media, equipment suppliers, concessionaries, etc. prior to the tournament.	❑	❑	❑
2. Employee and volunteer, orientation programs have been developed and implemented. (Safety rules, tournament/course layout, etc.)	❑	❑	❑
3. Golf cart battery charging areas secured and inspected for fire/safety hazards.	❑	❑	❑
4. Golf carts/mobile equipment checked for proper operation and inspected including signals, etc.	❑	❑	❑
5. Herbicide and insecticide controls are exercised and performed only during non-tournament hours.	❑	❑	❑
6. Previous year Incident Report Summary has been reviewed/ corrective action taken.	❑	❑	❑

Explain Deficiencies/Method to Correct:

Sample Risk Assessment Tool

Mark Twain Risk Management Service
Health, Fitness, Physical Activity, Recreation, and Sport Facility Survey

Facility Name:
Address:

Person(s) Interviewed:

Person Completing This Survey:
Date:

THE ONLY PURPOSE OF THIS DOCUMENT IS TO PROVIDE INFORMATION RELEVANT TO THE SUBJECT PROPERTY IT IS PUBLISHED WITH THE UNDER STANDING THAT MARK TWAIN RISK MANAGEMENT SERVICE (MTRMS) IS NOT ENGAGED IN RENDERING LEGAL, MEDICAL, OR OTHER PROFESSIONAL SERVICES BY REASON OF THE DOCUMENTATION OF THIS SURVEY

Thomas H. Sawyer, Ed. D., President
5840 South Ernest Street
Terre Haute, IN 47802
812/237-2186; FAX 812/237-4338
E-Mail pmsawyr@scifac.indstate.edu

I. Instructions

With this checklist the attempt is to be simple, while being as comprehensive as possible in the time given. The checklist items are written so one may simply check "yes," "no," or "not available" (" N/A"). Attach: 1) membership agreement/ contract, 2) brochures, if available, 3) equipment inventory, if available, 4) inside and outside photos (especially any hazardous areas), and 5) other pertinent material, if available.

In "comments" following each section, provide comments where further explanation is necessary and write the appropriate number and/or letter for the section that is applicable for the comment. If additional or general comments are appropriate, provide them at the end of the document in the space provided. While observing the facility, take slide photos or a videotape, including all different types of activities offered by the facility. Finally, on the last two pages, list (1) suggestions (changes that should be made), and (2) the recommendations (changes that must be made) which are essential to this facility and include relevant slides or video, where applicable.

The checklist must be signed and dated by person completing this survey.

Signature: Date:

II. General Introduction

Full organization name:
CEO name and title:

Years in this type of business:
CEO's experience and background:

List person(s) responsible for making and implementing business decisions, i.e., hiring, supervision, training:

1.
2.
3.

Current number of members/students (Male to female):
Minimum age required:
Current number of student athletes (Male to female):

Types of memberships available: Individual Family Corporate Other

New member orientation given: Yes No
Describe:

Number [#] of full-time employees/Coaches: Number certified:

Number of full-time coaches who have completed either a coaching endorsement coaching minor or coaching education course (either Indiana PACE or ACEP/NFCEP).

Subjects taught by coaches:

Number of part-time employees/Coaches: Number certified:

Number of part-time coaches who have completed either a coaching endorsement, coaching minor, or coaching education course (either Indiana PACE or ACEP/NFCEP).

What sports coached:

male coaches # female coaches
male coaches who coach girls what sports

Check certifications held:	ACSM	Dance Exercise		NFI
	NSCA	CPR	First Aid	WSI
	LG	NATA	Other	

Number of boys' sports: Number of girls' sports:

Number of ticket personnel: Are sellers bonded? Yes No

Is athletic director bonded? Yes No

Business manager? Yes No

Are there employees handling money who are not bonded (paid volunteer)?
Yes No

Annual gross receipts:

Circle the following:

Football
Soccer [B/G]
Cros Country [B/G]
Basketball [B/G]
Volleyball
Baseball
Softball
Wrestling
Golf [B/G]
Gymnastics
Swimming [B/G]
Track and Field [B/G]
Tennis [B/G]
Concessions
Proshop
Donations
Fundraising
Sponsorship
Licensing

Do you hold any gambling activities to raise money (e.g., 50/50 draws)?

What are your days and hours of operation?

M-F	a.m.	p.m.
Saturday	a.m.	p.m.
Sunday	a.m.	p.m.

Check the following which are offered at this location:

Aerobic classes how many per day?
Free weights (including barbells and dumbbells)
Square footage of area
Cardiovascular machines—how many?
Specify type: Sauna Steam room Showers Hot tub
Locker rooms Cold plunge Whirlpool
Body toning machines — how many?
Tanning beds — how many?
Racquetball or handball courts — how many?
Tennis Courts — Number indoor Number outdoor
Basketball courts — Number indoor Number outdoor
Jogging track: Indoor, size Outdoor, size:
Swimming pool(s): Indoor, size: Outdoor, size:
Is the depth? ft. shallow ft. deep
Is there a diving area? yes no
If yes what size diving boards: 1m 3m 5m platform
7m platform 1m platform
Is scuba diving offered? yes no
If yes, do you provide any of the following? snorkel mask
tanks air

Wrestling area, size:
Sport medicine/training room
Child care offered
Masseuse
Beauty salon

Dance studio
Gymnastics
Trampolines
Martial arts
Pro shop
Restaurant
Bar/lounge
Alcoholic beverages (sold or permitted)
Nutrition center or food supplements
Special events, i.e., camps, adventure excursions, dances, picnics, etc.
Specify:

Do you sublease any space to others? yes no
If yes, please describe:

III. Screening for Physical Activity Readiness

A. Profile on medical history
   1. Any health questionnaire used
   2. Physician release required for special participants
   3. Records maintained with health screening information
B. Any consent/waiver/release/assumption of risk form used
   [Attach copy(ies)]
C. Qualified staff to do exercise screening tests
   [Describe certifications held]
D. Exercise testing equipment properly maintained
   [Document procedures and forms used]
E. Emergency procedure in place for testing
   [Attach copy of procedures] Yes No N/A
F. Program and membership information include:
   1. Description of services [Attach a copy]
   2. Hazards/risks [Attach a copy]
   3. Disclaimer [Attach a copy]
   4. Minor consent (parent or guardian) [Attach a copy]
   5. Membership agreement [Attach a copy]
   6. Guests
G. Percentage of participants over 50 years of age:
H. Orientation for new members [Attach a copy]
I. Waiver/consent/medical forms used other than those provided by the IHSAA [Attach copies]
J. Do participants purchase injury insurance? [Cost:]

Comments:

IV. Emergency Plan

A. Are procedures in place for emergencies?
   1. Is there a written emergency evacuation plan?
B. Is at least one CPR certified person on duty during operating hours or on the field/court/track/pool?
C. Are emergency telephone numbers posted by each telephone (e.g., police, fire, EMS)? [Attach a copy]

D. Are staff members trained in emergency procedures?
[Document the training provided]
E. Is the expected response time less than 15 minutes?
F. Is there a manager/coach on duty at all times?
G. Are emergency equipment and supplies accessible, such as fire extinguishers, stretchers, sprinkle systems?
H. Is a first aid kit available and well-stocked?
I. Practice, drills and education
 1. Are drills documented?
 2. Are mock drills varied to match the most common and most serious potential emergencies the specific facility may encounter?
 3. Are all shift personnel involved in drills and emergency training?
 4. Are staff reviews of actual facility incidents done that involve injured patrons?
 5. Any emergency education training information given to staff?
 [Attach copies]
J. Is documentation of accidents incidents made? (e.g., form completed)
[Attach copies]

Comments:

V. Subleasing

A. Contracts executed with all independent contractors
[Attach sample copies]
B. Are subcontractors managed and supervised?
C. Are Subcontractors required to carry liability insurance coverage?
[How much:]
D. Any leasing by outside organizations for meetings?
[Provide a list of organizations]
E. Do you employ independent contractors (e.g., dance exercise instructors)?

Comments:

VI. Staffing and Personnel

A. Academic course work, degrees, or certification required for any staff?
Yes No
B. Experience required for any staff? Yes No
[Attach detailed listing & job descriptions]
C. Background and employment records checked on all prospective employees prior to hiring? Yes No
D. Special staff preparation requirements
 1. Nutritionist
 2. Physical therapist
 3. Athletic trainer
 4. Personal trainer
 5. Health promotion and/or special populations staff
 6. Massage therapist
 7. Babysitting/child care
 8. Beautician
 9. Golf professional
 10. Golf Course Superintendent
 11. Golf Course Maintenance and Grounds Supervisor

12. Other:

Comments:

VII. Facility Checklist

A. General overall facility
   1. Floors free of debris, standing liquid, and undamaged
   2. Entry/exits visible, marked
   3. At least two entry/exits present
   4. Floor coverings property secured
   5. Partitions functioning/undamaged
   6. "No Smoking" signs visible undamaged in hallways
   7. Are storage areas properly secured?
   8. Smoking areas specified
   9. Flammable or combustible materials properly stored
   10. [List and describe controls for these materials]
   11. Emergency power available
   12. Housekeeping satisfactory

B. Handball/racquetball/squash courts
   1. Entry/exits visible, marked unobstructed
   2. Walls clean, free of debris, and undamaged
   3. Walls smooth and undamaged
   4. Floors smooth (no cracks or warps)
   5. Lights functioning
   6. Eyeguard and safety rule signage visible, undamaged, and enforced
   7. Light switches undamaged and functioning
   8. Doors flush with walls
   9. Doors in good condition
   10. Movable walls
   11. Viewing window
   12. Valuable storage
   13. Glass walls on blank sides
   14. Second floor viewing area
   15. Acoustically sound

Comments:

C. Auxilary Courts (e.g., basketball, volleyball, badminton)
   1. Entry/exits visible, marked and unobstructed
   2. Signs visible and undamaged (safety, no smoking, exit)
   3. Floor free of debris and standing liquid
   4. Floors smooth (no cracks or warps)
   5. Backboards padded
   6. Gorilla rims
   7. Walls padded under baskets
   8. Scorers area wiring safe and secured
   9. Portable baskets can be stored and secured
   10. Bleachers are at least 10 feet from playing surface
   11. Stage area appropriately padded
   12. Drinking fountains are recessed
   13. Bleachers have side railings, entry aisles with railings
   14. Volleyball standards are padded

15. Retractable baskets are regularly inspected and maintained
16. Ceilings at least 20 feet tall
17. Adequate lighting that is protected
18. Seating capacity clearly marked
19. Safety glass in doors leading into area
20. Skylights
21. Adequate secured storage volleyball, badminton)

Comments:

D. Aerobic Area
   1. Separate classes for different levels
   2. Safety or warning signage posted
   3. Visible clocks
   4. Flooring made of shock-absorbent material
   5. Floors clean, free of debris, and undamaged
   6. Mirrors secured and unbroken
   7. Mats, aerobic steps, and other equipment stored properly
   8. Instructor certification(s) and training required
   9. Instructor covered by facility insurance
   10. Class size enforced, based on space restriction
   11. Target heart rate charts posted
   12. Area clear of obstructions
   13. All obstructions padded
   14. Telephone for emergencies purposes available
   15. Appropriate climate control and ventilation

Comments:

E. Cardiovascular/Circuit Training Area
   1. Signage (warning signs visible and undamaged)
   2. Climate controlled
   3. Non-slip flooring and drip mats
   4. Any restrictions for using area (e.g., age, handicapped)
   5. Housekeeping — infection controlled
   6. Machine and equipment maintenance exists [Attach reports]
   7. Is area supervised?
   8. All electrical wiring is concealed
   9. All treadmills start at zero MPH and 0% grade
   10. Telephone for emergencies available
   11. Manufacturer's guidelines followed

F. Strength Training Area
   1. Space allocation allows for easy access to equipment
   2. Signage
      (a) Instructional signs visible and undamaged
         (1) Signs emphasizing safety used
         (2) Safety, spotting, warning and acknowledgement of assumption of risk signs used
      (b) Entry/exits visible, marked and unobstructed
   3. Proper environment for weight training
      (a) Air exchanges and ventilation adequate
      (b) Lights functioning properly
      (c) Sufficient ceiling space for overhead lifts

4. Flooring
   (a) Non-slip
   (b) Shock absorbing
   (c) Easily cleaned, repaired, and replaced
   (d) Free of debris
5. Wall Covering
   (a) Mirror(s)
      (1) Positioned higher than largest weight plates
      (2) Secured and unbroken
      (3) Positioned away from activity
      (4) Above and away from dumbbell rack
      (5) Easily cleaned and replaced
      (6) Are cracked or distorted mirrors replaced quickly?
   (b) Walls free of protruding objects
6. Strength training equipment maintenance and service
   (a) Manufacturer-suggested maintenance program used
   (b) Manufacturer's guidelines for repair used
   (c) Are service contracts used?
7. Strength training equipment
   (a) Weight stacks protected by shields
   (b) Collars and clips
      (1) Properly stored
      (2) In proper working order
      (3) Corrosion-free
   (c) Do sitting or lying-resistance machines have correct body position illustrations and instructions posted on them?
   (d) Weight storage, dumbbell racks, adequately positioned, easily accessible
   (e) Benches
      (1) Braced firmly
      (2) Surfaces cleaned/disinfected regularly
   (f) Warning signs visible and undamaged on equipment
   (g) Staff in-service training conducted on equipment using manufacturer manuals
   (h) Strength machines, weight racks, and anchor points securely anchored to wall/floor, where required
   (i) Strength machines, squat racks have properly functioning safety stops
   (j) Strength machines, weight racks and pulley mechanisms
      (1) Cables not broken or frayed
      (2) Lubricated
      (3) No undue metal stress
      (4) Corrosion free
      (5) Non-slip material on pedals
      (6) Non-slip rubber grips on machines
9. Inventory of resistance training machines
   (a) Weight stacks
   (b) Hydraulic (e.g., Keiser brand)
   (c) Free weight machines-no chains or cables
   (d) Computerized/electronic
   (e) Other: specify:
10. New member orientation given

Comments:

G. Tennis Courts

1. Playing surfaces free of debris and undamaged
2. Tennis court nets in good condition
3. Wind screens in good condition
4. Fences and gates in good condition
5. Proper fighting- lights protected
6. Warning signs posted
7. Snow, ice, water removal adequate
8. Equipment securely stored
9. Necessary padding
10. Appropriate distances from endlines to fence
11. Adequate lighting

Comments:

H. Playing Fields

Baseball/Softball

1. Fields clear of debris
2. Fences in good condition
3. Playing surface in good condition
4. Baseball dugouts in good condition
5. Backstops in good condition
6. Storage area free of debris, organized, equipment stored, doors locked
7. Fences taller than six feet
8. Fences four feet or shorter are covered with a protective cover
9. There is a 10 foot warning track prior to fence
10. The softball team areas are protected by a fence
11. Easy transition from infield to outfield
12. Light poles outside of fence
13. Bleachers have railings and aisles
14. Bleachers are safe
15. Adequate lighting
16. Proper drainage

Football/Soccer/Field Hockey

1. Fields have a crown
2. Goals are padded
3. Benches are moveable
4. Scoreboard is located away from field of play
5. All fences are located at least 20 feet from playing field
6. Bleachers have railings and aisles
7. Bleachers are safe
8. Adequate lighting
9. Proper drainage

Comments:

I. Running Track

1. Indoor Outdoor
2. Proper signage (directional, safety, other)
3. Surface inspected regularly
4. Proper surface
5. Adequate lighting
6. Proper drainage, if outside

7. Proper and adequate storage
8. Appropriate landing pits
9. Fences at least 10 feet from the track surface
10. Appropriate separation of field events
11. Appropriate runways

Comments:

J. Pool
1. Pool area monitored
2. Pool area highly visible
3. Entry/exits visible marked and unobstructed
4. Adequate number of exits
5. Walkways undamaged, properly drained, free of debris, and standing liquid
6. Walkways slip-resistant
7. Emergency telephone or alarm equipped
    (a) Emergency phone numbers posted
8. Ceiling and pool lights covered and functioning
9. Signs (exit, no smoking, number of users, no diving, regulation, and safety rules visible and legible; no diving in depth less than feet or less than 25 feet of forward clearance)
10. Pool(s) vacuumed daily or, as needed
11. Water quality tested and daily pool H2O analysis log posted
12. Algae growth not visible in pool; water is not discolored from algae bloom
13. Water level acceptable
14. Water depth markings are plainly marked at or above the water surface on the vertical wall of the pool and on the edge of the deck
15. Light switches proper and functioning
16. Adequate ventilation no unpleasant, discernible odors
17. Diving board present
    (a) If present, does it have a slip-resistant Surface)
    (b) A or B board
18. Drains maintained and working properly
19. Ladders secured and undamaged
20. Chemicals:
    (a) Stored properly
    (b) Labels legible
    (c) Labels show appropriate hazard warning
    (d) Correctly dispensed into pool
    (e) Are employees trained in storage and use of hazardous chemicals
21. Storage area free of debris and uncluttered
22. Emergency equipment:
    (a) Ring Buoy (one each side)
    (b) Extension poles (one each side)
    (c) Shepherd's crook
    (d) Rescue tube (one each side)
    (e) First-aid kit well-stocked and easily accessible
23. Deck and floors leading to pool slip-resistant
24. Decks clean, sanitized twice weekly and algae free
25. Lifeguards
    (a) Possess appropriate certification What type?
    (b) Qualified in emergency procedures/rescue

    (c) Properly dressed/identifiable
    (d) Adequate number and positioning
    (e) Given frequent relief breaks and rotated
26. If no lifeguard on duty, is there a surveillance camera scanning pool area, proper signage, and rescue equipment

Comments:

K. Hot Tub
1. User age restriction
2. Temperature regulation
3. Timers functioning
4. Chemicals used correctly
5. Warnings list visible and undamaged
6. Emergency phone
7. Proper supervision

Comments: L. Sauna

1. User age restriction
2. Automatic temperature regulator to shut off heat when maximum temperature is reached
3. Timers functioning
4. Warnings list visible and undamaged
5. Emergency phone/panic button or alarm easily accessible
6. No locking or latching doors
7. Proper supervision
8. Proper maintenance followed
9. Users cannot touch sauna heater
10. Area clean and free of debris
11. Door opens out
12. Window in door

Comments:

M. Steam room
1. User age restriction
2. Automatic temperature regulator to shutoff steam when maximum temperature is reached
3. Timers functioning
4. Warnings list visible and undamaged
5. Emergency phone/panic button or alarm easily accessible
6. No locking or latching doors
7. Proper supervision
8. Proper maintenance followed
9. Users can't touch steam head
10. Area clean and free of debris
11. Door opens out
12. Window in door

Comments:

N. Therapeutic whirlpool
   1. Emergency procedures posted
   2. Timers functioning
   3. Daily inspection and water testing
   4. Proper surface (non-slip)
   5. Area free of debris and standing liquid
   6. Warning signs posted
   7. Inspection log kept
   8. Supervised
   9. Emergency phone or alarm

Comments:

O. Tanning
   1. Tanning beds placed in enclosed private area
   2. Emergency procedures and warning lists visible and undamaged
   3. Beds disinfected between uses
   4. Maintenance plan in place (e.g., check bulbs, for leakage)
   5. Strict adherence to manufacturer's suggestions on use of equipment
   6. Eye protection provided and required
   7. Waivers signed before use
   8. Timer coin operated token other

P. Dressing areas, locker/drying/shower rooms

Boys
1. Hallway and locker floors:
   (a) Non-skid surfaces
   (b) Free of debris
   (c) Proper drainage
2. Electrical:
   (a) Ground fault interrupters on outlets
   (b) Emergency power system available
3. Lockers
   (a) Corrosion-free
   (b) Free of rough or jagged edges
   (c) Secured to floor or immovable
4. Showers:
   (a) Easy temperature control
   (b) Non-skid floors
   (c) Signs noting caution
5. Locker room maintenance adequate (sinks, floors, mirrors, toilets, urinals sanitized)
6. No dripping water/leaks
7. Benches, tables, chairs secured
8. Adequate size locker rooms

Girls
1. Hallway and locker floors:
   (a) Non-skid surfaces
   (b) Free of debris
   (c) Proper drainage
2. Electrical:
   (a) Ground fault interrupters on outlets

        (b) Emergency power system available
    3. Lockers
        (a) Corrosion-free
        (b) Free of rough or jagged edges
        (c) Secured to floor or immovable
    4. Showers:
        (a) Easy temperature control
        (b) Non-skid floors
        (c) Signs noting caution
    5. Locker room maintenance adequate (sinks, floors, mirrors, toilets, urinals sanitized)
    6. No dripping water/leaks
    7. Benches, tables, chairs secured
    8. Adequate size locker rooms

Comments:

Q. Restaurant/bar/lounge/snack bar/concession stand
    1. Alcohol served or permitted
        (a) If alcohol is served, are state laws adhered to?
    2. Employees trained in serving alcohol
    3. Facility meets health inspection standards and permits kept up-to-date
    4. Cooking surfaces and kitchen have automatic fire protection system
    5. Area clean, free of debris and grease accumulation
    6. Proper refrigeration
    7. Any glass containers
    8. Pest control

Comments:

R. Off-premise activities: camps/adventures/excursions/special events
    1. Properly supervised
    2. Insurance coverage checked in advance and proof furnished by carrier
    3. Proper waiver and similar forms signed by participants. Specify:
    4. Risks properly explained and acknowledgement of risk forms signed
    5. Adequate transportation
    6. Transportation insurance obtained
    7. Warning signs properly posted

Comments:

S. Pro shop
    1. Sub-contracted
    2. Insurance covered
    3. Reputable, insured vendors
    4. Proper labels and warnings on products
    5. Proper security

Comments:

T. Beauty salon/masseuse
    1. Sub-contracted

2. Insurance covered
3. Licensed personnel (if required by state)
4. Proper security

Comments:

U. Nutrition Center, Food Supplements, Nutrition Advice
1. Instructors qualified (i.e., licensed nutritionist on staff)
2. Any diets recommended?

Comments:

V. Child care center
1. Give the staff-to-child ratio at this facility
2. Special staff requirements for employment
3. In-service training offered
4. Emergency care training provided to staff (Pediatric Medic First Aid-PEDS or Red Cross equivalent certification)
5. Adequate space allocation
6. Signage and rules posted
   (a) Language (simple)
   (b) Pictures
   (c) Placed at children's eye level
7. Flooring
   (a) Stain resistant
   (b) Non-slip flooring
   Specify type of floor:
8. Wall covering
   (a) Stain resistant
   (b) Washable
9. Communication available to front desk or other personnel
   Describe:
10. Security and records
   (a) All children clearly visible?
   (b) Restricted exit capability (escapable in case of fire or emergency)
   (c) Child registration (sign-in and sign-out)
   (d) Parental release for all children
   (e) Continuous supervision
   (f) Child's immunization record and medical history on file
   (g) Accident/incident records maintained
11. Housekeeping
   (a) Daily clean-up
   (b) Proper sanitation
12. Equipment/activities
   (a) Sink and toilet at appropriate heights
   (b) Refrigeration
   (c) Changing tables
   (d) Washable mats
   (e) Safe toys and games
   (f) Any type of exercise equipment

Comments:

W. Martial arts
   1. Is the program for competition training?
   2. Is the program for instructional purposes?
   3. Does your facility host competitions?
   4. Qualified and/or certified instructors
      Specify:
   5. Proper acknowledgement of assumption of risk, waivers, consent forms executed by students or parents
   6. Proper floor covering (e.g., resilient, extra carpet padding)
   7. Proper signage (contact rules, etc.)
   8. Class size enforced
      What is it?
   9. Any sub-contractors used?
   10. Any safety equipment required?
      Specify:

Comments:

X. Sports medicine/training room
   1. Location:
   2. Adequate space:
   3. Cleanliness:
   4. Ice Machine: (#)
   5. Telephone:
   6. Computer:
   7. Refrigerator: (#)
   8. Biohazard waste control:
   9. Storage
      (a) adequate
      (b) climate controlled
      (c) secured
   10. Adequate HVAC
   11. Team preparation area
      (a) Tables
      (b) Sink
      (c) Counter space
   12. Hydrotherapy (Wet) area
      (a) Whirlpool (#)
      (b) Hot water supply insulated
      (c) Electrical supply/GFI/receptacles
      (d) Tile floor
      (e) Tile walls
      (f) Proper drainage
   13. Rehabilitation area
      (a) Hydroculator packs
      (b) Ultrasound
      (c) Electrical stimulation
      (d) Free weights
      (c) Mechanized weights
      (f) Exercise bike(#)
   14. Athletic trainer
      (a) On staff
      (b) Under contract

- (c) Student trainers
  - (1) Education program (Attach a copy')

15. Health insurance (Limit:)

Comments:

Y. Transportation
1. School buses used
2. School vans used
3. Personally owned vehicles (POV)
4. Chartered bus
5. Drivers
   - (a) Professionally trained
   - (b) Coaches
   - (c) Parents
   - (d) Students
6. Transportation policy
7. Parental release

Z. Other Interscholastic (or golf) Issues
1. Interscholastic athletic (or golf) handbook
2. job descriptions
   - (a) head coach (golf professional)
   - (b) assistant coach (golf superintendent)
   - (c) athletic director (golf maintenance/grounds supervisor)
   - (d) business manager (golf business manager)
3. Athletic training handbook
4. Strategic plan
5. Risk management plan
6. Marketing plan
7. Financial development plan

VIII. INSPECTOR'S OVERALL RATING AND COMMENTS ABOUT THE FACILITY:

IX. SUGGESTIONS

Minimal changes that you think are necessary and should be made for this facility. If possible, please supply photos of each area or situation that you recommend a change to be made.

X. RECOMMENDATIONS

Minimal changes that you think are essential and must be made for this facility. If possible, please supply photos of each area or situation that requires a change to be made.

Bomb Threat Instructions & Checklist[1]

If you receive a bomb threat:

1. Stay calm and NO RADIOS.
2. Stay on the phone and be polite & patient.
3. Listen carefully and get the following information:
   a. date: time: a.m./p.m.
   b. When will the bomb go off? a.m./p.m.
   c. Where is the bomb right now? Bldg: Floor: Area:
   d. What does the bomb look like?
   e. Why are you doing this?
   f. Who are you?
   g. Caller's statement:
   h. Circle any that apply:

Caller	*Voice*	*Speech*	*Language*	*Accent*
male	loud	fast	obscene	local
female	soft	slow	course	regional
adult	rough	distinct	normal	foreign:
juvenile	educated	blurred	educated	
high	slurred			
low	stutter			

Manner		*Background Sounds*	
calm	deliberate	factory	party
angry	hysterical	traffic	quiet
rational	aggravated	music	voices
disturbed	humorous	office	other:
coherent	incoherent		

i. Other information:

NOTIFY DIRECTOR OF OPERATIONS, POLICE AND SECURITY

Name: ____

(officer taking call) (receiving phone)

1. See *supra* 180 at 302.

Huckleberry Finn Championship
Eighteen Hole Golf Course, Hannibal, MO
Insurance Review

Type	*Semi-Annual*	*Annual*	*Comments*
Health/Major Medical	❑	❑	
Dental	❑	❑	
Prescription Card	❑	❑	
Vision	❑	❑	
Life Insurance	❑	❑	
Disability	❑	❑	
Liability	❑	❑	
Fire/Casualty	❑	❑	
Car/Truck	❑	❑	
Bonds	❑	❑	
Workers Compensation	❑	❑	
Other:	❑	❑	

Huckleberry Finn Championship
Eighteen Hole Golf Course, Hannibal, MO
Maintenance Report

Maintenance Mechanic: ______________________________
Date: ______________________________

Item/Area	*Maintenance Report* Maintenance Completed	Returned to Full Service	*Comments*
Push Mowers	❑	❑	
Greens Mower	❑	❑	
Fairway Mower	❑	❑	
Triplex Mower	❑	❑	
Weed Eaters	❑	❑	
Utility Vehicle(s)	❑	❑	
Aerator	❑	❑	
Plugger	❑	❑	
Sand Dresser	❑	❑	
Sprayers	❑	❑	
Chippers	❑	❑	
Shop Area	❑	❑	
Golf Carts	❑	❑	
Fuel Area	❑	❑	
Chemical/Fertilizer Storage Areas	❑	❑	
Irrigation system	❑	❑	
Watering Closets	❑	❑	
Air Conditioners	❑	❑	
Rest Rooms	❑	❑	
Club House	❑	❑	
Kitchen Areas	❑	❑	
Aquatic Areas			
Pool Shell	❑	❑	
Pool Deck	❑	❑	
Pool Pump Area	❑	❑	
Pool Chemical Area	❑	❑	
Locker Rooms	❑	❑	
Other	❑	❑	

Huckleberry Finn Championship
Eighteen Hole Golf Course, Hannibal, MO
Inspection Monitoring Report

Inspector: ______________________________

Date: ______________________________

Item/Area	*Inspection Report* Satisfactory Condition	Unsatisfactory Condition	*Comments*
Push Mowers	❑	❑	
Greens Mower	❑	❑	
Fairway Mower	❑	❑	
Triplex Mower	❑	❑	
Weed Eaters	❑	❑	
Utility Vehicle(s)	❑	❑	
Aerator	❑	❑	
Plugger	❑	❑	
Sand Dresser	❑	❑	
Sprayers	❑	❑	
Chippers	❑	❑	
Shop Area	❑	❑	
Golf Carts	❑	❑	
Fuel Area	❑	❑	
Chemical/Fertilizer Storage Areas	❑	❑	
Irrigation system	❑	❑	
Watering Closets	❑	❑	
Air Conditioners	❑	❑	
Rest Rooms	❑	❑	
Club House	❑	❑	
Kitchen Areas	❑	❑	
Aquatic Areas			
Pool Shell	❑	❑	
Pool Deck	❑	❑	
Pool Pump Area	❑	❑	
Pool Chemical Area	❑	❑	
Locker Rooms	❑	❑	
Other	❑	❑	

Huckleberry Finn Championship
Eighteen Hole Golf Course, Hannibal, MO
Inspection Schedule

Item/Area	Scheduled Inspection				Comments
	Daily	Weekly	Monthly	Annually	
Push Mowers	❑	❑	❑	❑	
Greens Mower	❑	❑	❑	❑	
Fairway Mower	❑	❑	❑	❑	
Triplex Mower	❑	❑	❑	❑	
Weed Eaters	❑	❑	❑	❑	
Utility Vehicle(s)	❑	❑	❑	❑	
Aerator	❑	❑	❑	❑	
Plugger	❑	❑	❑	❑	
Sand Dresser	❑	❑	❑	❑	
Sprayers	❑	❑	❑	❑	
Chippers	❑	❑	❑	❑	
Shop Area	❑	❑	❑	❑	
Golf Carts	❑	❑	❑	❑	
Fuel Area	❑	❑	❑	❑	
Chemical/Fertilizer Storage Areas	❑	❑	❑	❑	
Irrigation system	❑	❑	❑	❑	
Watering Closets	❑	❑	❑	❑	
Air Conditioners	❑	❑	❑	❑	
Rest Rooms	❑	❑	❑	❑	
Club House	❑	❑	❑	❑	
Kitchen Areas	❑	❑	❑	❑	
Aquatic Areas					
Pool Shell	❑	❑	❑	❑	
Pool Deck	❑	❑	❑	❑	
Pool Pump Area	❑	❑	❑	❑	
Pool Chemical Area	❑	❑	❑	❑	
Locker Rooms	❑	❑	❑	❑	
Other	❑	❑	❑	❑	

Huckleberry Finn Championship Eighteen Hole Golf Course, Hannibal, MO

Inservice Education Schedule

Type of Training	*Monthly*	*Semi-Annual*	*Annual*	*Comments*
Chemical	❑	❑	❑	
First Aid	❑	❑	❑	
CPR	❑	❑	❑	
Life Guard	❑	❑	❑	
Pool Maintenance	❑	❑	❑	
Turf Maintenance/mgt	❑	❑	❑	
Equipment Maintenance School	❑	❑	❑	
PGA/LPGA Schools	❑	❑	❑	
Nat'l Golf Found Schools	❑	❑	❑	
Risk Management	❑	❑	❑	
Software upgrades	❑	❑	❑	
Other:	❑	❑	❑	

Huckleberry Finn Championship
Eighteen Hole Golf Course, Hannibal, MO
ADA Checklist[1]

Facility/Equipment	*Compliance* IN	OUT	*Comments*
Appropriate ramps to all bldgs and within bldgs (see chapter 26 for details regarding ramps)	❑	❑	
Necessary curb cuts made in sidewalks & entrances	❑	❑	
Repositioning of shelves			
Rearranging			
tables & chairs	❑	❑	
vending machines	❑	❑	
display racks	❑	❑	
Repositioning drinking fountains 48" high and 50% of all fountains must be accessible	❑	❑	
Adding raised marking on elevator control buttons & on doors	❑	❑	
Widening doors (32" minimum)	❑	❑	
Adding automatic doors	❑	❑	
Doors with closures must be set with the following pressure:			
Exterior doors 8 1/2 lbs	❑	❑	
Interior doors 5 lbs	❑	❑	
Fire doors must not exceed 15 lbs	❑	❑	
Installing offset hinges to widen doorways	❑	❑	
Eliminating turnstiles	❑	❑	
Providing alternative accessible paths around turnstiles	❑	❑	
Installing accessible door hardware (36" maximum to the centerline from the floor):	❑	❑	
Wheelchair access symbol mounted on all accessible doors	❑	❑	
Installing grab bars in toilet stalls	❑	❑	
Rearranging toilet partitions to increase maneuvering space (minimum space is 30" x 48")	❑	❑	
Lavatory doors at least 32" wide	❑	❑	
Toilet must be 34" high; urinal 17"	❑	❑	
Flush values on side	❑	❑	
Force to operate controls no more then 5 lbs	❑	❑	
Insulating lavatory pipes under sinks to prevent burns	❑	❑	
Installing a raised toilet seat	❑	❑	
Installing full-length bathroom mirrors	❑	❑	
Towel and soap dispensers must be located on side wall not above sinks no higher than 36"	❑	❑	
Repositioning the paper towel dispenser in bathrooms	❑	❑	

Repositioning the seat cover dispenser in stalls	❑	❑
Installing handicapped shower stalls (36" x 36")	❑	❑
hand-held shower device	❑	❑
Raising wash basins in bathrooms to accommodate wheel chairs	❑	❑
Creating designated accessible		
parking spaces 1:25	❑	❑
8" high	❑	❑
loading zone 60" wide x 20'	❑	❑
96" wide with an adjacent 60" wide path	❑	❑
appropriate signage	❑	❑
Installing accessible paper cup dispenser at an existing inaccessible water fountain	❑	❑
Removing high pile, low density carpeting	❑	❑
Installing vehicle hand controls	❑	❑
Accessible routes (48" wide) on golf course: (exception where there are handrails it needs to be 60")		
to bag drop areas	❑	❑
to teeing grounds	❑	❑
to putting greens	❑	❑
to parking lot	❑	❑
to club house & restrooms	❑	❑
to weather shelters	❑	❑
Putting greens and teeing grounds must be designed to:		
allow golf to enter	❑	❑
allow maneuvering room	❑	❑
allow exiting	❑	❑
Appropriately designed wheelchair lifts (see Chapter 26)	❑	❑
Repositioning telephones to 48" high	❑	❑
Repositioning light controls 36" high	❑	❑

1. The Building Owners and Managers Association International (BOMA) has developed an ADA compliance guidebook that explains the Department of Justice's Title III regulations. The guidebook is entitled *ADA Compliance Guidebook: A Checklist for Your Building* (1991). Also for an article outlining what a typical facility survey might entail, see Jay Murdoch and Michael Jawer (1992). The Foundation of ADA compliance: A building survey, 16 *Mental & Physical Disability L. Rep.* 101; see also Brian Lauder (1992). Conducting an ADA compliance audit: Identifying architectural barriers and determining solutions, in *Real Estate Aspects of the Americans with Disabilities Act* 117; finally, see United States Department of Justices, *Title III Technical Assistance Manual* (1992).

Huckleberry Finn Championship Eighteen Hole Golf Course, Hannibal, MO

Parking (Receipt) Ticket

The following information should be printed on the front or back of the parking receipt:

This ticket LICENSES the holder to part ONE AUTOMOBILE in this area. HUCKLEBERRY FIN CHAMPIONSHIP GOLF COURSE hereby declares itself NOT RESPONSIBLE for fire, theft, damage, or loss of any article left in same. ONLY A RENTAL OF SPACE LICENSE IS GRANTED HEREBY AND NO BAILMENT IS CREATED. Acceptance of this check constitutes acknowledgement by holder that he has read and agrees to the foregoing conditions.

Ticket VOID unless purchased upon admission to grounds. FOR YOUR SAFETY AND THE SAFETY OF OTHERS, THE FOLLOWING ITEMS ARE NOT ALLOWED: CANS, BOTTLES, STADIUM SEATS, FRISBEES, ICE CHESTS, VIDEO EQUIPMENT, PICNIC BASKETS, LAWN FURNITURE, TAPE RECORDERS, ALCOHOL, COOKING EQUIPMENT, CAMERAS, FOOD, WEAPONS, AND BEVERAGES.

Huckleberry Finn Championship
Eighteen Hole Golf Course, Hannibal, MO
Tournament Ticket Warning

The following warning should be placed either on the front or back of the admission ticket:

This ticket is a revocable license and admission may be refused upon refunding the purchase price appearing hereon. Unauthorized or unlawful resale or attempted resale is grounds for seizure and cancellation without compensation. Tickets obtained from unauthorized sources may be lost, stolen or counterfeit, and if so are void. Holder agrees by use of this ticket, not to transmit or aid in transmitting any description, account, picture or reproduction of the game, performance, exhibition or event (event) to which this ticket is issued. Holder grants permission to organization sponsoring event for which this ticket is issued and their designees to utilize holder's image or likeness in connection with any live or recorder transmission or reproduction of such event. This ticket is non transferrable or redeemable for cash. It is unlawful to reproduce this ticket in any form. DO NOT EXPOSE TO EXTREME HEAT.

WARNING: GOLF CLUBS, GOLF BALLS, GOLF CARTS, AND OTHER OBJECTS FLYING INTO SPECTATOR AREAS CAN CAUSE SERIOUS INJURY. BE ALERT AT ALL TIMES WHEN IN SPECTATOR AREAS. IF INJURED, NOTIFY USHER OR ATTENDANT FOR DIRECTIONS TO MEDICAL STATIONS.

Sexual Harassment
A Continuum of Unwanted Sexual and Gender-Directed Behavior Patterns

Visual	*Verbal*	*Written*	*Touching*	*Power*	*Threats*	*Force*
Ogling, leering	Request for dates	Love letters or poems	Violation of space	Retaliation	Quid Pro Quo Demands	Attempted or actual rape
Staring	Very personal questions	Obscene letters	Patting, rubbing	Using position to request dates or sexual favors	Conditioning of Grades or references for sexual favors	Attempted or actual assault
Posters, cartoons	Lewd comments	Cards, notes	Pinching	Gender-directed favoritism or disparate treatment	Retaliation for refusal to comply with requests	Pantsing
Graphics	Dirty/sexual jokes	Graphics	Bra-snapping	Hazing rituals		Stripping
Magazines, flyers	Whistling, cat-calling		Caressing	Lost job or school position		Extreme forms of hazing
Pin-ups	Obscene calls		Blocking of movement	Lost promotion		Stalking
Gestures	Sexual rumors		Kissing			Sexual abuse
Mooning			Groping			Physical abuse
Flashing			Grabbing			
			Hazing			

OFFENSIVE CONDUCT (may be illegal) .... DEMANDS (Illegal in all cases)

HOSTILE ENVIRONMENT (if severe and pervasive) .... QUID PRO QUO (Once is enough)

The less severe the form, usually the more it needs to be repeated before it is illegal sexual harassment. The more severe the form, the less it needs to be repeated before it rises to illegal sexual harassment from the perspective of a reasonable victim.

2000 adaptation from educational setting handbook by the *Harper Consulting Group* (301 South Oakes Street, Helena, MT 59601) from sexual harassment training materials developed by GENERAL ELECTRIC in "Sexual Harassment: It's No Game" by the Center for Women in Governance, Albany, NY, 1992.

Sexual Harassment Questionnaire #1

To check your knowledge of sexual harassment, circle True or False to the statements below.

T F It is okay for employees to tell dirty jokes and make sexually explicit comments to each other as long as it doesn't offend anyone else in the office.

T F Sexual harassment should be taken more seriously in a professional office than in a restaurant.

T F A cartoon cut from an adult magazine and taped to the wall behind the office copier constitutes a hostile environment.

T F A senior employee must demand sex from a junior employee before there can be a quid pro quo sexual harassment charge.

T F A sales representative for a retail computer store sexually harasses a young female customer when he tells her that he will get her a good deal on a computer if she goes out with him.

T F Employers would rather have an employee deal with another employee's inappropriate sexual behavior rather than file complaints because it is a headache to prove employee misconduct and enforce the sexual harassment policy.

T F Failure to promote someone who has complained about a hostile environment to the president of the company constitutes sexual harassment.

T F A junior partner in an architectural firm begins seeing another junior partner outside of the office. One of the senior partners, with whom the junior partner has previously had a relationship, blocks an opportunity for a promotion. This is sexual harassment.

Sexual Harassment Questionnaire #2

For each of these situations, indicate your personal opinion on the first scale of numbers and then what you think the legally appropriate answer should be on the second.

A young woman who is uncomfortable with her boss's sexually explicit jokes should ask for a transfer instead of creating waves by complaining. After all, it's not like he's demanding sexual favors. Do you agree?

1 2 3 4 5 6 7 8 9 10
Disagree Agree

1 2 3 4 5 6 7 8 9 10
Disagree Agree

A female office-supply vendor representative makes several suggestive remarks to a new female sales clerk at a card store. The representative's behavior embarrasses the sales clerk. The sales clerk begins to avoid the vendor representative whenever she's in the store. She fears she will have to quit her job because she believes there are no repercussions since the representative is a woman. Do you agree with her assessment of the situation?

1 2 3 4 5 6 7 8 9 10
Disagree Agree

1 2 3 4 5 6 7 8 9 10
Disagree Agree

A local restaurant that caters to college students employs mainly students. The students usually have a good time when they're working, and there is often a lot of bantering between both sexes. Managers put up with the behavior as long as it isn't disruptive and the customers don't hear or see it. Carol, a new server, is slapped on her bottom by Brad, another server. She talks to the manager about the incident, and the manager asks Brad to refrain from bothering Carol. Brad comers Carol in the kitchen and attempts to grab her this time, laughs and makes a rude comment about her size. Carol again goes to the manager. After a third incident, Carol files a sexual harassment lawsuit. She names Brad and the restaurant in the lawsuit since the manager didn't do anything to prevent the behavior after being made aware of it. Do you agree with Carol's actions?

1 2 3 4 5 6 7 8 9 10
Disagree Agree

1 2 3 4 5 6 7 8 9 10
Disagree Agree

Sample Employee Handbook Table of Contents

Kleiman, L. S. (2000). *Human Resource Management.* (2nd ed.) South-Western College Publishing.

Table of Contents

Free Legal Advice?

Where to find legal help on the Net

Source: You and the Law. Reader's Digest, 1997

If you want to do legal research on the internet, here some tips:

- Get a second opinion. Look at a couple of Web sites to see if they agree.
- Check the date of the publication. What is appropriate today may be illegal tomorrow.
- Look for the a name behind the Web address and information on who is writing the articles or running the site.
- Realize that laws are different in each state.
- Not sure if the information is complete and timely? Visit the law library at the county courthouse. Librarians there are trained to help you find information.
- If you are not 100% sure, call an attorney. Many will do free initial consultations.

A few good legal Web sites

Many Web sites provide legal information. Here are a few good general sites to get you started:

www.golflaw.com It has information regarding risk management and how gain legal assistance.

www.findlaw.com Perhaps the biggest internet legal site, it has links to commercial and institutional sites, including bar associations for every state.

www.lawguru.com It has links to statutes, the Constitution and other legal sites for every state and territory, along with a password-protected search engine.

www.freeadvice.com It has user-friendly explanations of basic legal issues, with "I want a lawyer" under every heading.

www.nolo.com Nolo press touts its self-help law books but also provides some basic information.

www.lectlaw.com The "lectric law library may look usual, but it has a dedicated following among lawyers.

www.abanet.org The American Bar Association's site has links to local bars and a lawyer directory. The ABA also is planning a links page to other legal sites.

www.pga.org This is the Professional Golfers Association Web site.

www.lpa.org This is the Ladies Professional Golf Association Web site.

www.ngf.org This is the National Golf Foundation Web site.

www.usga.org This is the United States Golf Association Web site.

www.gcsaa.org This is the Golf Course Superintendent's Association of America Web site.

Key Information Every Employee File Should Contain

Source: Indiana State University, Human Resources

All employees have the right to expect that any personal information will be kept confidential. An invasion of privacy lawsuit can result if the employee's right to privacy is violated.

This information should be separated into five files:

1. Medical
2. Financial
    - payroll
    - group life insurance beneficiary
    - company stock ownership
3. Personal
    - job description
    - job application
    - performance evaluation
    - letters of praise
    - awards
    - performance agreements and reprimands
    - certificates of training
    - miscellaneous personal information
4. INS I-9 file
5. EEOC file

How Long Do You Need to Keep These Files?

Most states require that employee records be kept for three years after the employee has left the company.

Guidelines for maintaining confidentiality and access of employee records

Employee:

- In most states, freedom of information laws give employees the right to have access to their personnel files in a timely manner.
- The federal Privacy Protection Study Commission recommends allowing employees to insert rebuttal information into their files.
- Employees cannot have access to a manager's personal personnel "working file."

Employer:

- Employers have the right to look into personnel files if they have legitimate business reasons:
    - to review performance evaluations
    - to prepare for performance evaluations

Every golf operation should have written policies to determine who has access to personnel files and under what conditions.

EEOC Guidelines for Testing Employees

1. General Rules of employee testing
   - Tests must be nondiscriminatory
   - Tests must be specific to required qualifications
   - Tests must be conducted "for cause"
   - Test results must be communicated only to those with a need to know
2. Combating the dangers of employee testing
   - Ensure nondiscrimination - look for validation studies on out-of-house tests; have validation studies done on tests developed in-house
   - Ensure testing is job-related - Take tests developed out-of-house yourself; compare job descriptions with test; conduct a criterion-related, content or validity study
   - Evaluate the need for the test - how does the test relate to the job; what factors are determined by the test; is the test justified; are the test results only one part of the selection criteria?
   - Ensure confidentiality - train test givers to protect applicants' privacy rights; develop guidelines on test security and data protection; keep test results separate from general employee files.

Drug Testing in the Workplace

Drug-testing policies should include:

- grounds for testing,
- procedure for the employee to notify the employer of prescription and over-the-counter drug use,
- grievance procedures for employees who refuse to take the test,
- types of tests and samples to be used,
- guarantees of confidentiality, and
- steps to be taken if test results are positive.

Lawful Interviewing and Hiring

Source: Indiana State University, Human Resources

Three Tips for Avoiding Discrimination Suits Stemming From Unfair Hiring Practices

1. Write job descriptions based on essential functions and skills needed
2. Write legally safe job advertisements and postings
   - Use descriptive language that mentions specific identifying factors—High energy, stable, sales representative, enjoys travel
   - Avoid descriptions that discriminate against protected classes
   - Follow good management practice guidelines for internal postings—Place the postings at a level where all employees can see them—Offer tape-recorded postings
3. Avoid application forms and screening techniques that have an unfair impact on any group of applicants

Avoid Making Promises That Can Be Viewed as Legally Binding Contracts

- Avoid making promises you don't intend to keep
- Avoid comments that are made to smooth over rough spots with an employee, such as, "Don't worry, you won't be laid off'
- Stress in all employee documents that employment is "at will"
- Add disclaimers to all documents
- Designate in the employee handbook officers who can enter into oral or written contracts with employees
- Make probationary period conditions clear
- Avoid using the phrase "just cause" as a grounds for termination

How to Develop Legally Safe Interview Questions

1. Keep all your questions job related
2. Ask the same questions of everyone

What can you ask?

Ensure that the questions don't violate Title VII of the Civil Rights Act of 1964 or Title I of the Americans With Disabilities Act of 1990.

Information you can ask for	Information you can't ask for
Name	Health or disability
Address	Union affiliation
Work experience	Language ability
Skills	Personal finances
Education	Arrest record
Employment references	Dependents
Criminal convictions	Marital status
	Sexual orientation

Legal Techniques for Gathering Information When You're Conducting Background Checks or Verifying References

You can legally verify any information that is given to you by the applicant if it is relevant to the job. This includes:

- Education
- Employment history
- Social Security number
- Letters of recommendation

How to obtain an in-depth reference check

- Ask candidate if you can call references in the evenings or on weekends
- Consider having candidate sign an agreement that would hold you and references harmless in case the candidate doesn't like the results
- Ask similar questions of the reference as you did the candidate in the interview
- Talk to current boss, previous bosses, peers and subordinates
- Investigate applicant's driving record if it is relevant to the job
- Investigate applicant's criminal convictions if they are relevant to the job

Index